Language, Culture and Linguistics

Language, Culture and Linguistics

Essays in Honour of Suniti Kumar Chatterji

Editors

Mina Dan
Aditi Ghosh

Orient BlackSwan

LANGUAGE, CULTURE AND LINGUISTICS: ESSAYS IN HONOUR OF SUNITI KUMAR CHATTERJI

ORIENT BLACKSWAN PRIVATE LIMITED

Registered Office
3-6-752 Himayatnagar, Hyderabad 500 029, Telangana, India
e-mail: centraloffice@orientblackswan.com

Other Offices
Bengaluru, Chennai, Guwahati, Hyderabad,
Kolkata, Mumbai, New Delhi, Noida, Patna

First published by Orient Blackswan Private Limited 2021

ISBN 978-93-5442-073-3

041767

Typeset in
Times New Roman 10.5/13 *by*
Le Studio Graphique, Gurugram 122 007

Printed in India at
Kensington Printing & Packaging, Noida 201 301

Published by
Orient Blackswan Private Limited
3-6-752 Himayatnagar, Hyderabad 500 029, Telangana, India
e-mail: info@orientblackswan.com

Contents

FOREWORD[1]

Pabitra Sarkar

I thank Honourable Vice Chancellor, University of Calcutta, the Head of the Department of Linguistics and President of the Session, my esteemed colleagues, distinguished and scholarly audience, other respected guests, and the organisers of this conference for the honour they have shown by inviting me to deliver this inaugural address. I am somewhat surprised at my selection for the role too, as I work mostly in Bangla, and have other engagements besides linguistics; and I might be distantly popular to most of those assembled here. With due humility, then, I proceed to present the following few observations to this audience.

Jubilees and centenaries are occasions for us to remember an event or a person who has contributed significantly to our intellectual and cultural history. The hundred and twenty-fifth year of Suniti Kumar Chatterji's birth has therefore presented us with an opportunity of not only just paying tributes to this stalwart but also appreciating him once again. It is more significantly an occasion to examine and evaluate the man and his works in the light of knowledge that has come to us later. This exercise will not overlook the historical and

[1] This foreword was delivered as an address at the two-day international seminar titled 'Revisiting Professor Suniti Kumar Chatterji as a Key to Feature of Indological Studies' on 26 November 2015, at University of Calcutta, West Bengal.

theoretical perspectives within which Chatterji worked, and the limitations in his achievements that may have been imposed by these. In spite of what we may say from a critical point of view, standing at a vantage point of further knowledge accumulated in the quickly changing field of linguistics, we must also acknowledge that he was a giant of a linguist, a monumental figure in the area, whose work can stand any close scrutiny and remain as impressive as ever. Secondly, this will also be an occasion for us to evaluate ourselves, our works, present and future, for which he has been a formidable role-model. One can easily be overwhelmed by his presence in the horizon and simply want to give up. But the better alternative will perhaps be to attempt, in spite of our own limitations, to work the way he did for linguistics and his other intellectual adventures—without mercy to himself. That is why we wait for such occasions to meet him face to face and seek guidance from him for what we may do in the area in which he was a great practitioner in India, nay, perhaps the world. This is, I hope, what we intend to do here.

This deliberation, in short, seeks to evaluate Chatterji's contribution to linguistics, in the specific context of the study of Indian languages, Bangla in particular. It also claims that the so-called 'paradigm shifts' do not and cannot drive important works done in the earlier traditions out of existence, and the latter's relevance continues beyond such shifts. A new paradigm does not always represent a better or a more perfect system, it may only be a shift in emphasis. Keeping the above points in mind, my attempt is to cover what Chatterji could and could not achieve.

As everyone knows, the 'Paradigm Shifts' à la Kuhn (1962) that from time to time occur in the world's intellectual history do not sweep everything incompatible with it out of its way, and therefore has a clean, paved road charted before it. Contending strands of thought recede in the background, but do not quite disappear. This I mention to keep things in proper perspective, as one finds overly enthusiastic terms like Copernican Revolution being tagged to what Chomsky did in linguistics by the middle of the last century. I don't know if Chomsky has objected to this in clear terms. But he has done it by implication. He has taken pains to emphasise the fact time and again that he has not cut loose his connection with traditional linguistics; he was, instead, very much a part of it. It was only descriptive linguistics of the American sort that he was out to reject. Copernicus, on the other hand, disproved and thereby discredited all the theories about the relationships of the earth and astronomical bodies current before him.

The Chomsky revolution follows the pattern set by Ferdinand de Saussure's prescription of the structural or synchronic study of language. His book put together, as everyone knows, was posthumously published in 1916. It was compiled from his notes and his lectures by his students, Charles Bally and Albert Sechehaye. But it did not seek to discredit, nor drive out of sight, what Saussure called the diachronic study of language. Significant studies of the diachronic nature continued being attempted, of which one of the best examples is Suniti Kumar Chatterji's University of London D.Litt. thesis (1921), 'The Origin and Development of the Bengali Language', ODBL for short, published in book form by the University of Calcutta in 1926 in two volumes.[2]

Suniti Kumar Chatterji's fame or reception stands on this book alone. His was a prismatic personality, emitting rays of light in many directions, as it absorbed light from many sources. I am tempted to say that to measure Chatterji's intellectual and expressive personality, one must take into account his works in Bengali as well—many of which, with serious critical studies on Tagore, hundreds of essays and lectures on diverse topics, cultural profiles of distant nations (which include countries like Ethiopia), travelogues, *belles letters* and all, show quite another aspect of his learning and erudition, and take him far beyond linguistics, to a broader area of culture. He was fond of quoting Terence's saying *Homi sum humani nil a mealienumputo*—that is, 'I am a man, and nothing human is alien to me'. One can, in this connection add that he had excellent skill in drawing, and the sketches he has left are proof of his ruminations that had his eyesight been stronger, he could have become a painter. He had an impressive presence in what is called the public sphere. He was the Chairman of

[2] Later he added a third volume, mainly of corrections and emendations, in the 1970 George Allen and Unwin edition (of the book).

the West Bengal Legislative Council for several years, President of the Sahitya Akademi and of International Phonetic Association, twice President of The Asiatic Society, Calcutta, and other such august organisations. He attended conferences all over the world, and was a member of the editorial board of the international journal *Phonetica*. As everyone knows, with his taste for good food (not 'healthy' food always though), including food that his and other's religions don't approve of, he was a gourmet and a glutton at the same time. Even the men who were instrumental behind, as well as results of, the arguably fragmented 'renaissance' of nineteenth century India, acquired and excelled in many skills. I will cite just one example. Rammohan Roy (1774–1883), for example, was an astute businessman and manager, a polyglot who translated copiously from Sanskrit, wrote and published in Persian, led the successful movement against the practice of *Suttee* or the custom of a Hindu widow being burned alive on her husband's funeral pyre, prevalent among the upper caste Hindus, and founded a new religion now known as Brahmoism. He was, in addition, also an expert singer and composer of north Indian classical music. Chatterji belonged to this tradition of the Bengal Renaissance, one of its later luminaries. The class of savants like Chatterji has become a rarity in our days of university-controlled, single discipline directed scholarship. Sukumari Bhattacharya's (1995) select list of his works will bear witness to that.[3] It contains twenty-four authored books in Bangla, thirty in English, six in which he collaborated with others. Books edited, singly or with others, are three in Bangla and four in English. And there are many articles that have not been presented in book form yet. While going over the list, one is astounded by the range of his interests and the volume of his writings, accomplished even with his feeble eyesight that plagued him right from his boyhood. He had an unending store of energy that has been reflected in the huge amount work he has done in English, Bangla and some other Indian languages. This energy was evident when one met him informally, undiminished even during his last years. He could speak for hours, and a survey of world languages

[3] Actually prepared by Subhendu Sekhar Mukhhopadhyay.

and culture—both longitudinal and latitudinal—would take place before the eyes of the spellbound listener. As we have already said, he was not merely a linguist; he was, in fact, a giant of an intellectual, with deep all-round human concerns. One has a feeling of one's own smallness, and one feels utterly intimidated, when one approaches this phenomenon, much larger than life.

He is of course known mostly as a linguist to the outside world, beyond the borders of the areas where Bangla is spoken. His magnum opus, ODBL, is one of the finest specimens of how the history of a language should be written. Others have followed his model, as he had followed the model of Jules Bloch's history of the Marathi language, but neither his own model, nor the works of his followers could match the massive range of his work. It looked as though he had already done much of the work for others, and they in fact are later found to begin their research taking Chatterji's homework on Indo-Aryan for granted.

Coming to the history of Bangla proper, one must say that at a time when published texts of the pre-modern stage of the language were not many, and dialects were not studied extensively, a book of some 1100 pages in fine print (we are told that he himself had made three hand-written copies of the dissertation for submission, as he was allowed to do so by the university authorities—he didn't have the money to have them typed), is definitely proof of his predilection for taking immense pains to achieve his objective. There was no short-cut for him, no cutting of corners. He would go all the way, whatever it may cost him in terms of physical efforts and intellectual diligence. As he says with humility in his preface, 'I have not stinted any labour'. One can see that he has not. It is not the size that confronts us so forcefully. It is the philosophy of doing everything possible and not sparing oneself any pains for what one has set out to do that we find hard to match.

It will be useless to give a graspable summary of the book. But a synopsis of sorts may be attempted. The 'Introduction' consists of 236 pages and briefly indicating the position of Bengali in the Indian linguistic milieu, he locates the non-Aryan group of languages that Bengali finds as its old neighbours, or languages of the substratum, then traces the former's evolution from the Indo-European to modern Bengali through a meticulous and pervasive survey of related languages and cultures along the way, marking the stages of evolution. In the course of that, Chatterji refutes Hoernle and Grierson's theory of 'Inner' and 'Outer' Aryan. At the same time, he relates Bengali to other Indo-Aryan speeches, marks the areas and features of four Bengali dialects [his student, Sukumar Sen (1939), added another to the number later], and those of the literary ones in addition. He then places five fully worked out appendices on vowel phonology of Indo-Aryan (A and B), on old place names (C), on classification of Bengali vocabulary—native and foreign and those in between (D), and finally on the sources of East Indian alphabets. The Introduction, to all intents and purpose, turns out to be a history of the NIA speeches of India.

The section on Bangla phonology, where he enters into the study of Bengali proper (while not stopping to refer to other Indian languages for comparison and supportive evidence), takes up the rest of the volume. He deals with both segments and supra-segments, and shows how both have evolved over the centuries. His 'Phonology' is diachronic in its approach, as could be expected. He begins with the changes through which the sounds of the OIA have undergone and traces the advent of sounds of Bengali. He discusses vowels, diphthongs and supra-segments from chapters I through IV, and then the consonants (chapter V). He uses the evolution of Bengali metres in order to trace the placement of Bengali stress and how stressed words and phrases are grouped, and his observation on the interrelationship of Bengali syllables and moraic patterns is illuminating.

His volume on morphology has five chapters. In it, he roughly distinguishes the derivational and the inflectional morphologies, and his discussion on formative affixes in chapter I belongs to the former. One is somewhat surprised by his omission of other processes of word formation in Bangla—compounding for example, or alternation of the stem vowels, of which a few examples exist. From chapter II, he moves right to the inflectional morphology of the language, and in this chapter, he discusses nominal declension, showing how the stems and various suffixes of gender and number came into being. In the same chapter, formation of cases is shown in great detail, where suffixes and postpositions get their due attention, as both—often together or alone—serve to form a case in the language. Chapter III treats Bangla numerals and their declensions. Chapter IV has Bangla pronominal forms as the main topic, and chapter V, the final one in the book, deals with the verb in Bangla and its numerous aspects—this is the largest chapter in the second volume and runs to 112 pages. The study of syntax was not thought important within his framework, hence there is no discussion of Bangla syntax here.

One should of course, add some of his other books that aid and reinforce the ODBL, as those which widen the linguistic map further. In the former category, we have his *Indo-Aryan and Hindi* (1940, second edition 1960), which however does not remain on track of building a history of Hindi, but goes out to investigate other areas like Indo-Hittite, Romanisation of Indian scripts etc. His book on Rajasthani (which I haven't been able to access), is probably the first historical treatment of the language, and his championing of Konkani as an independent language is well known. His work on Bengali phonetics drew praise from Leonard Bloomfield (see Hockett 1970: 178). This has finally taken shape as *A Brief Sketch of Bengali Phonetics* (1921), the first study of Bangla phonemes, following the Daniel Jones model.

I am, however, not going to repeat the list of his works, nor am I going to judge and evaluate each. I am hardly qualified for that. There may be, in fact there are, a few lapses or oversights even for a person like Chatterji, most of them due to the historical as well as intellectual framework within which he was working. Sarkar (2006: 93–107) has questioned some of his formulations as well as nomenclatures of rules given in the ODBL, but that can hardly make a dent in the greatness of the work. One can, in addition, even say that his plan and movement for Romanisation of Indian alphabet was not a realistic one, as traditional scripts arouse deep sociolinguistic emotions, and here science often has to submit to social forces (*see* Sarkar 1998: 128–38). His idea of a Bangla grammar has also been critically examined by Sarkar (2015). All these individual encounters with his work will go on, which he would have probably welcomed, had he been alive today. Any body of work is limited by the historical and theoretical perspective in which it is created, and new insights may arise later to mark some components as dated or falsifiable. We may therefore personally engage ourselves with some of his works, but such individual engagements, i.e. those of finding what is dated or incomplete or wrong in his work is not our objective here. I am not saying that this is not important for the progress of science, and I am sure many young scholars will continue the exercise. Had Chatterji been with us, he himself would have enjoyed the exercise most of all.

Dasgupta (2015) has shown another kind of engagement with Chatterji, that of either ignoring him or damning him with faint praise by some scholars with an American descriptive orientation. It is now widely, perhaps universally, agreed that Descriptivism of the American sort has been successfully demolished by Chomsky and his followers, as it has been proved that no description of a language is successful without referring to its history. One has to go beyond mere listing and classifying ('Items and arrangement') of items, and, instead of merely 'showing', one has to 'explain' forms that are there. The descriptivist's dependence on the 'performance' aspect of language has also been discredited. It can also be shown that without occasional referring back to history, most of the descriptive statement is either incomplete or simply wrong. As Dasgupta has shown, Chatterji was absolutely right in emphasising the point to the late Prabodh Pandit, who was probably a descriptivist with a vengeance. It is not, of course, unusual to be loyal to one's own schooling. It, however, doesn't hurt to keep one's mind open; Chatterji was one such person. That he was right in so many things, much more than the times he was wrong, is a kind of challenge that the young scholar today has the unenviable prospect of tackling.

Here we have assembled, instead, to have a communal engagement with him. By 'we', we do not mean linguists alone. We can marvel at how such an event, that of Chatterji, could happen, but that is not going to help us much. His life sketches do not shed much light on that. He came from an ordinary Brahmin family, somewhat indigent, as he had to study in a 'free school', Bengali medium at that, and there was no remarkable intellectual achievements recorded in any of his predecessors. He alone came out as an unusually bright boy, securing a high place in his matriculation (school leaving) examination.

If we want to reconstruct his developmental history step by step, I don't think we will succeed . But he is there, a figure like the Colossus of Rhodes, who invites us to approach him and understand how he grew, lived and worked. By us, again, I don't mean only linguists, nor do I mean only Indologists. He was a universal man in many ways, rising high above petty national, communal and social identities. And more often, his work crosses the boundaries of linguistics and Indology. It is the whole community of researchers scattered over linguistics and other disciplines of humanities, social sciences and even sciences, who can learn lessons from the works of this outstanding person. When we now see scholars narrowly pinned down to their own limited area of specialisation, no doubt prompted by the requirements of a teaching career dictated by the UGC or whichever agency that may rule his/ her country's higher education, we find that Chatterji's work is there to remind them that there are other areas of human knowledge—an exposure to which can have made his/ her research more meaningful. We can also tell the aspiring researcher that there are *ways* of doing a research, with a thoroughness and dedication, glimpses of which we can find in Chatterji's work. Also, research is not just going to the library or field, collecting material and writing a dissertation with accurate footnoting and an impressive bibliography, but it is something much more. It relates to the human existence in diverse ways. Chatterji had a broad human vision—that of appreciating others and other cultures, many of which had attracted his serious scholarly attention. He didn't limit himself to the study of more focussed and prominent Aryan world alone, as he also studied other, non-Aryan languages and cultures with equal love and respect. Himself a Brahmin, he was little prejudiced by the Brahmin orthodoxy in his academic interests. This broad outlook and vision is a serious need in India and other countries where plurality, whether in the academic or political, is being eroded.

I know that I have crossed the boundary of mere academia in saying this. But I am certain, that no serious encounter with Chatterji can ignore or avoid these deliberations.

Thank you. I wish the deliberations of this conference all success.

References

Bhattacharya, Sukumari. (1995). *Suniti Kumar Chattopadhyay*, 2nd edn. Kolkata: Paschimbanga Bangla Akademi (Bengali).

Chatterji, Suniti Kumar. (1926). *The Origin and Development of the Bengali Language*, volumes I and II. Calcutta: University of Calcutta.

Dasgupta, Probal. (2015). 'How Suniti Kumar Chatterji's legacy has been treated'. *Suniti Kumar Chatterji Revisited.* Kolkata: Gangchil and Kolkata Society for Asian Research, 66–94.

Hockett, Charles F. (ed.). (1970). *A Leonard Bloomfield Anthology*. Bloomington: Indiana University Press.

Kuhn, Thomas. (1962). *The Structure of Scientific Revolution*. Chicago: University of Chicago.

Sarkar, Pabitra. (1998). *Bhasha Desh Kal*, 2nd edn. Calcutta: Mitra & Ghosh Publishers Private Limited (Bengali).

____ (2006). *Bangla Byakaran Prasanga*. Kolkata: Dey's Publishing (Bengali).

____ (2015). 'Suniti Kumar Chatterji and Bangla Grammar'. Unpublished lecture delivered at Kolkata Society for Asiatic Research.

Sen, Sukumar. (1939). *Bhashar Itibritta*. Calcutta: Bardhaman Sahitya Sabha (Bengali).

Introduction

Suniti Kumar Chatterji (26 November 1890–29 May 1977) was a unique multifaceted personality whom the linguistic world reckons as the doyen of Indian linguistics; to the social scientists he is an eminent 'Culture Scientist', to a wider circle of people he is known as the National Professor, and also the Bhāṣāchārya—a title bestowed upon him by Rabindranath Tagore. His profound erudition, humanistic outlook, versatile knowledge, scientific insight, holistic approach and artistic sense made him 'a unique personality in the academic domain of the mid-twentieth century—a true ambassador of Indian scholarship and culture' (Sen 1980: 28).

Chatterji contributed plenteously to various fields of knowledge. Krishnamurti (1997: 7) provides a concise account of the quantity and diverse nature of his life-long contributions in print.

> SKC, during his over 60 years of active academic life, produced nearly 930 publications, written in four languages—English, Bengali, Hindi and Sanskrit. These include 41 books, 413 articles, 10 reviews and 321 miscellaneous items and short communications. He had five publications (excluding reviews and brief communication) on Indo-European, 32 on historical linguistics (Indo-European/Indo-Aryan), 93 on anthropological and ethnological themes, 10 on general linguistics, 51 on language problems and planning with special reference to India, 16 on philological studies, 19 on phonetics and phonology, 16 on morphology and grammatical topics, 15 on Hindi and Urdu,

> 55 on topics of literature with special reference to India, 10 on travel, 22 on art, and 102 on miscellaneous topics.

The expanse as well as the manifold aspects of diverse knowledge sectors present in the list appositely implies that it is quite impossible to do an apt evaluation of his huge contribution by a single person. The very task demands for intervention of experts from various fields of study. Krishnamurti's observation (1997: 7)—'The impact of his numerous writings on different fields of scholarship is yet to be assessed'—is pertinent even today. However, the value of his contributions may, to a degree, be understood from the various honours and recognitions bestowed upon him both nationally and internationally from time to time. To mention a few, at the national level, Chatterji was appointed National Professor of India for Research in the Humanities (1964), was awarded Padma Bhushan (1955) and Padma Vibhushan (1963), and also Deshikottama degree from Visva-Bharati (1966). He was conferred D.Litt. degree, Honoris Causa by the University of Delhi (1965), the Rabindra Bharati University, Calcutta (1968), Osmania University, Hyderabad (1968), and the University of Calcutta (1969). He was elected President of Sahitya Akademi (1969) and Asiatic Society (for two terms—1953 and 1970). He joined the West Bengal Legislative Council as an independent candidate from the West Bengal Graduates' Constituency and was elected the chairman thrice (1952, 1962 and 1965). Internationally, Chatterji was elected Honorary Member of the Asiatic Society of Paris (1946), American Oriental Society (1947), École Francaise de L'extreme-Orient, Hanoi, Vietnam (1949), Norwegian Academy of Sciences, Oslo (1954), Siam Society, Bangkok (1957), Linguistic Society of America, New York (1958), Italian Institute for the Near and Far East, Rome (1961), Permanent International Council of Phonetic Sciences, Helsinki, Finland (1961), University of Ceylon Linguistic Society (1963), and he was elected President of the International Phonetic Association, London (1969) . He was invited by the UNESCO to participate in the International Committee on the Braille Alphabet in Paris (1950) and in Beirut (1951), by the Soviet Academy of Sciences to visit Russia (1958), by Rome University to visit Rome (1961), by the Iran Government to the World Congress of Iranologists, Tehran (1966) and by the Asiatic Society, Bangladesh

(1972). He visited Kathmandu on special invitation of the king of Nepal (1963). As the representative of the Government of India, he attended the International Congress of Orientalists, Cambridge (1954), the Congress of Bahasa Indonesia, Medan, North Sumatra (1954), and the Commonwealth Parliamentary Conference, Canberra (1959). He was awarded Doctorate of Letters, Honoris Causa, by Rome University (1961) and a gold medal by Czechoslovakian Association for friendship with foreign countries (1967). A chronicle of Suniti Kumar Chatterji's life is available in Bhattacharya (2015). Needless to say that in all these visits and many more he delivered erudite talks on diverse pertinent topics.

The phrase 'many more' indicates to his travel list that includes numerous local, national and international tours, academic and otherwise. He was truly an avid traveller and explorer. His tours always went beyond the narrow boundaries of academia, as in all of his tours he keenly noticed and absorbed every detail of human life, society, culture, economy, politics and philosophy of the land and depicted them in his travelogues. This power of observation was one of the chief factors that made him a true culture scientist. The international travel list of Chatterji includes many countries all over the world—England, Austria, Hungary, Czechoslovakia, Germany, France, Greece, Belgium, Italy, Holland, Poland, Norway, Sweden, Finland, Bucharest, Dublin, Copenhagen, Riga, Russia, Turkey, Tashkent, Burma, Indonesia, Siam, Sumatra, China, Mongolia, Vietnam, Iran, Japan, Philippines, Jamaica, Mexico, New York, Michigan, Pennsylvania, Washington, Hawaii, Columbia, Egypt, Addis Ababa and Canberra to name a few. Within India too, he travelled extensively observing keenly the multidimensional faces of the land and its life. His travel list itself speaks for his wide-ranging first-hand exposure to various cultures that contributed directly to his development as a balanced culture scientist.

Expectedly, Chatterji as a person and as an academician have been the subject matter of numerous deliberations both in print and oral mode and in English and Bangla [cf. Kanjilal et al. 1970, Sen 1980, Mitra (ed.) 1985/2009, Bhattacharya 1989/1995, Singh and Padikkal (eds) 1997, Bhattacharya 2005, 2015, Dasgupta 2015, and Chattopadhyay 2017.]

The many facets of Chatterji as a scholarly human being and his pioneering contributions have already been highlighted in the volumes and articles mentioned above. Hence to pay homage to him on his one hundred and twenty-fifth birth anniversary we decided not to dwell on the areas already taken care of but to focus on significance of his work in contemporary linguistics and culture studies and on some current developments in linguistics. The Department of Linguistics, University of Calcutta, in 2015, organised an international seminar in two parts—first on 26–27 November and second on 22 December 2015. Some of the articles included in this volume were presented as papers in this seminar.

In this volume, we bring together eleven articles—including the foreword—not only enumerating Suniti Kumar Chatterji as a thinker and complementing his work but also articles on new developments in linguistics. Five of the articles requested for and received in the current volume are based on presentations made in the above-mentioned seminar, while the other six are collected from renowned scholars all over the world. The articles are grouped together in three sections based on three broad themes of the book. The foreword and first section of the book is devoted to contextualise Chatterji's contribution in the modern linguistic scenario. Here, we have three papers concentrating on re-evaluation of the great tradition set by Chatterji in the field of linguistics. The two other sections deal with diverse topics on language and culture. The second section tries to draw on Chatterji's legacy as a Cultural Scientist and explores various pertinent issues of language and culture of South Asia. The third section consists of studies dealing with different modern issues in Linguistics. A detailed description of the segments with brief summary of the chapters is given below.

The foreword 'Suniti Kumar Chatterji: The Contemporary Relevance of His Work' authored by Pabitra Sarkar was originally delivered as the inaugural address in the seminar. The essay primarily evaluates Chatterji's contribution to linguistics with special attention to the study of Indian languages (Bangla, in particular) and in the course of discussion fortifies the central claim of the paper, viz. the so-called 'paradigm shifts' in the field of linguistics do not and cannot drive important works done in the earlier traditions out of existence, and the latter's relevance continues beyond such shifts. Chatterji was a practitioner in the diachronic tradition of linguistics of the nineteenth century. Nevertheless, till date his colossal contributions survived the strong waves of the synchronic era and even the 'Chomskyan revolution'. The deliberation portrays Chatterji as a great intellectual figure as well as a Renaissance personality, both of which are reflected through the range and depth of his writings on various diverse topics. In conclusion, Sarkar draws our attention to Chatterji's biography and compares him to the figure like the Colossus of Rhodes who invites us to approach and understand him as he grew, lived and worked.

As mentioned earlier, the first section titled 'Reinstating Suniti Kumar Chatterji's Legacy in Contemporary Linguisties' is an appreciation of the academic contribution of Chatterji (in Linguistics in particular) and their relevance in contemporary academic scenario. This section aptly demonstrates Chatterji as an outstanding linguist whose significance thrives through the many metamorphosis in the field.

The first chapter 'Suniti Kumar and Rabindranath: Bangla Linguistics' by Krishna Bhattacharya is also based on a paper presented in the seminar. The paper chiefly dwells on the close and reciprocal relationship between Suniti Kumar Chatterji and Rabindranath Tagore, especially in connection to Bangla Linguistics. According to the author 'Rabindranath over-powered the mind of Chatterji with his uniqueness as a "Complete and Integrated Man, with a Mind of the widest perception" (Chatterji, 1961: 120) and as "one of the first successful investigators who sought to throw light on the character and the history of the Bengali language"' (ibid., 124). In the preface to his magnum opus *The Origin and Development of the Bengali Language* (ODBL) Chatterji acknowledges Tagore's original contributions to Bangla Linguistics. To come in contact with Rabindranath, an amazing personality with a life of a sage, was an inspiration, blessing and honour for Chatterji. Rabindranath too had great appreciation for Chatterji as an unparalleled linguist and valued his power of observation, analytical potentiality and fine eye for detail in language. Rabindranath himself read ODBL meticulously and wrote margin notes on its several pages. Moreover, with great admiration, he has immortalised the author and his creation in his novel *Shesher Kabita* ('The Last Poem'), where the protagonist was seen spending his vacation by reading Chatterji's ODBL.

The second chapter, 'Recuperating Suniti Kumar Chatterji's Opposition to the Structuralist Legacy' by Probal Dasgupta was delivered as the keynote address of the seminar, and is a contemporary appraisal of Chatterji's contribution in establishing priority of diachronic linguistics over different manifestations of synchronic linguistics. The paper points, on the one hand, to the fact that Chatterji was one of the few Indian linguists to resist structuralism with actual arguments, and on the other, identifies substantivism as an apt tool of study after the diachronic tradition to which Suniti Kumar Chatterji contributed abundantly both in quality and quantity. Structural linguistics with its generative, sociolinguistics and other successors share history-denying assumptions, while history denial is nearly as risky an enterprise as climate change denial. The paper reveals the limitations of the structuralist framework using a body of straightforward empirical evidence and also accuses structuralism of being detrimental to linguistic democracy, and side by side portrays subtantivism as the site of systematic resistance to structuralism. The author takes up the relation between the lexical parameters of Lalon Fakir's songs and the way the standard Bangla lexis has developed, with special reference to the question of defaults and corroborates the fact that while the structuralist view of a language L accords primacy to L's default items—an act that reflects dominations and hegemonies—the substantivist view interrogates the doctrine of default encoding itself, indicating that there are competing candidates equally qualified to gain the status of default within the same linguistic tradition. The author also touches upon the issue of pedagogy, which is for all time a negotiation and indicates that substantivism helps us to see that in the course of pedagogy, the learners and the teachers with them, evolve through successive settings; they do not get attached to any permanent defaults.

The second section titled 'Languages and Cultures of South Asia' broadens the focus from pure linguistics to encompass issues of culture, race and power-politics. The four articles in this section dwell on such issues relating to what may be called the Indian Subcontinent.

The third chapter, 'Exploring Odia Culture: A Study of Some Cultural Narratives in Odia' by B.N. Patnaik, throws light on some aspects of Odia culture based on a few minor cultural narratives in Odia tradition, viz. minor Puranic compositions and oral tales. Chatterji in his book *The People, Language and Culture of Orissa* (1966) illustrated an aesthetic dimension and a spiritual dimension of Odia culture represented by the best of medieval literature, the great temples and caves, and other artistic achievements like its sublime music and dance on the one hand, and on the other, the tradition of Jagannath Temple that totally rejects caste and caste-based pollution, all of which denote the most spectacular and most highly celebrated aspect with respect to Odisha. Contrary to this, the present paper aims to construct meaningful insights of cultural values and practices through a careful study of minor as well as neglected things like wise-sayings, naming system, idioms, proverbs, riddles, jokes, tongue-twisters and tales of the supernatural among others. The paper offers an analysis of less-studied cultural texts, written and oral, and a certain religious-cultural practice associated with the partaking of *mahāprasāda* and touches upon the issues like the inclusive nature and changing and disappearing traits of Odia cultural practices. The author concludes by addressing the issue of endangerment of culture and its preservation. The findings of the present paper reinforce and complement Chatterji's observations.

The fourth chapter 'Language, Violence and Power' by Tariq Rahman points to language as a power-tool, which brings in gratification, but when obtaining gratifications confronts curtailment, it yields violence. Chatterji, in his writings time and again, pointed to power, politics, violence and linguistic domination extant in human societies by drawing our attention to the downtrodden social creatures and features. In his book *Africanism: The African Personality* Chatterji (1960: 17) notes, 'It is the Black Africa which has been maltreated and ruthlessly exploited by the white peoples, of Europe and of Africa itself, and which is now crying for her right'; in *Indo-Aryan and Hindi*, he with great impartiality underscores the unpreventable appearance of the dominated non-Aryan traits in the dominating Aryan tongue and culture—'It is now becoming more and more clear that the non-Aryan contributed by far the greater portion in the fabric of Indian civilization...it was the Aryan's speech that became the dominant factor, although non-Aryan elements made very large inroads into its purity' (Chatterji 1969: 34). Based on current theories of linguistics, Rahman presents a fine elaboration on language as a power-tool and shows how it works in the linguistic scenario of Pakistan. The deliberation illustrates how, through its various uses, language relates to power and engenders violence. By conveying meaning language constructs systems of ideas and creates discourses, both of which are exploited as self-licensing tools to dominate and colonise others—humans as well as nature. Language also acts as a marker of identity. Based on the various aspects of language use we construct our social reality, which is largely hierarchical, where a few on the top exercise their power on others to remain in power and those who by means of language-based tools such as myths, ideologies, discourses, etc. are made to believe that they are inferior, receive violence. The chapter argues that the ability to manipulate the written word sanctions one power to run social institutions, while at the other extreme, there exist those who are the recipients of violence, who are taught to know their place, i.e. working classes, slaves, women, who are trained to accept patriarchy, and so on.

The fifth chapter 'Origin of Sinhala and Kālinga-Lanka Linguistic Affinities' by Sandagomi Coperahewa complements the observations of Chatterji on Sinhalese. Chatterji in the Introduction to ODBL, following Grierson, in the table illustrating development of the Aryan speech in India groups Sinhalese under the Praticya dialects (Gujarat etc.) of South-West with a question mark. In the text, Chatterji (1985: 15, point 18) states 'the first immigrants who carried the Indo-Aryan speech to Ceylon seem to have been from the Western India coast...Later, from the 3rd century BC downwards, Ceylon seems to have come in touch with Magadha, through Bengal, and traditions of intimate relations between Bengal and Ceylon are preserved in medieval Bengali literature...Sinhalese, by virtue of its position, has developed along its own lines, unlike the Indo-Aryan speeches of the mainland...'. Accepting Sinhala (Sinhalese in English) as a member of the Indo-Aryan family the current paper draws attention to (i) one of the lesser known aspects of Kālinga-Lanka relationship, the linguistic affinities between Sinhala and Kālinga, ancient Odisha,

(ii) the special position of Sinhala among the languages of South Asia because of its close affinities with two of the major linguistic families of the Indian Subcontinent, viz. Indo-Aryan and Dravidian, and (iii) the much debated Western and Eastern hypothesis regarding the origin of Sinhala. Taking into account the historical tradition and linguistic evidence the author comes to the conclusion that because of its origin from two different sources and also because of many streams of immigrants with their respective tongues from different parts of India affecting the language of the island, Sinhala exhibits a composite linguistic character.

The sixth chapter, 'Two Less-studied Chapters of Indology: Kirāta jana and Āhira jana' by Suniti Kumar Pathak rightly and timely invites attention to the synthetic nature of Indian culture, and to the factual essence of Indianism. The indologist in Chatterji in a number of studies, *Kirāta-jana-kṛiti, The Indo-Mongoloids: Their Contribution to the History and Culture of India* (1951/1974), *Bāngālā Bhāṣā-prasaṅge* (1975/1989) to mention a few, often indicated to the synthetic character of the Sanskrit language and Sanskrit/Indian culture. Chatterji (1974: 4) notes—'Sanskrit in its origin is an Indo-Aryan language...but...on the soil of India, the Non-Aryan peoples had a share in its development—in determining its tendencies and its history, helping to change its phonetics and its grammar and to modify and add to its vocabulary. It was thus a joint product of both Aryan and non-Aryan, so that it could become by 500 BC the most natural vehicle of a composite Indian-Aryan-cum-non-Aryan-culture.' Chatterji (1974: 4) also states—'Indian culture is, in fact, Sanskrit culture, or Sanskritic culture. It is expressed either through Sanskrit directly; or through Modern Indian languages of Aryan, Dravidian, Austric or Sino-Tibetan origin; or even through a highly Persianized Sanskritic language like Urdu, the Muslim form of Hindi, which may outwardly or formally ignore Sanskrit and the Sanskritic heritage.' Complementing Chatterji's view, this deliberation elaborates on the features of Indology and highlights the roles played by the two races, viz. Kirāta jana and Āhira jana, and underscores the following message—'Contributions of the above two groups among the Indian nationals today in developing unitary Indianism are to be reckoned thoroughly for developing "nationalism" of the peoples of India.'

The third section 'Essays in Modern Linguistics' presents some current approaches to study languages in different fields of Linguistics.

The seventh chapter, 'A Comparative Note on the Bangla Particle *to* and the German Particle *doch*' by Josef Bayer, highlights points of convergence between the two very distant Indo-European languages, viz. Bangla and German, with respect to the particles *to* and *doch* respectively, along with a series of concrete test cases. The paper explores the etymologies of the two particles, a dichotomy of autonomy and boundedness that can be found in *to* but not in *doch*, the semantic core of the particles, the shared properties in regard to information structure, the restrictions with respect to sentence mood, and a common core in their distribution in complex clauses. As regards convergence, among others, both *to* and *doch* display similarities in their usage—the Bangla *to* is found in different places in a sentence, it is a functional head; the German particle *doch* is also a functional element on par with negation and other grammatical elements, but it is not a clitic. Regarding the sentence mood, Bangla *to* and German *doch* attend to the same core restrictions. Both appear in declarative and imperative clauses, and they are strictly impossible in questions. The paper concludes with the suggestion that the convergence may be due to linguistic universality or to large-scale parametric properties, or may be, interestingly enough, due to the fact that the two elements under discussion emerged from a common Indo-European ancestral language.

The next chapter, 'Splitting and Recombining Abstract Lexical Levels in Contact Phenomena' by Carol Myers-Scotton is about the mechanism involved in across language re-structuring of lexical items. This paper puts forth the possibility of splitting abstract levels of lexical features from one language and combining them with the levels in another language. It deals with the words that have been re-structured in some way, and not just borrowed. The mechanism proposed is a feature of the Abstract Level Model, a model that identifies three levels of abstract lexical structure that underlie all linguistic elements, viz. lexical-conceptual structure, predicate-argument structure, and morphological realisation patterns. Examples are drawn from creole development and conversational codeswitching that yield such hybrid forms to illustrate the claim of the paper. In creoles, content morphemes from the lexifier language can be reanalysed to serve as grammatical elements and be combined with syntactic features from the substrate language. While in codeswitching, nonfinite verb forms from one language undergo reanalysis in some other language pairs so that they can appear with finite language inflections from the participating language, which is called the Matrix Language under the Matrix Language Frame Model.

The next chapter, 'Translation Theory as an Ever-Emerging Phenomena' by Udaya Narayana Singh deals with the indeterminate nature of meaning in relation to the domain of translation theory and thus fortifies the Theory of Indeterminacy to understand the complex act of translation. Starting with the Saussurian concept of the meaning of linguistic signs as a stable entity 'which does not change arbitrarily, or at a given individual's whim' the paper comments on the postmodern perception of it, i.e. sign is an unstable and fractured entity which can never capture the 'full' meaning of words. In the course of deliberation it brings in the views of various authors and philosophers like Derrida, Condillac, Orman Quine, Pym and Gayatri Chakravorty Spivak among others regarding the various aspects of written texts and their translation. The author also submits his views on the limitation of applicability of the theory of Iterability to literary texts that need to be translated. Focussing on translational challenges like handling of polysemy or contextually driven interpretations, expressions carrying unseen individual values, finding equivalences etc., all of which yield multiple interpretations of the same text, the author argues that a determinist position may be a quite disadvantageous one for the translation specialists.

The final chapter, 'Bengali Postlexical Rules: Lengthening and Shortening' by Aditi Lahiri deals with a few very productive phonological processes of Standard Colloquial Bengali. The author picks up some threads of phonology from Suniti Kumar Chatterji's *The Origin and Development of the Bengali Language*, the seminal study done in the diachronic tradition, and accounts for them in terms of the current tools of phonology such as the phonological feature system developed under the Featurally Underspecification Lexicon framework. The chapter highlights a few segmental processes that affect both features as well as quantity of vowels, viz. lengthening and nasalisation, and also of consonants, viz. gemination, degemination and deaspiration, and draws attention to their prosody governed identity with ample examples and meticulous explanation.

We acknowledge the debt of many people, without whose active contribution, it would not have been possible to bring together this volume. The idea for this volume came from the Seminar to commemorate the one hundred and twenty-fifth birth anniversary of Suniti Kumar Chatterji. A note of thanks is due to the members of the faculty, Department of Linguistics, along with the student volunteers and office staff who worked incessantly for days to organise the seminar. We acknowledge with thanks the comments and suggestions made by Professor Krishna Bhattacharya, Professor Saswati Mutsuddy, Professor Abhijit Majumdar, Professor Mau Dasgupta and Professor Aishwarya Biswas in the editing process. We are grateful to Rajeshwari Dutta, Aliya Halim and Madhura Sen for actively helping us in the making of this volume. Last but not the least, we would like to offer special thanks to Orient BlackSwan for publishing this book.

Chatterji's association with the Department of Linguistics (then Department of Comparative Philology), University of Calcutta, was long and rich. During this period, he taught in many other departments, produced many of his remarkable works, edited journals and actively participated in different pursuits of the department. With this volume of essays we are honoured to pay tribute to the great scholar in our humble way.

Editors

References

Bhattacharya, Krishna. (2005). *Suniti Kumar Chattopapadhyay*. Kolkata: Bangiya Saitya Parishad.

____ (2015). 'Suniti Kumar Chatterji as a linguist: His contribution and vision'. *Suniti Kumar Chatterji Revisited*. Kolkata: Gangchil and Kolkata Society for Asian Studies.

Bhattacharya, Sukumari. (1989/1995). *Suniti Kumar Chattopadhyay*. Kolkata: Paschimbanga Bangla Akademi.

Chatterji, Suniti Kumar. (1960). *Africanism: The African Personality*. Calcutta: Bengal Publishers Private Ltd.

____ (1961). 'Viśva-Manah Vāk-Pati'. *Rabindranath Tagore, A Centenary Volume 1861–1961*. New Delhi: Sahitya Akademi (5th printing), 120–26.

____ (1966). *The People, Language, and Culture of Orissa*. Bhubaneswar: Odisha Sahitya Akademi.

____ (1969). *Indo-Aryan and Hindi*. Calcutta: Firma K.L. Mukhopadhyay (First published by Pooran Press, Calcutta, in 1942).

____ (1974). *Kirāta-jana-kṛiti, The Indo-Mongoloids: Their contribution to the History and Culture of India*. Calcutta: The Asiatic Society (First published by The Royal Asiatic Society of Bengal, Calcutta, in 1951).

____ (1975/1989). *Bāngālā Bhāṣā-prasaṅge*. Calcutta: Jijnasa.

____ (1985). *The Origin and Development of the Bengali Language*. Calcutta: Rupa & Co (First published by the Calcutta University Press, in 1926).

Chattopadhyay, Lily. (2017). *Suniti Kumar Chatterji: The Journey of a Linguist*. Medinipur: Kabitika.

Kanjilal, Anil et al. (eds). (1970). *Suniti Kumar Chatterji—The Scholar and the Man*. Calcutta: Jijnasa.

Krishnamurti, Bh. (1997). 'Professor Suniti Kumar Chatterji: A centenary tribute'. In Udaya Narayana Singh and Shivarama Padikkal (eds), *Suniti Kumar Chatterji—A Centenary Tribute*. New Delhi: Sahitya Akademi, 7–12.

Mitra, Pallab (ed.). (1985/2009). *Samasāmayik Dṛṣṭite Suniti Kumar*. Kolkata: Parul.

Sen, Sukumar. (1980). *Suniti Kumar Chatterji—Scholar and Virtuoso*. New Delhi: Sahitya Akademi.

Singh, Udaya Narayana, and Shivarama Padikkal (eds). (1997). *Suniti Kumar Chatterji—A Centenary Tribute*. New Delhi: Sahitya Akademi.

PART I

Reinstating Suniti Kumar Chatterji's Legacy in Contemporary Linguistics

1

Suniti Kumar and Rabindranath

Bangla Linguistics

Krishna Bhattacharya

Abstract

Rabindranath Tagore overpowered the mind of Suniti Kumar Chatterji with his uniqueness as a 'Complete and Integrated Man, with a Mind of the widest perception' and as 'one of the first successful investigators who sought to throw light on the character and the history of the Bengali language.' Suniti Kumar considered himself blessed and honoured as he could come in touch with Tagore's artistic genius and great personality and also as he could obtain some experience from the sayings and life of a sage like Tagore.

Suniti Kumar admits that when he was a postgraduate student, the linguistic study of English was preparing him for a study of the history of his own mother tongue, Bengali, and of the sister Indo-Aryan languages of India. 'I was eager to get guidance in this matter; wherever I could receive it from—I discovered that Rabindranath himself, in his some remarkable essays (later collected and published as a book, *Śabdatattwa*), had made some very pertinent suggestions about the nature of the Bengali language in some of its salient characteristics.' Afterwards in the preface of *The Origin and Development of the Bengali Language* (ODBL), his magnum opus, Suniti Kumar acknowledges Rabindranath's original contributions to Bangla linguistics.

On the other hand Rabindranath also had great admiration for Suniti Kumar. He has celebrated the latter's work by the way in which Amit Ray, the protagonist of Rabindranath's novel *Shesher Kabita* ('The Last Poem/Farewell Song') used to spend his vacation by reading the ODBL. Rabindranath himself had read the ODBL meticulously and had written margin-notes on its many pages. The present paper aims at focussing on the relation between Suniti Kumar and Rabindranath in connection with Bangla linguistics.

INTRODUCTION

Suniti Kumar Chatterji and Rabindranath Tagore were two luminaries in the field of Bangla linguistics. A genius as well as the greatest writer-poet in Bangla—Rabindranath was self-trained and had the insight to visualise the character of the Bangla language. And Suniti Kumar was a brilliant student and a scholar of rare qualities with versatile interests, for whom Sukumar Sen has used the epithet 'scholar and virtuoso'. As a linguist, Suniti Kumar had the knowledge of the Indian grammatical tradition, its concepts and methods. After his stay in Europe, during 1919–1922, at the Universities of London and Paris, he became acquainted in the 'western methods of philological-historical investigation'.

From the writings of Suniti Kumar, it is known that Rabindranath overpowered the mind of Suniti Kumar with his uniqueness as a 'Complete and Integrated Man, with a Mind of the widest perception'(Chatterji 1961: 120) and as 'one of the first successful investigators who sought to throw light on the character and the history of the Bengali language'(ibid.: 124). In a letter (dated 29 December, 1976) to Professor Jailal Koul, Suniti Kumar writes 'I am an agnostic with imagination—being a follower of Tagore' (Chattopadhyay 1979: 86). Now questions can be raised whether Rabindranath was agnostic or not, but after his lifelong self-analysis, Suniti Kumar's submission was that he was a follower of Rabindranath. He considered himself blessed, satisfied and honoured throughout his life as he could come in touch with Rabindranath's great artistic genius and splendid personality and also as he could obtain his affection, blessings and some experience of the sayings and life of a sage like Rabindranath (Chattopadhyay 1979: 86).

It is known that Suniti Kumar had the opportunity to come in close contact with Rabindranath for a long period, for some thirty years. As a result of this long association he gained the confidence of Rabindranath—not only as a linguist, but also as a trustworthy person. Rabindranath asked Suniti Kumar to take part in different administrative works of Visva-Bharati. Rabindranath appreciated Suniti Kumar not only as an unparalleled linguist he also noticed and highly valued his power of observation, perception of phenomena around him, his power of analysis as well as description of the details and his expertise in language as a litterateur. It is not possible to describe all these aspects of Suniti Kumar's personality with the obvious limitation of space and time. So with a view to concentrate on a particular aspect of his personality, the aim of the present work is to focus on Bangla linguistics as was dealt with by them and their mutual appreciation for each other.

The History of their Acquaintance

In his unfinished autobiography titled *Jiban Katha*, Suniti Kumar writes (Chattopadhyay 1979: 61) that at the age of fourteen when he was a school boy, he was introduced to the poems of Rabindranath. Later he got the opportunity to see Rabindranath in person afar in some meetings in connection with the nationalist movements, particularly the movement against the partition of Bengal (op. cit.: 87). In an unpublished article in English titled 'Rabindranath Tagore: What I received from him—what he gave to India—how he served humanity' (op. cit.: 87–88), Suniti Kumar states, 'I had never any occasion to exchange any word with him [Rabindranath] before, I believe, the year 1911. At that time I was a student of the

MA class, preparing for my MA Degree Examination in English Language and Literature, with a lot of Old and Middle English and Germanic linguistics as my special subjects. This linguistic study of English was preparing my mind for a study of the history of my own mother tongue, Bengali, and of the sister Aryan languages of India. I was eager to get guidance in this matter wherever I could receive it from. Naturally, whatever was written in Bengali and in English, I read as and when I could lay my hands on it, and I discovered that Rabindranath himself, in some of his remarkable essays, had made some very pertinent suggestions about the nature of the Bengali language in some of its salient characteristics'(ibid.). At that time Rabindranath was in Bolpur and was busy running his school of Santiniketan. Suniti Kumar went to Santiniketan to meet Rabindranath. After getting a very cordial reception he discussed with Rabindranath about his interest in linguistics and became surprised to know how Rabindranath himself was interested in the subject. While visiting the library of the school Suniti Kumar discovered some more evidences of Rabindranath's interest in the subject. He found that Rabindranath had read carefully the English translation in four (five?) volumes of Karl Brugmann's *Elements of the Comparative Grammar of the Indo-Germanic Languages*. He also noticed the occasional notes and markings in pencil in Rabindranath's own hand on the pages of the book. Suniti Kumar himself admits that it was a very heavy book to read and at the same time he wondered to find Rabindranath's single-minded devotion to scholarship. Rabindranath also critiqued the *Grammar of the Bengali Language: Literary and Colloquial* (Oxford Oriental Series) by John Beames who is known as the father of modern Indo-Aryan linguistics for his seminal book *The Comparative Grammar of the Modern Indo-Aryan Languages*. Gradually, Suniti Kumar became a close associate of Rabindranath. From a letter written by Rabindranath from Santiniketan in the July of 1918 to Pramatha Choudhury, it is known that he gave Suniti Kumar a recommendation letter certifying him as an uncommonly competent scholar. He was also invited to attend the symposiums of 'Vicitra' established by Rabindranath at his house in Calcutta. Thus he had attended many lectures and readings which Tagore held here

(Sen 1980: 13). Suniti Kumar accompanied Rabindranath on his tour to Indonesia and Thailand. After which, Suniti Kumar's relation with Rabindranath deepened. Thus in course of time Rabindranath began to depend on his decisions in many matters like Bangla spelling, designing of new letters for Bangla script etc. From *Rabijībanī* ('Life of Tagore') by Prashanta Kumar Paul and *Rabindra-Patrābali* ('Letters by Tagore') edited by Gaur Chandra Saha it is known that in the course, Rabindranath also started to ask him to take part in different administrative works of Visva-Bharati. Rabindranath wrote six letters to Suniti Kumar on different matters and there are seventeen letters by Rabindranath where Suniti Kumar is referred to in various contexts. After the publication of *The Origin and Development of the Bengali Language* in 1926 Rabindranath became a great admirer of Suniti Kumar. From 1927 onwards their relation became very close as is known from different letters and writings.

In this connection we can refer to the deliberation between Rabindranath and Suniti Kumar regarding the Bangla synonym of the English word 'culture'. Suniti Kumar (Chattopadhyay 1976: 15–16) mentions that though the word *kṛṣṭi* was in use at that time as a synonym of the English word 'culture', but Rabindranath did not like this word as in the Vedas this word was used in the sense of 'tribe' or 'people' though he used this word several times in his dance drama called *Taser Desh* ('Land of Cards') but in a negative way. Suniti Kumar further says that in 1922 he first noticed the usage of the word *saṃskṛti* in Marathi as a synonym of the English word 'culture'. It also came to his knowledge that this word occurs in Brahmana literature. There *saṃskṛti* means that by which something becomes refined or polished or improved. Incidentally, Suniti Kumar was informed by Durgacharan Chattopadhyay, one of his former students, that in Buddhist Sanskrit the word *kṛṣṭi* had been used in the sense of 'civilisation' or 'culture' and the word *utkarṣa* derived from the same root was used in Sanskrit in the sense of 'development'. Anyway, as Rabindranath approved the word *saṃskṛti* instead of *kṛṣṭi*, this word was unanimously accepted and started to be used regularly.

Grammarians' Attitude towards Bangla Language

The period under discussion is that of the last part of the nineteenth century and the first two to three decades of the twentieth century. Some Bengali intellectuals who paid attention to the nature of Bangla language and forwarded some valuable observations are Rammohan Roy [grammar (English in 1826; Bengali in 1833)], Shyamacharan Sarkar [grammar (English in 1850; Bengali in 1852)], Shyamacharan Gangopadhyay [an essay on Bengali, Spoken and Written (1877 in *Calcutta Review*)], Chintamani Ganguli [grammar (1881, in Bengali)], Nakuleshwar Vidyabhushan [grammar (1898, in Bengali)] and Hrishikesa Shastri [grammar (1900, in Bengali)]. This is not the place for a long discussion on their observations on Bangla; but mention must be made of two great intellectuals, Haraprasad Shastri (1853–1931) and Ramendrasundar Trivedi (1864–1919) who were contemporaries of Rabindranath. As Suniti Kumar says (Chatterji 1961: 124) they wanted to introduce a rational approach to the study of the Bangla language. Haraprasad Shastri was quite conscious about the different nature of Bangla as a language though it developed from Sanskrit in an extended sense. He clearly stated that Bangla grammar should be prepared on the basis of its own individual characteristics, not following either the Sanskrit model or the English model.

Haraprasad Shastri's essay, 'Bangla Vyakaran' read in the meeting of Bangiya Sahitya Parishat in 1907 made a huge impact on the Bangla scholars of that time. Ramendrasundar was also interested in studying the internal nature of Bangla and wrote essays on some aspects of Bangla structure with a systematic and objective outlook. Rabindranath's thoughts were along similar line. Suniti Kumar states that probably Rabindranath took notice of these problems before them (Chattopadhyay 1972: 56). He did not support the orthodox school that was in favour of preparing a Bangla grammar after the model of Sanskrit grammar. His approach was modern as well as objective; though he had no formal training in linguistics, his dealing with the language reminds us of the state of the modern approach to language analysis in the history of linguistics in the western world.

Suniti Kumar on Rabindranath's Contribution to Bangla Linguistics

Suniti Kumar mentions *vyakaraniya* ('grammarian') Rabindranath as the pioneer in the area of Bangla linguistics (Chattopadhyay 1972: 72–73). He points out that it was Rabindranath who first understood the need of the analysis of the modern colloquial Bangla and initiated the linguistic analysis of it (op. cit.: 46). This statement reminds us of the dichotomies forwarded by Ferdinand de Saussure. Beside some stray references to Rabindranath's insights for the structure of Bangla in his different essays and books, Suniti Kumar has written three separate articles on Rabindranath, the linguist. These are 'Vyakaraniya Rabindranath' (Chattopadhyay 1972: 43–47),'Vakpati Rabindranath'(op. cit.: 48–52) and 'Rabindranath o Bangla Bhasha'(op. cit.: 52–60). And in 'Rabindranath' (op. cit.: 66–73) Suniti Kumar has expressed that he was personally indebted to Rabindranath for directly and indirectly taking part in developing his insights. He further says that his association with Rabindranath had a great role in the development of his own personality, one aspect of which is that of a linguist. In 'Viśva-Manah Vāk-Pati' (Chatterji 1961: 120–26) Suniti Kumar depicts Rabindranath as *viśva-manah* ('one with Universal perception') and *vāk-pati* ('lord of speech'). He says that Rabindranath's attitude to language and literature was scientific. 'He was one of the greatest artists in language' and we are fortunate enough that he looked at the language with an analytical outlook to discover the nature of the spoken language. In the preface to ODBL (1985: xvi) Suniti Kumar has acknowledged Rabindranath's original contributions to Bangla linguistics.

> The first Bengali with a scientific insight to attack the problems of the language was the poet Rabindranath Tagore, and it is flattering for the votaries of Philology to find in one who is the greatest writer in the language, and a great poet and seer for all time, a keen philologist as well, distinguished alike by an assiduous enquiry into the facts of the language and by a scholarly appreciation of the methods and findings of the modern Western philologist. The work of Rabindranath is in

> the shape of a few essays (now collected in one volume) on Bengali phonetics, Bengali onomatopoetics, and on the Bengali noun, and on other topics, the earliest of which appeared in the early nineties, and some fresh papers appeared only several years ago. The papers may be said to have shown to the Bengali enquiring into the problems of his language the proper lines of approaching them.

According to Suniti Kumar, the essays collected in *Śabdatattwa* ('Science of Words') (later *Bangla Śabdatattwa*, third edition published by Visva-Bharati, 1984) are the first scientific treatment of Bangla linguistics (Chattopadhyay 1972: 57). He refers to the article first published by Tagore, called 'Bangla Uccaran' ('Bangla Pronunciation') (BS 1292, c. 1885) where the anomalies between the spelling and pronunciation of Bangla have been treated and given first some rules regarding the pronunciation of the word-initial letter 'a' in Bangla. Suniti Kumar writes (Chattopadhyay 1972: 50) though Rabindranath has mentioned that he did not undertake any training like a professional linguist, but his *sadhana* was unparalleled. He cites examples of 'Rabindranath's serious study of the science of Linguistics and of the Comparative Grammar of the Indo-European languages'. He writes that Rabindranath read meticulously 'the monumental work on the subject by the great German scholar Karl Brugmann in its English translation in 4 volumes.' Suniti Kumar has seen 'one of these volumes in the library at Santiniketan with pencil marks and notes by the poet himself' (1961: 125). He also refers to the fact that Rabindranath wrote an appreciative criticism of John Beames' Bengali grammar. From the essays collected in *Śabdatattwa* it is evident that he was introduced to all works related to Bangla linguistics, available in his time. I quote, 'he collected materials and examples, and deduced for the first time some of the fundamental laws of Bengali phonology which were operating in the standard spoken form of the language' (Chatterji 1961: 124). Thus Rabindranath made it clear that without a complete description of the spoken language, any grammar or historical description of a language cannot be written (Chattopadhyay 1972: 47). In *Bhashar Katha* ('About the Language') and in *Bangla Kathya Bhasha* ('Colloquial Bangla') Rabindranath has expressed the need for studying and comparing the Bangla dialects and their comparison. Suniti Kumar classifies the essays collected in *Śabdatattwa* into four categories. These are:

1. phonological—related to pronunciation, spelling and metre;
2. morphological—both inflectional and derivational;
3. syntax—word order in sentences, and
4. etymology of words and semantics.

(Chattopadhyay 1972: 57)

Besides the pronunciation of the word-initial 'a' Rabindranath discussed about the pronunciation of the vowel 'e', discussed about the three forms of the *sadhu* ('literary') definitive classifier [ṭa] as [ṭa], [ṭe] and [ṭo] in *chalit* ('colloquial') Bangla and discovered the rules of vowel harmony or vowel height assimilation (Sarkar 1992: 62). In the criticism of Beames' Bangla grammar also there are some important observations on Bangla pronunciation. In *Bhashar Ingit* ('Symbolism in Language') Rabindranath has dealt with the symbolic nature of Bangla language. The onomatopoetics in Bengali (*dhwanyatmak shabda*) are a characteristic speech-element or speech-habit which Bengali shares with all other languages in the Indo-Aryan family (in Assamese, Odia, Hindi, Nepali) and also with the Dravidian (in Tamil, Telugu, etc.) and Austric (in Santali, Mundari etc.) speeches. Rabindranath was the first to consider the nature and action of this class of words. Suniti Kumar refers to Bangla *shabdadwaita* ('word reduplication'), Bangla *krit* and *taddhit* ('primary and secondary suffixes'), *sambandhe -kar* ('-*kar* in the genitive form'), Bangla *bahuvacan* ('plural forms in Bangla'), Bangla *nirdeshak* ('Bangla definitives'), Bangla *vyakarane tiryakrup* ('oblique forms in Bangla grammar')—papers on Bangla morphology. The amount of actual contribution made by him may not be very extensive. But what is valuable in these essays is the sound beginnings and the precise orientation which lie to the credit of Rabindranath (Chatterji 1961: 124–25). Rabindranath thought about the meta language in Bangla also. Along many other words the Bangla words viz. *ābaśyik* ('compulsory') and *aicchik* ('optional') are his contribution (Chattopadhyay 1972: 60). He created the word *sumantrasabhā* as a synonym of 'advisory council of senior members'. Rabindranath also gave his own interpretation of the complicated topic of Bangla versification (Chatterji 1961: 125).

As Suniti Kumar says, Rabindranath in his *Bhashar Ingit* has categorically mentioned that 'Prakrit Bangla' has its own characteristic nature and a Bangla grammar should be prepared identifying and theorising this nature (Chattopadhyay 1972: 47).

In 1938, a book called *Bangla Bhasha Parichay* ('Introduction to the Bengali Language') was published which contains a collection of Rabindranath's later studies and papers on the Bengali language in a collected form. Suniti Kumar says 'with the true humility of the scholar who knows the science and of the poet who has an intuitive sense of the language, described himself as a traveller who is doing his journey on foot. ...he has been wandering in the highways and by-ways of language and recording his observations, only with a view to create a similar Wanderlust in the domain of language-study among his readers. ...he has thus both the sense of wonder for the mystery of speech on the one hand, and the conscious desire and attempt to explain that mystery' (Chatterji 1961: 126).

I am tempted to refer to a passage from the *Rigveda* as quoted by Suniti Kumar, which he uses for Rabindranath:

Utatvaḥpaśyan, nadadarśavācam;
utatvaḥśṛṇvan, naśṛṇotienām;
utotuasmaitanuaṃ vi sasre—
jāyevapatyauśatīsu-vāsāḥ

Suniti Kumar's translation:

Although a man is seeing, he does not see Speech;
Although a man is hearing, he does not hear Her;
But to another man She has shown Her beauty,
Like a well-dressed and loving Wife to her Husband.

Suniti Kumar says that it is Rabindranath who saw and heard Speech with a true vision and insight. So Suniti Kumar honours him with the title *vak-pati* ('lord and lover of speech') (Chatterji 1961: 126).

Rabindranath on Suniti Kumar's Contribution to Bangla Linguistics

Rabindranath's interest in language is first noticed in his article titled 'Prachin Kavyasamgraha' ('Collection of Old Poetics', 1881). Before that as he says in 'Jivansmriti', ['Loken Palit' chapter, *Rabindra-Rachanavali* ('Complete Works of Rabindranath Tagore'), 1961: 82] when Tagore was studying in the London University College (1878–1880) along with Loken Palit at the age of seventeen, Bangla linguistics was a regular topic in their discussion. The reason was, as he mentions, in London he tried to teach Bangla to a non-Bengali speaker and many 'unexplained difficulties began to raise their heads. This set him thinking, and he collected materials and examples, and deduced for the first time some of the fundamental laws of Bengali phonology which were operating in the standard spoken form of the language' (Chatterji 1961: 124).

Incidentally, it can be mentioned that Suniti Kumar offered a copy of ODBL to Rabindranath with his signature on the title page. Rabindranath read the book in two volumes meticulously. It is found in the copies preserved in the Rabindra Bhavan that he wrote margin-notes on different eighteen pages by his own hand in pencil. The pages are as follows: volume one—198; volume two—655, 658, 662, 663, 664, 666, 668, 677, 678, 679, 684, 685, 686, 695, 706, 712 and 713. Rabindranath wrote his comments in margin-notes on these pages. All are good examples of his profound analytical mind. Some of these are mentioned here with reference to the page numbers. On page 194 (ODBL, first volume) Rabindranath has given a red mark below the word *pāik* ('a foot soldier') and written the word *padātik* in the margin. Suniti Kumar derived the word from the Iranian word *pāīk*. But from the margin-note it appears that Rabindranath was in favour of the Sanskrit word *padātik* to be the source. On different seventeen pages of the second volume, Rabindranath's comments are documented and it is to be mentioned that all are related to the derivational morphology. On page 655, Suniti Kumar gives examples of words with the suffix *-(a)ti/(a)tī* as in *paṛti* ('decline'), *bāṛti* ('surplus'), *ghāṭti* ('shortage') etc. and says that it forms abstract nouns of action and manner. Rabindranath raises a question regarding the status of *parti* and *ghāṭti* as nouns and that is why he has written 'adjectival' and 'adverb' respectively in the margin-notes for these two words. On page 399, in the context of diminutive suffix *-ni/ -uni*, Suniti Kumar gives examples like *nācuni* ('a dancing girl'), *chāuni* ('roof'), but *chā̃kni* ('a strainer'). He has already discussed about the effect of vowel harmony in Bangla. So Rabindranath has rightly mentioned the word *chā̃kuni* in addition to *chā̃kni*. Again on page 662, in connection with the words like *corāi* ('stolen'), *bāmnāi* ('practice of a Brahmin'), *kholtāi* ('having a good show') etc., by writing 'becoming' as a margin-note Rabindranath possibly wants to refer to a process. On page 663, Rabindranath has written 'flying' as meaning of the word *udhāo* which is translated by Suniti Kumar as 'running out of one's sight'. Next, on page 666, Rabindranath has given a compound word viz. *nākānicobāni* ('continuous embarrassment') as an example in addition to the words like *cobāni* ('dipping'), etc. On page number 668, Rabindranath has given one question mark only in the margin. The suffixes *-āra*, *-āri* [as in *payāra* ('a metre'), *jhiyāri* ('daughter'), etc.] derived from the word *ākāra* ('shape') are discussed in this section. Maybe Rabindranath had some query about this derivation. On page 684 Suniti Kumar discusses the use of the suffix *-jā* derived from the word *jāta* ('born') and mentions that this suffix is used with some surnames like *ghoṣjā* ('belonging to the family of Ghoshes'), *bosjā* ('belonging to the family of Boses'), etc. Rabindranath adds an example and comments that it occurs 'only in case of these Kayasthas'. On page 685 Suniti Kumar provides examples like *dhõyāṭ*, *gholāṭ* (now obsolete) with the suffix *-ṭ*. Rabindranath writes two familiar forms of these two words—*dhõyāṭe* ('smoke-like') and *gholaṭe* ('slightly muddy or dull'). On page 686, Rabindranath justifiably adds the definitive *-ṭuku* to the list of *-ṭa* and *-ṭi*. Finally, mention can be made of the page number 695. Here Suniti Kumar discusses the usage of the feminine suffix *-(ā)nī* to indicate the female of a particular caste or profession, for example, *dhobānī* ('washerwoman'), *sekrānī* ('wife of a goldsmith') etc. Rabindranath raises a question in the margin-note—why not *ukilnī* ('wife of a lawyer') or *byārisṭārnī* ('wife of a barrister'). In this way Rabindranath's scientific attitude towards the Bangla language is expressed. As to the comments made by Rabindranath on his book, Suniti Kumar's own feelings in his own words are: 'He has done me the great honour of reading my book *The Origin and Development of the Bengali Language*, and for me it was one of the crowning glories of my life that he appreciated and approved my approach and my method as well as my conclusions, and this appreciation he expressed in some of his writings' (Chatterji 1961: 125–26). Below is given the title page of the copy of ODBL presented to Rabindranath along with another page containing the margin-note in Tagore's own handwriting.

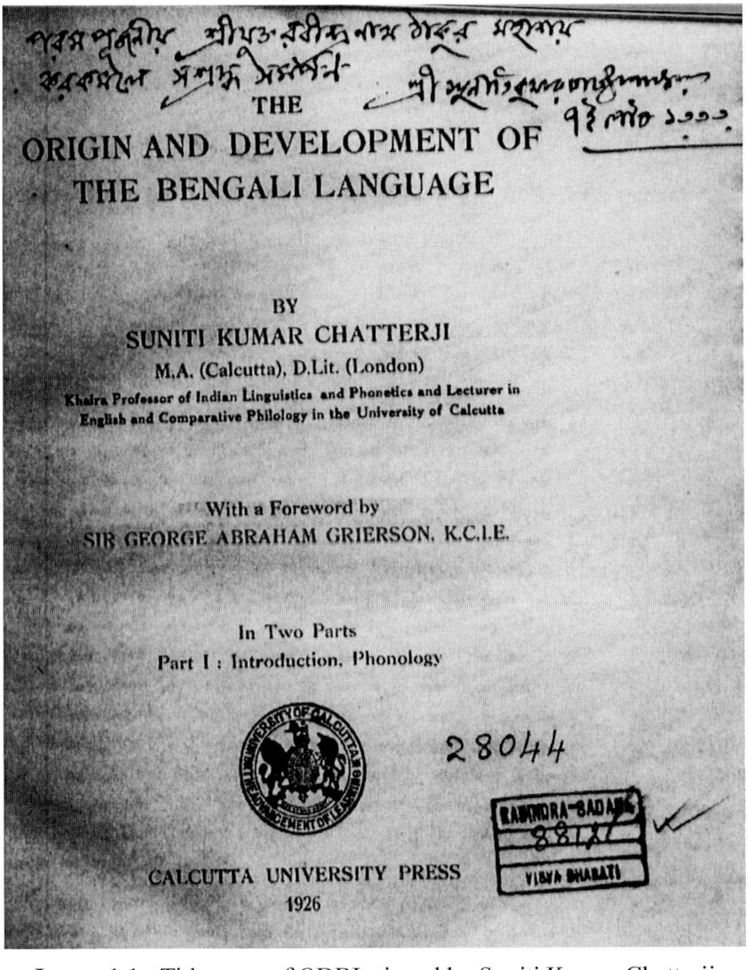

THE ORIGIN AND DEVELOPMENT OF THE BENGALI LANGUAGE

BY

SUNITI KUMAR CHATTERJI

M.A. (Calcutta), D.Lit. (London)

Khaira Professor of Indian Linguistics and Phonetics and Lecturer in English and Comparative Philology in the University of Calcutta

With a Foreword by

SIR GEORGE ABRAHAM GRIERSON, K.C.I.E.

In Two Parts

Part I : Introduction, Phonology

CALCUTTA UNIVERSITY PRESS

1926

Image 1.1: Title page of ODBL signed by Suniti Kumar Chatterji

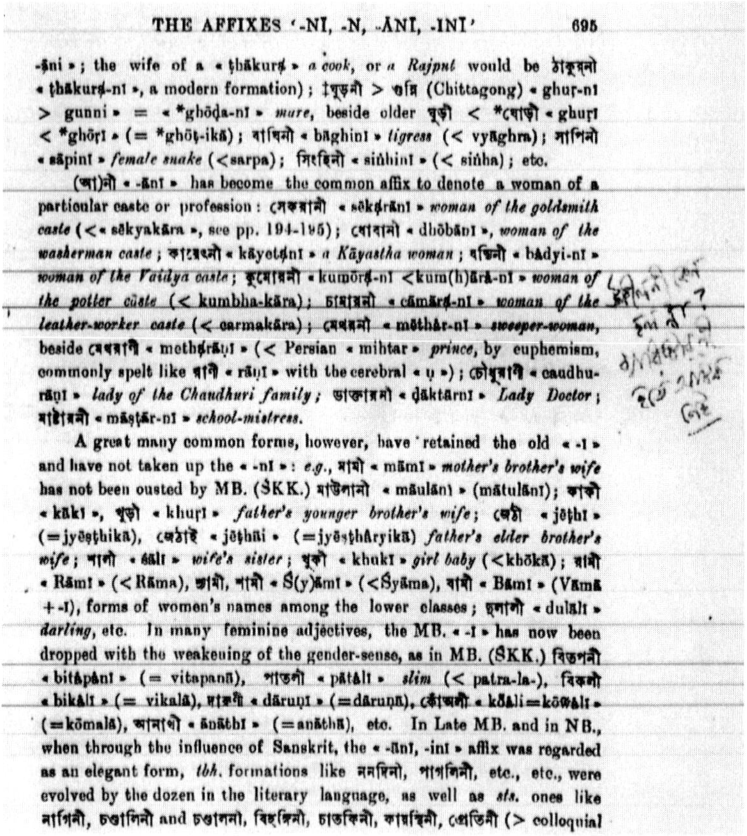

THE AFFIXES '-NĪ, -N, -ĀNĪ, -INĪ' 695

-ṛni »; the wife of a « ṭhākur » *a cook*, or *a Rajput* would be ঠাকুরনী « ṭhākurṛ-nī », a modern formation); ‡ঘুড়নী > ঘন্নি (Chittagong) « ghuṛ-nī > gunni » = « *ghōḍa-nī » *mare*, beside older ঘুড়ী < *ঘোড়ী « ghuṛī < *ghōṛī » (= *ghōṭ-ikā); বাঘিনী « bāghinī » *tigress* (< vyāghra); সাপিনী « sāpinī » *female snake* (<sarpa); সিংহিনী « siṁhinī » (< siṁha); etc.

(আ)নী « -ānī » has become the common affix to denote a woman of a particular caste or profession: সেকরানী « sēkṛānī » *woman of the goldsmith caste* (<« sēkyakāra », see pp. 194-195); ধোবানী « dhōbānī », *woman of the washerman caste*; কায়েতনী « kāyetṛnī » *a Kāyastha woman*; বদ্যিনী « bādyi-nī » *woman of the Vaidya caste*; কুমোরনী « kumōrṛ-nī <kum(h)ārā-nī » *woman of the potter caste* (< kumbha-kāra); চামারনী « cāmārṛ-nī » *woman of the leather-worker caste* (< carmakāra); মেথরনী « mēthār-nī » *sweeper-woman*, beside মেথরাণী « methṛrāṇī » (< Persian « mihtar » *prince*, by euphemism, commonly spelt like রাণী « rāṇī » with the cerebral « ṇ »); চৌধুরাণী « caudhu-rāṇī » *lady of the Chaudhuri family*; ডাক্তারনী « ḍāktārnī » *Lady Doctor*; মাষ্টারনী « māṣṭār-nī » *school-mistress*.

A great many common forms, however, have retained the old « -ī » and have not taken up the « -nī »: *e.g.*, মামী « māmī » *mother's brother's wife* has not been ousted by MB. (ŚKK.) মাউলানী « māulānī » (mātulānī); কাকী « kākī », খুড়ী « khuṛī » *father's younger brother's wife*; জেঠী « jēṭhī » (=jyēṣṭhikā), জেঠাই « jēṭhāi » (=jyēṣṭhāryikā) *father's elder brother's wife*; শালী « śālī » *wife's sister*; খুকী « khukī » *girl baby* (<khōkā); রামী « Rāmī » (<Rāma), শ্যামী, শামী « Ś(y)āmī » (<Śyāma), বামী « Bāmī » (Vāmā + -ī), forms of women's names among the lower classes; দুলালী « dulālī » *darling*, etc. In many feminine adjectives, the MB. « -ī » has now been dropped with the weakening of the gender-sense, as in MB. (ŚKK.) বিতপনী « bitāpānī » (= vitapannā), পাতলী « pātālī » *slim* (< patra-la-), বিকলী « bikālī » (= vikalā), দারুণী « dāruṇī » (=dāruṇā), কৌঅলী « kōāli=kōmālī » (=kōmalā), আনাথী « ānāthī » (=anāthā), etc. In Late MB. and in NB., when through the influence of Sanskrit, the « -ānī, -inī » affix was regarded as an elegant form, *tbh.* formations like ননদিনী, পাগলিনী, etc., etc., were evolved by the dozen in the literary language, as well as *sts.* ones like নাগিনী, চণ্ডালিনী and চণ্ডালনী, বিহঙ্গিনী, চাতকিনী, কাদম্বিনী, প্রেতিনী (> colloquial

IMAGE 1.2: A page from ODBL with Tagore's margin-notes

There are many other instances which prove that Rabindranath recognised and appreciated Suniti Kumar as a scholar in the 'science of words'. Rabindranath has used three words for the present day 'linguistics'—*Shabdavidya*, *Shabdavijnan* and *Śabdatattwa*.

Rabindranath considered Suniti Kumar most worthy of solving all problems related to the language viz. problems related to the structure of Bangla, spelling of Bangla, designing of new Bangla letters and so on. In reply to Bimalnarayan Choudhury's letter [published in *Vicitra*, Bhadra, 1339 (c. 1932)] regarding the spelling problems of Bangla, Rabindranath comments that we are not worthy of this work. This work suits people like Suniti Kumar. In the same letter, Tagore further says that once he requested Suniti Kumar to prepare a dictionary of 'Prakrita Bangla', i.e. colloquial Bangla and in that connection if he fixes the norm of Bangla spelling, many problems will be solved. Some final decisions will come out. Again in a letter written to Debaprasad Ghose [published in *Pravasi*, Shravan, 1344 (c. 1937)] Rabindranath states that standardisation of the spelling of Prakrit Bangla forms is the need of the day and that is whý he appealed to the authority of Calcutta University to systematise the rules of Bangla spelling immediately. He requested Suniti Kumar to take an initiative in this matter and Suniti Kumar prepared a draft of rules for Bangla spelling. But he says that finally rationality was defeated by the strictness of the orthodox group. Rabindranath felt the need of new letters to be introduced to the Bangla script for writing foreign loan words in Bangla. Rabindranath gave this responsibility to Suniti Kumar. In this connection we get a letter dated November 25, 1927, by Rabindranath (Saha 1984: 266) to Suniti Kumar. Image 1.3 shows a few lines of this letter.

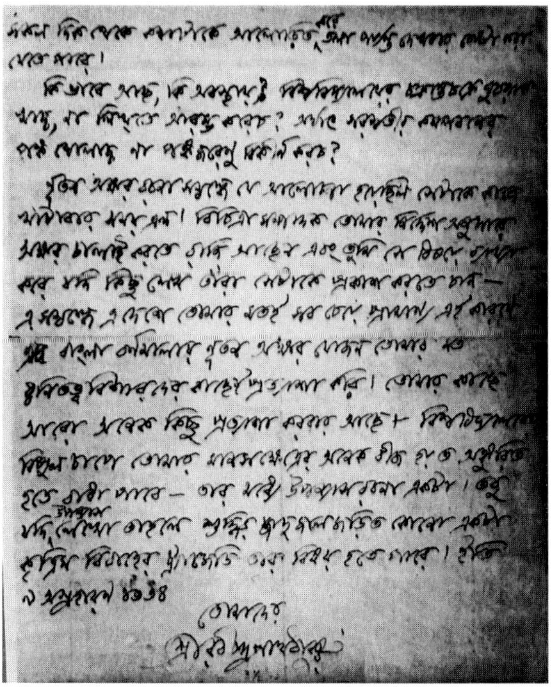

Image 1.3: Excerpts from Tagore's letter to Suniti Kumar Chatterji

But Rabindranath did not agree with all the opinions of Suniti Kumar. He critically reviewed the opinion of Suniti Kumar with regard to the time of the origin of Old Bengali. Rabindranath was not in favour of using the word *jOnmo* ('birth') in connection with 'origin'. To mark the time of the beginning of something which is in the state of gradually being exposed from the condition of not adequately exposed is very difficult. According to Rabindranath the Bengali language has flourished for centuries. We cannot fix a specific century as the starting point of Old Bengali. Again he saluted the scholarship of Suniti Kumar in the context of diachronic development of the Bengali vowels from Middle Indo-Aryan. Rabindranath coined many new words mainly from Sanskrit as these sometimes become necessary to express some ideas. Being inspired by Suniti Kumar he submitted all these technical terms to Suniti Kumar for publication. On the initiative of Suniti Kumar these were published in *Sahitya Parishat Patrika*. While writing *A Bengali Phonetic Reader* (1928) Suniti Kumar acknowledges Rabindranath thus: 'Dr Tagore kindly went through the sections on Intonation (sec. 61–63) with him and expressed his agreement with the views given there, as well as with the charts, as giving correct enough representation of the intonation of the sentences used for illustration.' Rabindranath appreciated Suniti Kumar by conferring several titles on him. He was surprised by Suniti Kumar's power of minute observation and power of expression in a language which comes out naturally—flows like spring-water not like tap-water which is regulated, controlled. He pronounced Suniti Kumar *lipivacaspati* ('writer master of letter') or *lipisarvabhauma* ('emperor in letter writing') or *lipichakravarti* ('supreme letter-writer') (*Java-Yatrir Patra*: 616).

Rabindranath dedicated his own book *Bangla Bhasha Parichay* ('Introduction to the Bengali Language') (1938) to Suniti Kumar and gave the sobriquet of *bhashacharya* ('master of speech').

উৎসর্গ

ভাষাচার্য শ্রীযুক্ত সুনীতি কুমার চট্টোপাধ্যায়

করকমলে

Let me quote Suniti Kumar's feelings in his own words: 'an informally awarded title or degree which I value so much and which I use with my name with pride' (Chatterji 1961: 126). Regarding this book Rabindranath expressed his own view and at the same time praised Suniti Kumar in the following way:

> My book describes the form and not the theory. Suniti Kumar looks at the language like an expert geographer whereas my viewpoint is like that of a pedestrian. Suniti Kumar knows the minute details of the world of vocabulary and can put forward his hypotheses and proofs systematically; but I express my thoughts on the language which originate from my own experience.

Suniti Kumar composed the grammar of Bengali called *Bhasha Prakash Bangala Vyakaran*. After its publication by the University of Calcutta in 1939 (re-published by Rupa & Co. in 1988) Rabindranath wrote a letter dated 24 October, 1939, to the Registrar of the University applauding Suniti Kumar.

> We have been waiting long for a comprehensive grammar of Bengali language. Our expectation has been amply fulfilled by the appearance of *Bhasha Prakash Bangla Vyakaran* by Dr Suniti Kumar Chatterji for which I offer him grateful blessings.

Conclusion

Suniti Kumar believes that Rabindranath's affection for him was not rooted in his appreciation of his 'linguistic investigations undertaken with the objective approach of a scientist.' Rather, it was rooted in Rabindranath's sensing that Suniti Kumar's interest in language was closely interwoven with his interest in Man and in the surroundings of Man. Suniti Kumar says that he himself was vaguely conscious of it and Rabindranath discovered it for him. Suniti Kumar concludes that it was Rabindranath's 'love for Man—which was the motive force behind his own interest in language, in both its origin and its functioning.'

Suniti Kumar cherished Rabindranath's affection for him as the greatest treasure in his life. In an article he writes that he found one facet of Rabindranath's multifaceted genius in which only the poet and he were present; there was no room for anyone else. In this connection he mentions what Tansen in a Dhrupad song referred to his adored God as *bahuvallabha* ('dear to many') but in his case He was *ekavallabha* ('dear to one only'). This was the aspect of Rabindranath as *vyakaraniya*, ('grammarian').

Acknowledgements

I would like to thank Professor Tapati Mukherjee, the-then Adhyaksha, Rabindra Bhavan, Visva-Bharati for giving me the necessary permission to collect the photocopies from the audio-visual unit, Rabindra Bhavan. I would also like to thank Professor Ramkrishna Bhattacharya for his help.

References

Bhattacharya, Krishna. (2015). 'Suniti Kumar Chatterji as a linguist: His contribution and vision'. *Suniti Kumar Chatterji Revisited.* Kolkata: Kolkata Society for Asian Studies, 9–65.

_____ (2014). 'Suniti Chatujjer Bangla bhashar sabdatattva o Rabindranath'. In Probal Dasgupta (ed.), *Alochona Chakra*, 37, 8–21.

Chattopadhyay, Suniti Kumar. (1972). 'Vyakaraniya Rabindranath'. *Manishi Smarane*. Kolkata: Jijnasa, 43–47.

_____ (1972). 'Vakpati Rabindranath'. *Manishi Smarane.* Kolkata: Jijnasa, 48–52.

_____ (1972). 'Rabindranath o banglabhasha'. *Manishi Smarane.* Kolkata: Jijnasa, 52–60.

_____ (1972). 'Rabindranath'. *Manishi Smarane.* Kolkata: Jijnasa, 66–73.

_____ (1976). 'Itihas o sanskriti'. *Sanskriti, Shilpa, Itihas*. Kolkata: Jijnasa, 15–16.

_____ (1979). *Jiban Katha*. Kolkata: Jijnasa.

Chatterji, Suniti Kumar. (1961). 'Viśva-manah vāk-pati'. *Rabindranath Tagore, A Centenary Volume, 1861–1961*, 5th print. New Delhi: Sahitya Akademi, 120–26.

_____ (1985). *The Origin and Development of the Bengali Language*. Calcutta: Rupa & Co (First published by University of Calcutta, in 1926.)

Das, Nirmal. (2000). *Bangla Bhashar Vyakaran o Tar Kramavikash*. Kolkata: Rabindra Bharati University.

Tagore, Rabindranath. (1961). 'Jivansmriti'. *Rabindra-Rachanavali*, volume 10, Birth Centenary edn. Kolkata: West Bengal Government.

Saha, Gour Chandra. (1984). *Rabindra-Patravali: Tathyapanji*. Kolkata: Dey's Publishing.

Sarkar, Pabitra. (1989). 'Rabindranath Tagore: The Linguist'. *125th Tagore Birth Anniversary Commemoration Volume*. Bolpur, West Bengal: Visva-Bharati, 193–206.

_____ (1992). 'Rabindranath Thakur'. *Bhashamanan Bangali Manisha*. Kolkata: Punascha, 54–78.

_____ (1992). 'Suniti Kumar Chattopadhyay'. *Bhashamanan Bangali Manisha*. Kolkata: Punascha, 140–62.

_____ (1997). 'Suniti Kumar Chatterji as a grammarian'. In Udaya Narayana Singh, and Shivarama Padikkal (eds), *Suniti Kumar Chatterji—A Centenary Tribute*. New Delhi: Sahitya Akademi, 15– 23.

Sen, Sukumar. (1980). *Suniti Kumar Chatterji—Scholar and Virtuoso*. New Delhi: Sahitya Akademi.

2

Recuperating Suniti Kumar Chatterji's Opposition to the Structuralist Legacy

Probal Dasgputa

Abstract

Linguists working after Chatterji's time have based their assessment of his work on history-denying assumptions shared by structural linguistics with its generative, sociolinguistic and other successors. But history-denial is nearly as risky an enterprise as climate change denial. Structuralist assumptions have led later commentators to sideline not just Chatterji's practices and his underlying methodological assumptions, but also his explicit opposition to structural linguistics. Continuing a conversation with him from the early seventies, it is now appropriate to retrieve the thread of that opposition, placing it on a foundation that is indebted to his work for some of its methodological postulates.

The approach to the legacy of Suniti Kumar Chatterji that prevails among commentators today takes it that he fought a pointless rearguard action against progress in linguistics, that he lost the war, that the structuralists and their various successors were and are basically right and that he was basically wrong on matters where they differed, but that nonetheless we should be kind to this pioneering giant because of what he accomplished even though he was out of date.

This view is an indefensible Whig history. To see how out of touch it is with the facts, it helps to revisit an anecdote that Chatterji was never tired of recounting. The pivotal figure in that narrative was Prabodh Pandit; the context was one of the workshops held at Deccan College, Pune, under the joint auspices of the Government of India and the Rockefeller Foundation, from 1952 onwards. Many bright young men and women from all over the country were trained there in several brands of linguistics. Some of those who did well at these workshops were given fellowships for higher studies in the United States or Britain.

Now, apart from the foreign professors teaching at those workshops, the faculty, in some of the workshops, included several established Indian linguists as well, such as Chatterji himself, his professional partner Sukumar Sen, and some of their juniors, such as the Gujarati scholar Prabodh Pandit who worked at Deccan College, Pune. Among the students at those workshops who later established themselves were Ashok Kelkar, Braj Kachru, Yamuna Keskar (who married Braj and is remembered as Yamuna Kachru), Debi Prasanna Pattanayak.

The whole enterprise was run by Sumitra Mangesh Katre, the generous and thoughtful director of Deccan College who was equally at home in the Paninian tradition of Sanskrit grammar and in the synchronic linguistics that had by then become prevalent in several western countries. Katre had written an account of his mother tongue Konkani along the lines of Chatterji's pioneering work. Katre, like Chatterji, wished for healthy dialogue between the old scholars and their successors. It was in this milieu that Chatterji, one fine morning, asked Prabodh Pandit a tricky question.

He initiated the exchange fairly simply: "Prabodh, could you go over the basics of that phoneme theory of yours, please? There's one little point on which I would like to ask you something."

Pandit said, "Well, it's like this. We all agree that one sound can appear in slightly different forms in different contexts without losing its unity as a sound. In order to make this point clear, we structuralists have introduced a couple of technical terms. In your mother tongue Bengali, for instance, the three words /alta/ 'lac dye', /lalce/ 'reddish', /ulTo/ 'opposite' show three variants of the phoneme /l/; structuralists call them three different allophones of this phoneme. The allophone that occurs in /alta/ is dental; the one in /lalce/ is palatalised; the allophone you find in /ulTo/ is retroflex. But Bengali has one and only one /l/ phoneme through all this diversity. Or consider Marathi, where the single phoneme /c/ has two allophones. Preceding the vowels /e, i, i:/ or the semivowel /j/, we find the default palato-alveolar allophone [c], as in /pra:ci:n/ [pra:ci:n]; but if the following vowel is /a, a:, o, u, u:/ then Marathi uses an unusual allophone, the alveolar affricate [ts], as in /ca:Mgla:/ [tsa:ŋgla:] 'good'. Is the phoneme theory clear to you now, sir?"

Chatterji replied, "I think I've managed to get that point, thank you, Prabodh. But I'd like to go one step further and ask you another question now. The question is about the numerals in Marathi. My memory is a bit rusty, could you please repeat the cardinal numerals for me from one to ten?"

Pandit obliged him: "[ek don ti:n ca:r pa:ts saha: sa:t a:Th nau: daha:]".

Chatterji now asked his question: "I thought I heard you say that the phoneme /c/ is manifested as the palatalised allophone [c] only when it immediately precedes /i, i:, e, j/, and that to the left of /a:/ you get the allophone /ts/ instead. Now, you just pronounced the numerals for me, and the way the word for 'five' is pronounced fits your theory perfectly, given the fact that a slow rendering would give us [pa:tsa] with a short [a] after the [ts]; but the word for 'four' surprisingly came out as [ca:r], not [tsa:r]. Can you please explain that surprising fact for me in terms of the phoneme theory?"

Pandit found that he could not answer this question at once; he said, "I'll think about it and let you know—I should be able to get back to you tomorrow." Chatterji told me, in the early seventies, twenty years after the conversation, that Prabodh Pandit's 'tomorrow' never did arrive. Pandit's intellectual progeny, as the oral and written records show, matched his own non-performance on this front. Neither Pandit nor his associates return to the negotiating table with Chatterji, or to the question itself, at any point in their career. By the time Chatterji was reporting this stonewalling of his question to me, twenty years had already passed after he had asked it, and he saw clearly that he would never receive a reply.

To return to that conversation, Chatterji was not the kind of person who would accept stonewalling without comment. The moment Pandit asked for a postponement, Chatterji said to him, "Your wanting to continue this conversation tomorrow is perfectly okay, Prabodh, but you might want to know right now what my analysis of the data looks like. I take it that there came a time, in the history of Marathi, when a particular sound change occurred. As long as that process was active, those pre-back-vowel affricates of yours shifted from a palato-alveolar to an alveolar point of articulation. But the word for 'four' resisted that change. Why? Because at that point in the diachrony of Marathi the word was not [ca:r], but [cia:r]. So the sound change left it intact; the [c] was protected by that [i]. Later, when the depalatalisation process had become a spent force, the word for 'four' dropped its [i], leaving just [ca:r], whose palato-alveolar was no longer in danger of getting alveolarised. That is why the facts look the way they do in today's Marathi. You know all this, Prabodh. You have studied historical linguistics yourself. Knowing what you do, you surely do not propose to swallow what these illiterates are offering? Are you seriously going to take a giant step backwards and carry all your students with you into such unwillingness to face obvious facts?"

Prabodh Pandit had already made that kind of agreement with the architects of the new ethos, namely the Structuralists. When he moved from Deccan College, Pune, to Delhi University and took over the university's nascent linguistics department, he recruited those from the new generation of linguists who would adhere to this new field and encouraged specific pursuits by them in such a way as to ensure that whenever the 'mainstream' in the United States shifted its course from path A to path B, the teachers and students in Delhi University's linguistics fraternity would provide them empirical confirmation from many Indian languages. This was purposefully done to showcase Indian scholarship that fitted American research. Their originality claims were limited to a few quirks that they found, here and there, and they hoped to gain recognition within American academia, even if only as footnotes.

What am I driving at? Let me spell it out pointwise, bowing to the cultural fact that irony is often misunderstood. Point one, structuralism in its various formalistic and functionalistic incarnations was installed in the Indian academic establishment in large part by the non-accountable Prabodh Pandit, ignoring the contestation by Suniti Kumar Chatterji that I am reporting to you. Point two, the overwhelming majority of practitioners of Indian linguists in and outside India take it for granted, to this day, that these views merit the paradigmatic status they have acquired, regardless of the mendacious methods that were used to stonewall, silence and sideline all opposition. Point three, Chatterji was one of the very few Indian linguists who had the energy to resist structuralism with actual arguments and to seek debate, a privilege that was denied to him by the coalition of the willing 'led' by Prabodh Pandit, if what he did merits the honorific epithet 'leadership'; the mantle of this 'leadership' in due course passed into the hands of other Indians who enthusiastically emulate their non-accountable and illiterate neo-colonial sponsors instead of calling their bluff. Point four, we urgently need to resume Chatterji's campaign against structuralism today if we wish to arrest the erosion of democracy under the neo-liberal regime in the sector of labour known as linguistics.

For a socio-politically oriented take on why structuralism is inimical to democracy, I refer you to Dasgupta (2015). In the present study, I stick to linguistic contestation of a type that retains continuity with Chatterji's own concerns. I begin with a body of straightforward empirical evidence that undermines the structuralist framework and its successors roughly the way the celebrated obstruent voicing data from Russian once undermined the notion of the taxonomic phoneme.

It is an instructive exercise to juxtapose the particles /jodi/ 'if' and /tObe/ 'then', observed in (1), with /jodio/ 'though' and /tobu/ 'yet', exemplified in (2).

(1) jodi bhebe thako ora aSbe, tObe bhul bhebecho
    if think.cjv aux they come.fut then wrong have thought
    'If you thought they would come, you were mistaken.'

(2) jodio jante ora aSbe na, tobu cole jaoni
though knew they come.fut neg yet away didn't go
'Although you knew they wouldn't come, yet you didn't leave.'

If we analyse /jodio/ 'though' as the result of applying the associative focus particle /o/ 'even, also' to /jodi/ 'if'—a description rendered plausible by their Sanskrit counterparts /yadi/ 'if' and /yady-api/ 'though' (note that /jodi/ counts as a *tatsama* 'adaptation of the Sanskrit particle' /yadi/ to Bangla phonology)—then we have a satisfying account of (2). However, such a move leads to trouble at example (3).

(3) jodio jante ora aSbe na, tobuo cole jaoni
though knew they come.fut neg yet.foc away didn't go
'Although you knew they wouldn't come, yet you didn't leave.'

If we stick to the story that /tobu/ 'yet' in (2) is the result of attaching the associative focus particle /o/ to /tObe/ 'then' seen in (1), then the problem at (3) is that its particle /tobuo/ counts as exhibiting two occurrences of that /o/ element in a row, in a language that never allows two focus particles to appear next to each other.

Under the assumptions prevalent in synchronic structural linguistics—whether one invokes its classical structuralist incarnation or the supplementary assumptions of generative grammar with or without sociolinguistic add-ons, it doesn't matter—one would solve the problem by claiming that the real focus particle /o/ appears only in the word /tobuo/ in (3); that it does not in fact occur in the /tobu/ of (2); and that, by parity of reasoning, the particle /jodio/ observed in (2) and in (3) doesn't contain an instance of the focus particle /o/ either. The generalisation that two focus particles never occur in immediate succession in Bangla can thus be maintained across the board.

The difficulty with this simple looking analysis is that it is simplistic. If we consider a wider set of examples in which old focus particles have, through linguistic change, been integrated into the host word to the point of making the focus particle unrecognisable—let us call such an obscured focus particle an 'augment' for expository convenience—we systematically find that an augment can be followed by another, 'real' focus particle, but that this only becomes possible when the augment is indeed not recognisable as a focus particle. Thus, when one looks at the pair /Emoni/ 'thus indeed' vs /emni/ 'spontaneously, ordinarily', the augment /i/ in /emni/ permits the addition of a focus particle: /emnio/ 'even ordinarily', /emnii/ 'simply spontaneously'; but such a supplement is not tolerated with /Emoni/ 'thus indeed', where the dissociative focus particle /i/ remains recognisable.

When we examine the indefinite series /keu/ 'someone, anyone', /kichu/ 'something, anything', /kothao/ 'somewhere, anywhere', /kOkhono/ 'some time, any time', diachronically derived by attaching the associative focus particle to the interrogative series /ke/ 'who', /ki/ 'what', /kothae/ 'where', /kOkhon/ 'when', we find a slightly more nuanced generalisation. The fact that some of the ex-focus particles are less obviously recognisable than others seems to make no difference as far as resistance to attachment of the dissociative focus particle /i/ is concerned. Thus, one can freely say /keui/ 'anybody at all', /kichui/ 'anything at all', /kothaoi/ 'anywhere at all', /kOkhonoi/ 'any time at all'. However, attaching the associative focus particle /o/ is a different matter; such attachment is licit only where the ex-focus particle has indeed undergone significant change and become an augment not recognisable as having ever had anything to do with the focus particle system. Thus, one can say (4) or (5).

(4) ar-keuo parbe na
else-anybody.foc will be able not
'Nor will anybody else be able to do it.'

(5) ar-kichuo caini
else-anything.foc wanted not
'Nor did I want anything else.'

In these cases, the old focus particle has turned into the different looking augment /u/. But one cannot say (6) or (7):

(6) *ar-kothaoo jabo na
else-anywhere.foc will go not
'Nor will I go anywhere else.'

(7) *ar-kOkhonoo jabo na
else-any time.foc will go not
'Nor will I go at any other time.'

Why don't (6) and (7) work? The problem seems to be that attaching a new /o/ to an old /o/ has the effect of producing a glaring sequence of two /o/ particles, which offends the contemporary speaker's ear.

This would make sense if Bangla were to otherwise allow a host to be followed by a synchronically active associative focus particle /o/ and then an active but formally distinct disssociative focus particle /i/. But the generalisation is quite robust: word-o-i and word-i-o are completely ruled out where the -o-i and -i-o sequences instantiate a succession of distinct focus particles. Thus, the indefinite series facts presented above do not lend themselves to a purely synchronic explanation.

Going back to the data concerning /jodi, tObe/ 'if, then' and /jodio, tobu/ 'although, yet', we have to conclude that the asymmetry between /tobuo/ 'yet.foc', which is permitted, and */jodioo/ 'though. foc', which is not, reflects a sharp prohibition against a succession of focal /o/ elements. This prohibition, which can only be stated in hybrid language that mixes synchronic with diachronic labels, suggests that even augments still exude some residual focal aroma; and that the intensity this aroma has to do with the degree of fossilisation.

After these preliminaries, I now move to substantivism, the site of systematic resistance to structuralism; I shall present a substantivist case study in the context of renewing and extending Chatterji's opposition to the structuralist counter-revolution. This is hardly the place to provide a quick summary of how substantivists have configured this struggle over the decades; readers interested in those matters may consult Dasgupta (1993) for the core idea, which is that structuralism and its successors have worked for the code cultivation enterprise, whereas a serious take on language needs to engage with discourses and to keep in view the power-laden character of the negotiations between the spoken and the written. In the current intervention, our main target is the structuralist inclination towards extreme naturalisation. The structuralist view of a language L accords primacy to L's default ('most natural, least marked') items and default subsystems. This portrayal represents dominations and hegemonies in the inappropriately neutral guise of scientifically diagnosable quasi-natural facts about the structure of L and about other structures surrounding L—thus sidetracking energies that would otherwise be available for real opposition to the dominations leading to the undermining of discriminatory and chauvinistic views and to the establishment of genuine neutrality. In classical structuralism those neighbouring structures were taken to be cultural; in generative and allied cognitivist work and its spillover into contemporary sociolinguistics those neighbouring structures are viewed in the light of human cognition, however articulated with biology; it is frustrating to see how little these variations matter when the chips are down. Structuralism in all its variants, including its putatively very different successors, amounts to an encoding of the expectations of the colonial masters of the episteme and the neo-colonial inheritors of their riches. It is likely that some individuals taking part in the enterprise will wish to dissociate themselves from this portrayal at the level of subjective intentions; certainly; but the effect of the enterprise is objectively to reinforce the epistemic structures sponsored by colonialism and neo-colonialism (this and related claims are unpacked in Dasgupta 2014). Thus, objectively speaking, the need to oppose even those successors to structuralism, who personally wish for a decolonised world remains on our agenda.

Substantivism is one mode of intellectual and moral labour that has consistently opposed the structuralist encoding of the needs of the North; it has engaged with this adversary both in sociolinguistics and in grammar. It has consistently linked the terms of reference of this struggle with the resistance to the hegemonic strand in the otherwise magnificent Paninian oeuvre in early India.

In the present intervention, by way of extending Chatterji's opposition to structuralism, we take up the relation between the lexical parameters of Lalon Fakir's songs and the way the standard Bangla lexis has developed, with special reference to the question of defaults, and keeping in view the secular imperative to which the contemporary academic imagination often adds a positivist flavour. As we work towards a genuine neutrality, we need to eliminate this positivist flavour and to put in place a seriously articulated secular standpoint that does not amount to chauvinist hegemonies operating by other means.

The fact that the authentically, iconically neutral author Lalon Fakir's legacy is not recognised as canonical in the received codifications of modern Bangla is a fact not only about religious, literary or artistic codification, but about language as well. To place this particular fact under the substantivist lens becomes an important task in the context of moving away from a culture-describing structuralist approach that seeks to confine the Third World to its ethnic ghettoes and towards a history-making orientation that recognises the rationality of the spaces of what has come to be called the global South; hence our decision to pitch this intervention at the level of lexical inquiry, one of the hitherto less explored sectors of substantivist research.

The type of Bangla that has been hegemonic since the nineteenth century (and has therefore been portrayed by its votaries as 'natural') may appear to many of us to just happen to be stuck with the coincidental predicament of having to carry a predominantly Sanskritic burden. This common sensical viewpoint is of a piece with the structuralist belief that a language is an arbitrary set of arbitrary signs, and that this fundamental arbitrariness precedes and grounds all questions of history. From such a viewpoint, it may seem appropriate to ask whether the Perso-Arabic lexical inheritance that Bangla was also entitled to went missing due to arbitrary vagaries of cultural history, which could have turned out otherwise (and which, on such a view, need not be seen as a history that addresses us and should ideally elicit an active response from us as we do our further history-making today). This structuralism-inspired question carries the subtext that questions about the contingent diachronic road that we happen to have travelled by are optional, although of course they can quite naturally be pursued by diachronic linguists and other antiquarians who happen to be 'into' them.

Taking those questions seriously at the level of textual diachronicling (we hesitate to endorse the tendency to call it 'history') will mainly involve looking at the transmission of a literary and religious sub-tradition from Lalon to Tagore. The details of such interrogation must be left to Tagore scholars. The part of that inquiry taken up here has to do with the lexical composition of Lalon's own texts.

Analysts who wish to bring the resources of philology and related diachronic disciplines to bear on this issue will rightly regard Shaktinath Jha's (1995) work as an invaluable resource (I pause to record my debt to Partha Majumder, who gave me access to this and other Lalon Fakir books for my research). Jha reproduces the orthography of Lalon's original manuscripts, thus advancing the cause of exact textual study in this domain. He also applies the apparatus of traditional Bangla grammar to the corpus and provides a survey of relations between verbs and factors or actants, and of types of compounds occurring in the corpus. His characterisation of these structural features of Lalon's oeuvre will also be invaluable for research focused on those issues.

However, if an analyst wishes to consider Lalon's diction in terms of the overall legacy that Bangla has inherited, with principles of general linguistics in mind, then focussing too intensely on fine points of the original orthography, warts and all, may prove counterproductive. This consideration leads me to rely on Shah (2000a) for the purposes of working towards a linguistic characterisation of Lalon's lexis. Future work—apart from looking at a larger set of examples, drawing on Shah (1998, 2000b)—will certainly take Jha's meticulously produced philological results on board as well.

To be sure, some readers of Shah (1998, 2000a, b) may also wish to apply Jha's criteria to this version of the oeuvre. They may note, in this spirit, that *noirekar* (Shah 2000a: songs 18, 20), contrasting as it does with the standard word *nirakar* 'formless' (song 22), is to be construed as a distinctive personal synthesis, based on such a word as *noiraMtto* 'selflessness' and on *nirakar*.[1] A similar variant occurs

[1] The transcription system used here deploys capitalisations in a way that seeks maximal intelligibility; it is somewhat eclectic (but based on practices that have been prevalent in Indo-Aryan linguistic studies for several decades); we are sure readers can cope.

in song 29: the passage *nirete niranjon ache* 'in the water is the one devoid of attributes' deploys a distinctive coinage *niranjon* where a reader who belongs to our time and is lexically anchored in our 'standard' language would expect the form *nirOnjon* 'the one devoid of attributes'. The effects of such entropy on the shapes of words do deserve attention. The context renders plausible a reading of *nila* in song 18 as a variant of *lila* 'divine play'—one that familiar *n*/*l* alternations across dialects of Bangla suffice to explain. An elaborate engagement with the minutiae of the text will certainly be required for certain specialised purposes. But it pays to emphasise yet again that those are not the purposes salient in the present study, which concentrates on the traffic of Perso-Arabic and Sanskrit-derived elements in Lalon's lexis.

If one takes a look at the Perso-Arabic words in the very first song by Lalon in Shah (2000a), it becomes clear that they are not all indices of Islamic thinking here: *lagao* ***kinare*** [take (it) to the **shore**], ***jaher*** *ache triSONSare* ('is **visible** in all three spheres'), *abar tara* ***khalaS*** *pabe* ('they will be **free** again'), are clearly religion-neutral. But several Perso-Arabic words in that song do betoken the Islamic context (to save space, from this point onwards only key words shown in boldface are glossed):[2] ***alla badSa alanpOna*** ('God, emperor,

[2] The reader interested in the core issues of the present paper may wish to scrutinise syncretistic religious figures whose work is available in other languages that the reader can parse. My decision to limit my glossing here to key words—in tune with the fact this is a lexical study—can be seen as one response to the need for truly serious renderings of the longer passages. If an author, who lacks the specialist's intimate familiarity with the spiritual traditions Lalon invokes, rushes in where theologically sophisticated translators fear to tread, even if he labels his hasty renderings as merely rough and ready glosses without claiming any validity for them, they run the risk of being treated as serious translations. The only way to avoid such an undesirable scenario is to rigorously avoid translating the passages. Other readers who need theoretically sophisticated clarifications about the decision not to translate entire passages from Lalon into English here will perhaps consult Dasgupta (2011) for a take on translation theory pertinent to this issue.

lord of the universe') *tumi Dubaiye bhaSaite paro*; *nuhu name Ek* ***nobi****re* (***nobi*** 'prophet') *na mane jara*, ***moahed kafer*** ('unregenerate infidels') *tara*... ***behiSab dozOkhe*** *jabe* ('their wantonness will take them to hell').

At this phase of the enterprise, it is already clear that one will eventually have to ask: Is one comparing two theologies associated with two source traditions? Or is the investigation merely about the numerical preponderance of Sanskrit versus Arabic (filtered through Persian) as source languages for Bangla? Although this question does count as important, it is heuristically optimal for the investigation to proceed without any hasty answers. Components of a valid response will emerge as the analysis progresses, in this study and in sequels by other scholars.

The words *kinar* and *khalaS* are current even in contemporary Bangla, although poets today do not use *khalaS* particularly often. While *jaher* may not elicit instant recognition, once one is told that Arabic treats /e/ and short /i/ as allophones, one identifies *jaher* as the *jahir* that occurs today only in the fixed phrase *jahir kOra* 'to give publicity to' in standard Bangla—as far as West Bengal is concerned, we obviously cannot speak for Bangladesh.

Song two contains the passage *bhObonodir* ***tuphan*** ('storm') *dekhe/ bhOYe pran keMpe oThe*—the word *tuphan* is familiar, and even in our period of history is still a tool that poets freely use. However, the story of the Perso-Arabic component of song two is limited to this *tuphan* and one occurrence of *kinara* 'shore'. At song three, we draw a blank: not one word of Perso-Arabic provenance. We hit gold at the fourth song, in the form of *ciz* 'stuff', an ordinary Persian word devoid of religious accoutrements, which makes us ask, with some optimism: perhaps the secular linguistic analysis project can be disengaged from religion after all?

Such naive hopes do not survive scrutiny, however. The key word *ciz* is embedded in the following syncretistic passage: *jante hOe* ***adom*** ('Adam') *chobir addo kOtha/ na dekhe* ***ajajil*** ('God') *Se/ kirup adom goThlen Setha./ aniye* ***jeddar*** ('Jeddah') *maTi/ goThlen* ***borkha*** ('integument') *poripaTi/ mittha nOe Se kOtha khaMTi/ kon* ***cize*** ('substance') *tar goThlen aMtta./ Sei je adomer dhORe/ Ononto kuThori gORe/ majhkhane hatone kOl juRe/ kirtikOrma boSlen*

Setha./ admi hoile adom cene/ Thik namae Se ***del*** ('heart') ***korane*** ('the Qur'an')/ *lalon kOe Siraj SaiMr gune/ adom OdhOr dhOrar Suta.*

This is a *fakir* speaking, from the *silsila* of narratives emanating from the Qur'an Sharif and related scriptures, providing the cosmogonic backdrop to his spiritual quest. The Perso-Arabic words, even such an item of daily use as *ciz* that can indeed mean 'thing' in some contexts, become carriers for the invocation of the Quranic tradition here, with appropriate deployment of a few terms from Hindu traditions to keep the project of syncretism going.

In contrast, the fact that we found only a *tuphan* and a *kinara* in song two is to be read in the context within which these words, set in boldface, occur: *eSo dOYal, amae par kOro bhOber ghaTe/ bhObonodir* ***tuphan*** *dekhe/ bhOYe pran keMpe oThe./ pap punno jOtoi kori/ bhOroSa kebol tomari/ tumi jar hOo kanDari/ bhObo bhOe tar jae chuTe./ Sadhonar bOl jader chilo/ tarai kul* ***kinara*** *pelo/ amar din Okajei gElo/ ki jani hOe lOlaTe./ purane Sunechi khObor/ potitpabon namTi tor* (*tomar*)/ *lalon kOe aj ami pamor/ taite dohai dei bOTe*. This clear invocation of Hindu traditions, carried by the use of Sanskritic words and the disappearance of Perso-Arabic diction, continues in song three, which is not cited here.

It is important not to lose sight of Lalon's larger picture. His emphatically original vision invoked the ethos, otherwise unavailable in his time, of a public discourse released from sectarian chains: *Emon manob SOmaj kObe go srijon hObe/ jedin hindu muSolman bouddho khriSTan/ jati gotro nahi rObe* ('when will such a society come into being/ where Hindus, Muslims, Buddhists, Christians, castes and *gotras* will cease to be?') is a passage that presents the vision explicitly. Another is *bhObe manuSguru niSTha jar/ SOrbo Sadhon Siddho hOe tar* ('all strivings are fulfilled if one's loyalty in this world is to the preceptor who gives access to the inner man'). The issue is not whether Lalon was preaching humanism; of course he was. The question is just how he spoke to the empirical humans in his time and place, and what inner core of humanity he invoked through esoteric teachings about *moner manuS*.

His discourse picked up threads familiar from earlier discourses pertaining either to Islam or to Hinduism, as was surely inevitable.

His aim was to get devotees to pay the kind of attention that constitutes devotion. This meant working with narratives, which were embedded in particular sub-traditions either Hindu or Islamic. The songs rested on the narratives, and each narrative presupposed a particular religious background, carrying distinctive lexical items in its train—which is where the distinctive lexical emphasis of our intervention becomes relevant.

Given the context of the enterprise here, it becomes appropriate to wonder if this picture of compartmentalised, tradition-hugging modes of spiritual striving preached in two parallel tracks by one preceptor is not refuted by the evidence of songs 18 and 19, which may invite a syncretistic tradition construal.

The text of song 18 runs: *na chilo aSman-jomin pObon-pani/ SaiM tOkhon nirakare./ ilahi almin, sadratul ekin/ kudroti gach pOeda kOre./ gacher chilo car Dal/ holo hajar Sal/ Ek Ek Dal, ki hal/ chilo tar kOtoi dure./ Sottor hajar Sal dhore/ gacher pOre Sadhon kOre/ baritalae hokum holo, nur jhorilo/ jhoriya donee sriSTi kOre./ Ekdin Dimbo bhore, bheSechilo noirakare/ lalon bOle hae ki khEla, kader mOola/ koreche nila Opar pare.*

Song 19 continues this unusual cosmogonic narrative: *Ekakare huhuNkare mere/ apni SaiM rObbana./ Ondhokar, dhOndokar, kuokar,/ noirekar SOb lina./ kun bole Ek SObdo kOre/ Sei SObde nur jhOre/ chOTi guTi holo tate/ Sono go tar bOrnona./ Sei chOe guTi hote/ chOeTi jiniS pOeda tate/ aSman-jomin srijonite/ mone tar hOe baSona./ chOYete tosbi holo/ Sei tosbi jOp korilo/ koranete proman rolo/ lalon kOe Sono Thikana.*

Colleagues in religious studies may wish to read songs 18 and 19 as a prolegomenon for a potential merger of the traditions Lalon Fakir was heir to. It is important to consider, or alternatively to eliminate, the possibility that these songs provide the first few moves in a syncretistic cosmogony amounting to a warrant for a serious third spiritual path, neither Hindu nor Muslim, that Lalon might be taken to have been recommending. If such a construal of these songs does indeed prove to be appropriate, then any linguistic comments will have to work with that understanding of the theological contours of Lalon's enterprise.

Such a construal does not survive scrutiny, however. Lalon himself insists on some measure of denominational purity in each session of any individual seeker's meditation. In song 37, he explicitly suggests that a seeker who wishes to use the Islamic path must follow what the Prophet has laid down, and that an improvised yoga that imitates some superficial features of Islam will not get a spiritual seeker anywhere: *bhulo na mon karo bhole/ rasuler din Sotto mano/ Dako SOdae alla bole./ khoda prapto mul Sadhona/ rasul bine ar keu jane na/ jaher batun upaSona/ rasul dara prokaSile./ dEkhadekhi Sadhile jog/ bipOd ghoTbe baRibe rog/ jejon hOe Suddho Sadhok/ nobir phOrmane Se cOle.*

Scholars who wish to confute this interpretation of song 37 will no doubt look for resources to do so. Philological experts may cast doubt on the authenticity of this item in the Lalon corpus, for instance. Or perhaps some scholar will focus on a passage from song 34—*kholifa auliya roile/ je ja bojhe diyo bole/ lalon bOle rasuler je/ nochihOt jari*—to argue that Lalon was in favour of allowing listeners to interpret any input in whatever way they are moved to do so. However, Lalon's oeuvre as a whole clearly suggests that it is important to preserve the spiritual integrity of each path.

In song 46, for instance, it becomes clear that the method of meditation associated with the Baul movement's best known brand, the *SOhoj manuS* motif ('the authentic inner man', if a rough and ready rendering will do as a temporary gloss, given that this key concept of Baul mysticism has no established translation associated with it), is not being projected as a site for free mixing of materials from various paths. Lalon's basic text is the Qur'an. He speaks explicitly of *namaj* in the text of song 46: *SOhoj manuS bhoje dEkh na re mon dibboggEne/ pabi re Omullo nidhi bOrtomane./ bhOjo manuSer cOron duTi/ nitto bostu pabi khaMti/ morile SOkol maTi/ ei bhed tOrae nao jene./ mole pabe behestkhana/ ta Sune to mon mane na/ bakir lobhe nOgod paona/ ke chaRe ei bhubOne./ assalatul mirazul momenina/ jano Sei namajer bena/ biSSaSider dEkhaSuna/ lalon kOe ei jibone.*

This line of interpretation is confirmed by the following passage in song 49: *ki kalam paThalen amar SaiM dOYamOe/ Ek Ek deSer Ek Ek bhaSa/ kOe khoda paThae./ Ek juge paThae kalam/ onno juge hOe kEno haram/ emni dekhi bhinno tamam/ bhinno dEkha jae./ jodi Eki khodar hOe rOcona/ tate to bhinno thake na/ manuSer SOkol rOcona/ taite bhinno hOe./ Ek Ek deSer Ek Ek bani/ paThan ki SaiM gunomoni/ manuSer rocito jani/ lalon fokir kOe.*

What then is one to make of song 33? Does the occurrence of a *rasul* ('messenger') here and a *khoda* ('God') there, amidst a deluge of Sanskritic words like *dOYal* ('compassionate'), *bondhu* ('friend'), *Sotto* ('truth'), *lokkho* ('goal'), betoken a theologically syncretistic path? Such hopes are dashed again; it suffices to read the text of song 33 as a whole: *tomar moto dOYal bondhu ar pabo na/ dEkha diye ohe rasul/ cheRe jeYo na./ tumi to khodar dosto/ Oparer kanDari Sotto/ toma bine parer lokkho/ ar dEkha jae na./ asmani Ek ain diye/ amader SOb anlen rahe/ Ekhon moder phaMki diye/ cheRe jeYo na./ amra SOb modinabaSi/ chilam jEmon bonobaSi/ toma hote gEn peYechi/ achi Santona./ tumi bine erup SaSon/ ke korbe ar diner karon/ lalon bOle ar to Emon/ bati jolbe na.*

This song too functions within the Islamic tradition, then. A couple of neutrally used Sanskritic words are able to appear precisely because they carry no theological baggage. Lalon is not departing from his policy of denominational differentiation—of deploying Perso-Arabic words in an Islamic context and seriously Hinduism-laden Sanskritic words only in the context of spiritual practices continuous with narratives or motifs from the Hindu traditions.

If one tries to make sense of words in Lalon's songs indiscriminately, without reference to context, one can get into real trouble. One example of such a risk appears in song 30. The song opens by invoking fundamental elements: *nire Suni nirOnjon holo/ nur chilo ki paMja paMja/ era kon nure elo./ kon nure hOe aSman jomi/ kon nure hOe* ***pObon pani****/ kon nure bhaSilen goni/ Se nure kon nur aSilo*. After such a beginning, a typical reader accustomed to the standard colloquial Bangla prevalent among non-Muslims can perhaps be forgiven for assuming that an occurrence of the word *haWa* in this song should count as synonymous with the boldface item *pObon* ('air, wind') that appears above alongside *pani* ('water'). However, this assumption breaks down at once, when one reads *adom bOlo kon nure hOe/* ***ma haWa*** *ki Se nure nai/ kOe roti nur* *jhOre kothae/ ihar bhed khule bOlo*. Here the word *ma* ('mother') helps make sense of the name *haWa*.

A Bengali not familiar with Islam who encounters the word *haWa* would normally assume that it means 'air, wind'. But the wind-god Pavana is not called a mother in any tradition. The text we are looking at actually invokes the primordial couple of the Semitic religious traditions, known as Adam and Eve in English. The name 'Eve' looks so different from its Arabic equivalent that it is hard for non-Islamic readers accustomed to the English form alone to recognise *haWa* as a rendering of the same name. It is much easier for an uninstructed reader to identify *adom* with 'Adam'. Unless one is told that an *admi*, a 'man', is built in Adam's image and that likewise an *aurat*, a 'woman', is made in Eve's image, one cannot, from the perspective of contemporary non-Muslim speakers of Bangla in a country like India, readily associate the form *haWa* with 'Eve'.

The common noun *haWa* ('wind, air') is a neutral word available to all Bengalis. But the proper noun *haWa* ('Eve') in Lalon's texts and elsewhere, to this day, is not simply a marker of the Islamic tradition—the homonymy of the word for 'wind, air' with this particular form of the marker creates a specific difficulty for some of our contemporaries trying to read Lalon or other Islam-rooted texts.

That particular lexical choices correlate with the traditions invoked by specific songs does not of course mean that Lalon never allows the two streams of his legacy to meet. One place where he does allow this is song 53: *o mon bOlo re SOdae lailaha illalla/ ain bhejilen rasul ulla./ namer Sohit rup/ dhiyane rakhiya jOpo/ beniSanae jodi Dako/ cinbi kirup ke alla./ la-Sorik janiya take/ pORo kalam dele mukhe/* ***mukti*** *pabi thakbi Sukhe/ dekhbi re nur tajella./ lailaha nophi Se hOe/ illalla Sei din dOYamOe/ nOph ejbat jahare kOe/ Sehi to ebadOt ulla./ boleche SaiM alla nuri/ ei jekerer darja bhari/ Siraj SaiM tai kOe pukari/ Son re lalon belilla.*

One point to be made here is that the entire theological baggage in the passage just quoted comes from Islam, as the lexical choices indicate, but that the goal is specified as *mukti*, the Sanskrit word for 'liberation', set in bold type above to make it salient.

The second point is as follows. Even an uninitiated reader sees that this text points to the spiritual unity at the level of goals that cut across denominational differences. However, the text clearly says, *beniSanae jodi Dako/ cinbi kirup ke alla* ('if your invocations are badly aimed/ how will you recognise who God is?'). One is urged to meditate on the name and the form held together in one's consciousness: *namer Sohit rup/ dhiyane rakhiya jOpo.*

It pays to dwell on this point. This mode of *japa* ('chant') based on a *naama* ('name') has been used by seekers both Hindu and Muslim; it can be seen as one place where these traditions become allies, so to speak. However, the logic of name-chanting needs to be borne in mind. Alliance is not merger. When meditating on a name, one considers elements of narratives associated with it. Hindus and Muslims cultivate traditions that cherish distinct religious narratives. The names one chooses to chant determine one's narrative itinerary and correspondingly one's preference for a Sanskritic or a Perso-Arabic mode of speech.

In other words, while the logic of name-chanting concentration does make for Hindu-Muslim alliance-building, and renders salient unity of the seekers' spiritual goals, the contextual specificity of the words they deploy also becomes a salient factor.

Suppose we pursue the thread of song 53, then, and ask just how the key words in the passage *ei* ***jekerer*** ('idea') ***darja*** ('level') *bhari* ('this idea belongs to a sublime level') managed to go missing in the Bangla spoken by Hindus—in contrast to what took place in the lexical history of Hindi, where *zikr* continues to mean 'thought' and *darjaa* still means 'class, grade (e.g. as in elementary schools)' regardless of the religious affiliation of particular speakers of Hindi—then we must take our investigation away from language per se. The crux of the matter has to do with the narratives setting the context. Within song 53, in the passage *la-Sorik janiya take/ pORo kalam dele mukhe*, the option *del* becomes the obvious word to use for 'heart', rather than *mon* or *hridOe*, because of the company it keeps in this diction, words like *kalam* and *la-Sorik*, and this lexical pattern reflects the default status of one particular set of underlying narratives.

One take on this state of affairs might be that it pays to notice that educated speakers of Hindi today say *dil* rather than *hriday* for 'heart' and *dimaag* rather than *mastiSk* for 'brain'. It is necessary to address the fact that Bangla did not follow a similar trajectory and thus cannot relate to Lalon's use of *del* as directly as Hindi can.

There is no gainsaying the importance of this question. However, the investigation of the mystical strand of religious writings—with a view to attaining a sustainable perspective on neutrality—is perhaps not the right context for raising it with the kind of seriousness called for. Let us move to the general level of discourse that that larger question resonates with, reach some sort of tentative closure on that front, and return to our Lalon.

That the linguistic history of northern India is sharply different from that of Bengal has to do with the fact that within the Hindi-Urdu speech community the social ties between the Hindu elite and the ashraf Muslims remained unbroken during the core period of modern history.[3] The milieu in which that Farsi-tinged, Hindi-Urdu-speaking elite practised their social and verbal arts also made a deep impression on the culture of ashraf Muslims in Bengal. One consequence was that when the Muslim elite in Bengal did come into its own, it found it necessary to use a few Perso-Arabic words—current in Hindi-Urdu—as a gesture betokening its affinity to the elite of Northern India.

In contrast, the intellectuals in the Bengali Hindu elite, having been through a trajectory marked by *Navya-Nyaya* and similar preoccupations, had attained a regional ascendancy that made them socio-culturally independent of northern India. As is well known, English replaced Farsi as the administrative language of Bengal only in the nineteenth century; before this, educated Hindus did learn Farsi in order to cope with the challenge of the administrative world, but they did not let Farsi into their own intellectual space. The rise of English marks the moment that has been described as the Bengal Renaissance.

Just what made Sanskrit words inundate Bangla as part of the renaissance process, is a complex question that our scholars have not

[3] What happened after that core period is summarised and analysed in Dasgupta and Sardesai (2009), q.v.

yet begun to face. A few remarks here maybe in order. In a politically subjugated community, it obviously made sense for the elite to seek to maintain a modicum of its prestige and to gather inner strength in the hope of regaining glory. Besides, the project of terminologically careful translation of English textbooks for the new school system left the elite with no choice but to use Sanskrit equivalents on a large scale (Qayyum 1982).

There were other factors at work. The BBK[4] coalition had a relatively cosy modus vivendi with the British rulers. That coalition's deployment of a Sanskritic diction as a marker of its *bhadralok* identity served two purposes. On the one hand the BBK were saying, our circumstances may compel us to fake a certain loyalty to the British, but of course we are not really like this, our fealty is to our indigenous tradition. On the other hand they were also saying, our adversaries are those who have wrested cultural ownership of these modern times; in order to resist them we must master modern intellectual tools; to this end we need to survey points of similarity and difference between Western thought and the ancient Indian tradition, which means retaining the Sanskritic weapons in our arsenal.

One possible construal, then, is that the need to devise an episteme that would enable modern resistance to a modern hegemon pushed the nascent modern elite in early nineteenth century Bengal towards an English-Sanskrit lexical tie-up. This elite saw itself as bearing a moral status for which it deployed the distinctive term *bhadralok* that has gained currency in anglophone social scientific and even journalistic commentary today. This elite also saw itself as the repository of a linguistic standard; this is what particularly concerns us in this paper. The proposal that standard speech is to be regarded as an epistemic default was first made by Patanjali, the major commentator on Panini's grammar of Sanskrit (the *Ashtadhyayi*); his commentary gave rise to one strand in the work of Bhartrihari, whose oeuvre is responsible for much of the substantivist (Dasgupta 2011) brand of linguistics; we hope that this quick reminder about

[4] A reference to the three most powerful castes in Bengal—Brahmins, Baidyas, Kayasthas.

the ancient Indian background that informs substantivist inquiry will plug some obvious gaps in this exposition; a single exposition can obviously never adequately represent its research programme; readers interested in getting a sense of the programme as a whole will have to look beyond one particular exposition.

The responsibility for worrying about the origin, development and dismal prospects of the *bhadralok* species—whose defaults are often paraded in reference works as if they were settings shared by the entire community, a quasi-sharing process known as hegemony—can be left in the able hands of social scientists, who have been exerting themselves in this domain. Consider for instance Dipankar Gupta (2010), who deploys the tools of mainstream sociology to make sense of the current vagaries of the *bhadralok* species. Gupta is worried at the decline of true *bhadra* ('gentle, polite') behaviour in India's gentry. In the final analysis, such moral and behavioural sophistication is undoubtedly related to the custodianship of standard speech and writing. In the present context, however, one is engaging in decidedly non-final analysis, and concentrating on the polished use of language.

What does substantivism have to say about such language use?

A standard mode of speech is mainly characterised by its version of the doctrine of default encoding. In other words, a few places in the language are privileged under the rubric of 'this is not merely one way to put the matter, this is the normal way to say it'. Thus words like 'boat' and 'letter' become default terms, while a word such as 'vessel' or 'epistle' counts as expressing some sort of stylistic taste. The default taste is not a taste; it is nature itself. The point that interrogating this play of less natural and more natural is the central interrogation of substantivist linguistics—with the twist that there are competing candidates for maximal naturalness at any given point on the history curve—is the only tenet that needs to be highlighted for the purposes of this intervention.

One aspect of the advent of the Sanskrit borrowings in nineteenth century Bangla was the fact that they began to count as default signifiers for those signifieds. A second axis had to do with the work that these recombinations or redeployments of Sanskrit elements were designed for in the context of the translation-coupling of English with

Bangla. Since then, the community of literate users of Bangla has been regulating its existence on the basis of an interlexical contract involving components of modernity and a certain Sanskrit-laden reading of ancient Indian history. Not a single phase of the British Indian trajectory, not a single phase of the freedom struggle produced an alternative lexicalisation strategy for implementing the discursive technology of a modern social existence. If any intervention today or later is to modify the default settings in the lexicon of Bangla with respect to the words borrowed from Sanskrit, such an initiative will involve renegotiating that interlexical contract.

There are no effects without causes. For a change of such magnitude to become feasible, new forces will need to come into play that go beyond just talking about words. Such forces will have to be effective at the level of action involving the serious setting of verbal defaults.

It is at this point in the argument that Lalon addresses us. Some of us, to be sure, have made no investment whatever in the conceptual or spiritual content of mystical poems or songs. Despite our illiteracy, nonetheless he addresses even us.

When Lalon states that valid devotion can follow more than one path but that these paths are equivalent, the point is that one must retain the integrity of one's quest. Surely there is no reason to construe his proposition as applicable to spiritual striving alone. Other readers of his oeuvre are free to take his point on board in their own projects as well.

Consider those of us who are wedded to the modernist gospel and have conceded that the discourse of science, in particular, deserves the hegemony it has attained, and must dominate the curriculum in any serious educational effort; this issue is pertinent because linguistics is a major adviser to the educational planners of a modern nation-state. Notice that it is this unquestioning acceptance of the hegemony of the positivism-laden forms of scientific inquiry that is responsible for the burden contemporary Bangla has to bear—the burden of an authoritative terminology that looks Sanskritic but is in fact an import-substituted version of the English terminological system.

Suppose we modernists—pondering the default status we have granted to this English-derived episteme, and using the apparatus of substantivism to re-examine this default—take a leaf out of Lalon's book and ask if it is in our power to choose to regard this lexical path as optional, as equivalent to other paths that we may be able to find to the same goal. Such a choice, if available, might set us free, might give us a certain *mukti*. Once we taste such liberty, that epiphany of ours might stop us from deriding the everyday register of speech as a mere informal dress that our thinking wears when it inhabits the space of ordinary public conversation. Such an epiphany might stop us from imagining that it is certain lexically formal-looking technical formulations that alone are qualified to carry the rigorous, specialised meanings of modern discourse, if by modern discourse we mean one that is subject to critical canons of scrutiny and accountability.

If we taste that liberty, we will stop being able to imagine, for instance, that implementing a literacy mission on the basis of standard principles—bowing to the exigencies imposed by passively accepted and unchallenged networks of scientific terms in contemporary Indian languages—is a straightforward way of doing good to the poor.

We shall begin to see, instead, that missions of the 'education for all' genre—sponsored by the United Nations and other venues of hasty 'international' confabulations not nourished by any critical cogitation reflecting the experiences and self-articulated needs of the South in general and its subalterns in particular—actually need to be recast as sites of cultural, cognitive and educational renegotiation.

Serious renegotiators, once they succeed in making their presence felt at such sites—overcoming the pressure to give in to mobilisations imposed from the commanding heights of the global decision-making system (which is governed by a not exactly accountable plutocracy)—will be able to get the cultural and educational systems to take notice of a fundamental point made by authors such as Bleich (1988).

The point is that both the adults involved at any serious site of 'Education for all' and the elders ethnically responsible for the children of indigenous peoples being schooled in a hurry through such systems, in order to make the global summiteers feel good about their millennium development goal performance, must be seen not as recipients of aid, but as sources of knowledge, from whom the 'educators' had better know how to learn. Bleich's point is a special case of the much older principle that a true teacher must be more teachable than the students s/he teaches (readers are hereby encouraged to discover for themselves who enunciated the principle in this form in 1951). If the hard-pressed persons who happen to have been given the responsibility of carrying out the mission under the supervision of more knowledgeable individuals, and on the basis of curricula designed by even more knowledgeable individuals, then this responsibility devolves on those sets of knowledgeable individuals.

It would be a mistake to read the rhetoric employed here as simply a notational variant of Rabindranath Tagore's *Opomane hote hObe tahader SObar Soman.*[5] The point is not just moral, but intellectual as well. It is intellectually crucial that we should arrive at a new deal in negotiations involving both ordinary language and the extraordinary cognitive cartography that underwrites that ordinary language, and that these negotiations should rigorously reference the dealings between the intended recipients and the purveyors of all this literacy largesse that the world proposes to unleash on its poor.

Why does this begin to look crucial after an epiphany makes available to us the insight that science is not a unique crucible for discursive coherence?

Such a reperception takes place because, once one has dethroned science from the presumption of unique authenticator status, the conceptual basis of the literacy service provider's scholastic pride dissolves. The point then becomes, for a secular scholar who used to base his or her cognitive coordinate system on Western and specifically anglophone premises, to relativise and contextualise, rather than to submit to the will of God or to the will of one's sponsors located in the global North. The point instead is to share one's scholastic knowledge with true humility with non-academic members of the public in the mode of discursive negotiation with fellow citizens far removed from one's own background.

---

[5] The full sentence, *he mor durbhaga deS, jader korecho Opoman/ Opomane hote hObe tahader SObar Soman*, is translated as followed by Gayatri Chakravorty Spivak: 'My unfortunate country, you will have to be equal in disgrace to each and every one of those you have disgraced millennially' (Spivak 2012: 318 and 568n8).

This involves allowing one's interactions with them to reshape one's understanding of the public space. Under the managerial conception that has lapsed into a default, the public space looks like an arena where one either manipulates or is manipulated. If one has not dislodged this default, seriously inclusive perceptions do not become available. Substantivism, an approach that encourages inquiry to place all defaults under scrutiny, pushes our argument in this direction, and bears on the issue of neutrality/ extremism via the fact that an 'education for all' mission targeting the world's poor is bound to target many Muslims, who have become one of the important recruiting grounds for practitioners of certain brands of extremism. Given the current balance of epistemic power, western-trained educational missionaries routinely try to stuff 'modern' knowledge down Muslim throats without exhibiting any inclination towards humility or dialogue. Substantivist reasoning, focussed on the fact that we have inappropriately allowed specific western traditions to occupy the default niche in our epistemic space, leads us to reconsider the basis for our default settings; we find that there actually is no defensible basis; we conclude that it is obligatory for would-be educators of the Muslim poor to start an ecumenical dialogue with the Islamic intellectual and moral tradition.

What are the specifiable intellectual reasons for such a request for humility and dialogue, if this is not a moralistic or political harangue hiding behind an intellectual facade?

The reasons have to do with the inappropriately dialogue-excluding mode of specialisation that soi-disant 'professional' parameters have imposed on rigorous inquiry within the western tradition, even if we consider it in isolation from cross-civilisational dialogue. Such academic overspecialisation, by minimising the search space for valid criticisms, has reduced Popper-falsifiability, thus reducing the scientific content of hypotheses. Re-establishing the public space means making a targeted effort to maximise falsifiability and enhance scientific content again, breaking out of the managerial economy's abridgement of the enlightenment. For a critical epistemological elaboration of this argument, see Dasgupta (2000). To the extent that specialisation fosters pride, this intellectual argument has moral implications as well, which leave its intellectual core intact.

Such an argument can only acquire teeth in a suitable social context. For us to be convinced that an inappropriately interpreted image of science drives the hegemony of English-backed Sanskritic-looking technical discourse in Bangla makes no difference per se. This conviction butters no parsnips. Do we have the resources to actually move out of the clutches of this scientism—this scientifically indefensible view of science as a unique site of valid statement?

One alternative to the default scientism of our current public discourse is articulated in Sarukkai (2002), who argues that scientific writing deploys a multisemiotic symbolic system. Elaborating on his work, it has been argued (Dasgupta 2011) that narrative and analytical discourse are intimately linked in the form itself of scientific writing. A science paper uses prose, equations, schematic diagrams and photographic representations in a multisemiotic set-up driven by the logic of narrative. Just as literary scholars have a duty to pay attention to at least the popular register of scientific discourse, producers and users of scientific writing too have a parallel duty to pay attention to the way narrative works in science writing without discontinuity from the role it plays in journalism. Readers who comprehend the geometry of this mutual accountability will notice at once that claims for the unique validity of scientific criteria in fact represent an unwillingness to face the burden of intellectual accountability.

None of us who have been targeting scientism have the slightest intention of undermining science; on the contrary. The point is to dethrone the obscurantist and indefensible claim that the scientific method is a unique path to novel and true propositions of cognitive interest in the public domain. Proponents of that position refuse to carry out Sarukkai-type studies themselves or even to perform the obvious duty of reading the studies that exist. That they avoid the reading any serious enterprise of rational discourse would require them to do, is vitiating the possibility of an accountable public debate regarding science. As it stands, soi-disant 'scientific' discourse has lapsed into an 'obscure and intuition-bound' (these words are used by Chomsky 1957: 5, in a different context) discursive formation that serves primarily commercial interests. Its proponents have no intention of becoming accountable, and use every means at their disposal to prevent the growth of accountable debating practices about their modes of inquiry.

Points related to these are familiar to readers who have been exposed to the writings of Tagore or Gandhi. Earlier in this intervention, there was a suggestion that it might make sense to revisit Tagore. Given the way the argument has in fact developed, it is appropriate to revisit Tagore's interface with science and terminology.

Tagore's overall stance on scientific terms closely hugs the popular lexical ground. The point was to empower ordinary speakers and bring them closer to the language of science, and science closer to the public. The terms he used for 'positive' and 'negative', for instance, were *hEM-dhormi*, *na-dhormi* ('yes-property-bearing, no-property-bearing'). Certain readers may anxiously point out that the traditional terms *dhonaMttok*, *rinaMttok* ('wealth-like, debt-like') are still used by scientists writing in Bangla; surely we are not suggesting that they abandon these and switch over to Tagore's coinages?

There is no call to be anxious. The needs of a beginner and those of a professional adult may well be different. Perhaps distinct chambers of the mansion of science will need distinct terms. That beginners are an essential part of the scientific community, that pedagogy is continuous with doing science—was a central tenet of Richard Feynman's take on physics. Feynman or Tagore, like Bleich, reminds us that a pedagogy is always a negotiation, and involves a continuum, not a rigid cluster of yes-no settings. Substantivism helps us to see that in the course of a pedagogy, the learners and the teachers with them, evolve through successive settings; they do not get attached to any permanent defaults. Once we drop the assumption that the anglophone scientism underlying most well-meaning, secular, modern inquiry into these matters is defensible as a foundation, we begin to take this negotiation at heart of pedagogy much more seriously. And we learn that a set of technical terms represents only one niche in an intricate ecology of scholastic labour connected to the public space of communication.

Tagore, however, did not have an interface with science alone. His dealings with spiritual seekers were so intense that calling these dealings an interface would be an understatement. For most readers, he just was a spiritual seeker. Now, corresponding issues arise in that domain. How far do ordinary people's everyday needs match those of the spiritual seekers who take on the role of icons for the community? Does the ordinary pedagogy of children share anything at all with what spiritual masters have to offer us? Is there some sort of continuum to learn about there as well? These perennial questions were central not only to Tagore as a poet and as a seeker, but also as an educator and a democratic articulator of public opinion. His oeuvre as a whole proposes that spiritual seekers too count as teachers, whose pedagogy the community must take seriously (without of course agreeing with everything that every pedagogue offers in this or any other mode).

To be sure, many of us value a strictly denomination-free education; ghastly experiences have made us justifiably suspicious of any proposal that seems to mix education with sermons of any type. Such rigorously secular readers sometimes fail to notice that secularism is not best served by steering clear of all contact with anything spiritual, but by exposing learners ecumenically to what teachers of several persuasions have to say. The latter view at least deserves equal time. The current state of affairs gives undue primacy to soi-disant conceptualisers—arrogating to themselves the right to asymmetrically educate all educators—whose positions, despite significant internal variation, converge on a view of humankind as deserving to be encouraged in the pursuit of its greedy essence. That a culture of unbridled impulses of gratification undermines the possibility of education itself, by weakening the affective basis of all learning, does not seem to matter to these prophets. At the very least, the other side of this debate deserves a hearing in the halls of education and culture.

The context for the present discussion is neutrality and the ethos that declares war on it. Most anti-neutralist ideological stances emanate from radicalised versions of philosophies—ranging from various religions to socialism—that negate greed; this is one reason that their extreme versions attract certain young minds. Once 'secular' intellectuals begin to live up to their responsibility to formulate credible philosophies that either (a) offer a viable[6] defence of their default preference to let greedy people feel justified in remaining greedy or (b) arrive at the conclusion that the quest for intellectual truth and moral integrity requires some fundamental bridling of the pursuit of gratification, it becomes possible to work in the context of a truly critical debate between moderate positions of the greed-negating type (religious or socialist) and the so-called neutral positions that are in fact anything but neutral.

Thinkers who wish to combat anti-neutralist extremism or its origins owe it to themselves, and to their intended beneficiaries, to work towards such an opening up of the space of secular, public discussion. The present study, on the basis of principles we need to inherit from Suniti Kumar Chatterji, has mainly tried to show that the substantivist research programme in linguistics is one of the tools that may come in handy for workers in this domain, and that Lalon Fakir's oeuvre is a useful object of study that these tools can help illuminate. That other readers will disagree with many points proposed here goes without saying. The point is that such disagreements need to be aired in a way that can take the discussion forward; and such an exercise involves looking at one's own preprogrammed defaults as critically as one can. One of our early culture heroes, Suniti Kumar Chatterji, never allowed himself to cultivate the defaults his forefathers had bequeathed him, and immersed himself in historical processes in the hope that Bengal, India and the world—his sense of community was cosmopolitan, as we see from the company he kept—would have the energy and the vision to take them forward. May we inherit his resolute refusal to get trapped in inappropriately accepted inheritances.

---

[6] In this context, viability must include at least a credible response to the normally sidelined point that a culture of unbridled impulses of material gratification (both sensual and pecuniary count as material gratification) undermines the possibility of education itself, by weakening the affective basis of all learning.

References

Bleich, David. (1988). *The Double Perspective: Language, Literacy, and Social Relations*. Evanston, IL: Northwestern University Press.

Chomsky, Noam. (1957). *Syntactic Structures*. The Hague: Mouton.

Dasgupta, Probal. (1993). *The Otherness of English: India's Auntie Tongue Syndrome*. New Delhi/ Thousand Oaks/ London: Sage.

____ (2000). 'The post-missionary condition: Towards perceptual reciprocity'. In Sherry Simon and Paul St-Pierre (eds), *Changing the Terms: Translating in the Postcolonial Era*. Ottawa: University of Ottawa Press, 289–305.

____ (2011). *Inhabiting Human Languages: The Substantivist Visualization*. Delhi: Samskriti (On behalf of the Indian Council of Philosophical Research).

____ (2014). 'Judges and grammarians in Britain's liberal pedagogic performance: A diglossic approach to colonial Bengal'. *Droit et Cultures*, 67, 151–86.

____ (2015). 'Dialects, literature and thin description'. *Humanities Circle*, 3/1, 117–27.

Dasgupta, Probal, and Madhavi Sardesai. (2009). 'Sociolinguistics in South Asia'. In J. Martin Ball (ed.), *The Routledge Handbook of Sociolinguistics around the World*. London/ New York: Routledge, 81–88.

Gupta, Dipankar. (2010). 'Manners make the middle class: How we interact with people around us reveals a lot about our socio-economic progress'. *The Times of India*, 11 October, 16.

Jha, Shaktinath. (1995). *Fakir Lalon Sai: Desh Kaal Ebong Shilpo*. Kolkata: Sangbad.

Qayyum, Muhammad Abdul. (1982). *A Critical Study of the Early Bengali Grammars*. Dhaka: Asiatic Society of Bangladesh.

Sarukkai, Sundar. (2002). *Translating the World: Science and Language*. New York: University Press of America.

Shah, Fakir Anwar. (ed.). (1998). *Lalon-Sangit*, volume 3. Kushtia: Lalon Mazhar Sharif o Seba-Sadan Committee.

____ (2000a). *Lalon-Sangit*, volume 1, 2nd edn. Kushtia: Lalon Mazhar Sharif o Seba-Sadan Committee.

—— (2000b). *Lalon-Sangit*, volume 2, 2nd edn. Kushtia: Lalon Mazhar Sharif o Seba-Sadan Committee.

Spivak, Gayatri Chakravorty. (2012). *An Aesthetic Education in the Era of Globalization*. Cambridge, MA.: Harvard University Press.

PART II

Languages and Cultures in South Asia

3

Exploring Odia Culture

A Study of Some Odia Cultural Narratives and Practices

B.N. Patnaik

Abstract

For Suniti Kumar Chatterji, Odia culture has an aesthetic dimension and a spiritual dimension. The best of medieval literature and the great temples and caves, among others, of Odisha represent the former and the tradition of Jagannath temple that totally rejects caste and caste-based pollution represents the latter. This paper sets aside the spectacular objects and studies instead some minor puranic compositions and oral tales to understand Odia culture. Its findings reinforce Chatterji's observation about Jagannath culture and by extension, Odia culture. Culture is not static and the paper mentions instances of culture change and discusses in some detail a particular religious-cultural practice that is in the process of change. The paper maintains that endangerment and preservation are notions that apply to both language and culture and makes some remarks on how certain Odia cultural practices can be preserved. Without engaging with these notions in much detail, the paper observes that a community can be said to have an 'aspirational culture' and a 'lived culture'. The former could be viewed as a set of values and objects that the community celebrates more as memory than as representing real life. The paper suggests that 'lived culture' can be arrived at, from a study of the food and dress culture, recreational activities, beliefs, taboos, naming system, day-to-day linguistic interactions, among such others. Both the aspirational and the lived cultures are important and these together offer an understanding of the culture of a community.

In his characterisation of Odia culture, Suniti Kumar Chatterji in *The People, Language and Culture of Orissa* (1966), suggests that the following be taken as its representative features: 'Jagannath(a) cult', as he calls it, which singularly rejects caste considerations and caste-based pollution; artistic achievements, including the caves of Khandagiri and Udayagiri—with their carvings on secular themes—which is remarkable; and the great temples—the most celebrated being the Konark temple; great literature written in both Odia and Sanskrit; sublime music and dance; maritime achievements in the past and history of resistance to invaders and the gentleness and simplicity of the people. Chatterji arrived at his conclusions by looking at, what are clearly the most spectacular and the most highly celebrated, with respect to Odisha. However, there are things hidden under their shadows and we believe that a careful study can lead to meaningful insights. These neglected things include wise sayings, naming systems, idioms and proverbs, riddles, jokes, tongue-twisters, tales of the supernatural, *brata katha*s ('tales associated with fasts') and *mahatyam*s ('narratives that celebrate places, months, trees and plants, etc.'). Pursuing this broad approach, this paper deals with some less studied cultural texts and a certain religious and cultural practice that is presently undergoing change.

The paper is organised in four parts. The first part makes some general introductory observations about culture and the way a community negotiates with its cultural values and practices. It suggests that culture may be conceptualised at two levels: the collective and the individual. These may or may not always converge. The second part offers an analysis of the selected written and oral texts and the third, of a practice—undergoing change—associated with the partaking of *mahaprasad*, the consecrated food offered to Shri (Lord) Jagannath (henceforth, Jagannath, following informal discourse in Odia). The fourth deals with the issue of the endangerment of culture and its preservation, an issue that arises in the context of language as well.

I

A literate community with thousands of years history, like many in India, recalls its past through its epics, *lokakatha*s ('folktales'), *lokagita*s ('folk songs'), riddles, proverbs, *bacana*s ('wise-sayings'), kinship terms, naming practices, tongue-twisters and the like, and also non-linguistic expressions such as painting, dance and music, and certain practices associated with the celebration of festivals, observance of ritual fasts, partaking of sacred food, among others. There are then community performances with both linguistic and non-linguistic features, such as *dandanacha* ('a type of folk dance'). All these are carriers of world views, belief systems, ethical codes, modes of living, and many other kinds of knowledge systems in terms of which the ancestors of a community had made sense of their world and negotiated with it on a day-to-day basis. The thoughts, beliefs, rituals and other practices, the artistic creations and other artifacts, which have stood the test of time, can be viewed as constituting the cultural repertoire of that community. Drawing from this repertoire, members of a community often make sense of their world and assign meaning to their experiences. When it does so, the community, often unawares, re-lives its past, and this it does in several ways. When Odia parents, even today, hesitate to name their girl child 'Ganga' or when one tries to comfort someone suffering for no fault of his, saying *bhagya dose ramachandra gale banabasa* ('because of destiny Ramachandra went on exile to the forest') or either fondly or otherwise calls an obese child Bhima, one re-lives one's cultural past.

Homogeneity is often not the feature of a community, especially when it is large; thus what some members of a given community might count as belonging to their culture, others of the same community might not—not as strongly at least. Members of a cultural community do not assign the same meaning or significance to each cultural entity that is part of the total cultural repertoire of a community. Such differences, however, are likely to be rather minimal in the case of small organisations, for instance, a sports body like the East Bengal Football Club or a cultural organisation like the Ramakrishna Mission. Culture may be conceptualised at two levels: the collective and the individual, like language. A given sentence, say a code-mixed sentence, may be viewed as a sentence of his language by one native speaker, but not so by another. When one rejects a code-mixed sentence as not belonging to his language, X, one is conceptualising X at an individual level, but to the extent that he considers that sentence with respect to his language in order to make that judgement at all; he is arguably thinking of language as a social entity in some sense. Thus there is no contradiction when two speakers of Odia offer contradictory judgements about, say, the status of an Odia-English code-mixed sentence and assert that they are the speakers of the same language, Odia. This makes Odia an abstraction. Similarly, there is no contradiction when two persons asserting their membership of the same cultural community, say, Odia (using the same term for both the language and the culture), differ with respect to whether touching menstrual blood or a dead body is polluting or not. Thus Odia culture is an abstract notion, and specific cultural ideas and their realisations in the form of artefacts, attitudes, observances and the likes, are particular concretisations of this abstract notion.

Odia culture can be said to be a composite of at least the following subcultures: Hindu—which constitutes the base, Jagannath, Islamic, Western and north Indian. The underlying concept of Jagannath subculture, as noted by Chatterji, is inclusiveness; it rejects caste and upholds equality and its ritual system integrates beliefs and forms of worship of various sects and communities, such as the tribal, Shaiva, Shakta, Brahminical and Vaishnava. Interaction of Hinduism with Islam has resulted in the worship of *pira*s ('Sufi spiritual guide') by both Hindus and Muslims, the worship of *satyapira* ('corresponding roughly to Satya Narayan of the Hindus'. Satya Pir was a seventeenth century Sufi saint of Odisha. He was worshiped by both the Hindus and the Muslims) and the creation of a body of stories called *satyapirakatha*s (in which Satya Pir corresponds to Satya Narayan of the Satya Narayan Puja of the Hindus) that describes his glory and power. In some (setting aside details) *palas*, a performance reminiscent of *harikatha*, a *satyapira* story is ritually recounted in Odisha. This interaction has also given rise to, among others, a form of satirical farce called *mogalatamasa*, which emerged in the eighteenth century in Northern Odisha. The impact of the Western values and lifestyle on the population under reference has been pervasive; it is evident at the level of beliefs and attitudes and of daily life, which are too well-known to detail here. In many domains of day-to-day life, interaction between tradition and Western culture has created interesting hybrid beliefs and practices. It is these that probably constitute the most interesting instances of the westernisation of the native Odia culture. For instance, not many Odias remember the Odia New Year, but on the first of January a large number of people visit temples for an auspicious start to their new year. *Prasad* ('food offered to gods') is still considered sacred food, but instead of partaking of it on the floor as stipulated by tradition, educated city dwellers prefer to have it on their dining table for reasons of hygiene. The influence of north Indian culture—which is a recent phenomenon—has resulted in new practices, such as the burning of the effigy of Ravana, Kumbhakarna and Indrajit on the day of Dussera. In the process, one story of the destruction of the negative forces, of *adharma*, is substituted by another story, borrowed from another tradition, with the same theme. In Odisha this day is associated, primarily with the destruction of evil in the form of the powerful demon Mahisasura by Goddess Durga, and only secondarily with the killing of Ravana, representing *adharma*, by Rama. *Hanuman Chalisa* ('couplets celebrating Lord Hanuman') is immensely popular as is *Tulsi Ramayan*, written in Hindi, but people know almost nothing about the Odia Ramayana—*Dandi Ramayana*, also called *Jagamohana Ramayana*—composed by the sixteenth century poet Balarama Dasa. As new gods become popular, new places of worship and new *satsanga*s ('gatherings of devotees to deliberate on the doings of their favourite gods or sages') come into existence. In Odisha, with Santoshi Mata in the 1980s and more recently, Shirdi Sai Baba, new narratives have arrived from outside and have found their place in the growing repertoire of Odia cultural narratives.

This paper maintains that inclusiveness is one of the most important Odia cultural values and analyses two minor puranic compositions, two oral narratives and a certain cultural practice in order to support this assertion. The last three are connected with the ritual system in the Jagannath temple in Puri. None of the above five is spectacular. The main reason we choose to discuss two minor puranic compositions here rather than any of the three major and celebrated ones, namely, Sarala Das's *Mahabharata*, Jagannatha Dasa's *Bhagabata* and Balarama Dasa's *Jagamohana Ramayana*, is to show that important insights into Odia culture can be obtained from a study of the minor works as well. The events in these two narratives centre around two related central characters: Lakshmi, the goddess of prosperity, in *Lakshmi Purana* and Alakshmi, the goddess who is her opposite, in *Kartika Mahatmya*. *Kartika Mahatmya* is an eighteenth century composition by Mahadeva Das, and *Lakshmi Purana*, a sixteenth century composition by Balarama Dasa. These narratives are simple in structure, their content is simple and they are limited in terms of scope and vision. Of these, *Lakshmi Purana*, is more didactic; it spells out a moral code, outlining what one should or should not do in order to live a virtuous life. Such minor works, which are close to the *loka sahitya* ('folk literature') in spirit, appear to inform us about the 'lived culture' of the people better than the celebrated *purana*s ('a class of Sanskrit writings not included in the Vedas'), which deal with a wide range of topics and issues of great complexity in a serious, reflective and sophisticated manner. They can be said to represent what can tentatively be called the 'aspirational culture' of the people.

Although called a *purana* by the poet himself, *Lakshmi Purana* is not a *purana*, lacking in the vast scope, the comprehensiveness and the depth of insight, which characterise a purana. It is actually a *brata katha*. A *brata katha* is a story associated with ritual observances of the worship of a god or goddess, more often a goddess, such as Lakshmi, Mangala, Shashthi, etc. and with ritual fasting. In addition to *brata kathas*, there are *osha kathas* as well, similarly associated with the worship of goddesses and with fasting. The differences between them are beyond the scope of this chapter. The story in these two categories of puranic compositions is always about how one suffers when one— however wealthy or mighty, deliberately or otherwise—offends a certain goddess, say Lakshmi or Mangala, and then about how the person becomes even more prosperous than he was before when he surrenders to the goddess and observes the *brata* or the *osha* associated with her. At the same time most of these narratives provide a list of what—more often than not—a woman must or must not do in order to lead a virtuous life, from which one gets a glimpse into the social and belief systems of those days.

II

The story of Alakshmi is an important creation of Mahadeva Das. The concept of 'alakshmi' is the same here as in the puranic literature in Sanskrit. However here, unlike in the classical tradition, there is an attempt to accommodate her in the order of things and in discourse as well. There seems to be no narrative in classical puranic literature devoted to her and this might be due to the common belief, still existing, that telling her story or listening to it might bring misfortune to both narrator and listener. Sage Narada once observed, as goes the saying, that Alakshmi is beautiful when she leaves (and Lakshmi is beautiful when she arrives), which one might interpret to mean that it is best for a narrative to avoid even mention of her. In fact, Alakshmi has been the great taboo of classical puranic literature. Against this background when the story of Mahadeva Das is viewed, one cannot fail to acknowledge the poet's courage to break the tradition in times unsympathetic to such efforts and bring the hitherto taboo, namely, Alakshmi, into puranic discourse. His narrative recognises the negatives of the reality, accepts their existence and tries to find a way to accommodate the same in life—*tamas* ('darkness or ignorance') has a place in life and cannot be wished away. *Lakshmi Purana* is viewed here as an attempt, on the one hand, to create a belief system in order to restrict the woman's space in the society and, on the other, to legitimise her need for space in her own terms. As for the oral narratives—one is about Goddess Rai and the other is about a ghost in the temple town of Puri. To the best of the author's knowledge, neither of these, whose origins are unknown, has been the subject of academic deliberations so far. These four narratives are interpreted here as highlighting the inclusive nature of Odia culture. Each is a complex discourse in the sense that each juxtaposes contrasts and tries to find a way of accommodating them both. It may be viewed as the acceptance of this 'different other', embodied in these discourses, that we suggest is the hallmark of Odia culture.

The Alakshmi episode can be viewed as a narrative of counter-culture. Both the dominant culture and its counter-culture are part of the repertoire of Odia culture, as of many others. This narrative projects a perspective on the good and evil that is different from the one in puranic literature, which can be roughly summed up as follows: these two forces are at war with each other, in which evil may win initially but would eventually be annihilated through the intervention of the divine. In the 'Swargarohana Parva' in *Sarala Mahabharata*, when Arjuna is persuaded to surrender to God Agni his weapons, to which he was deeply attached, the god told him that he would return them to him when, in another *yuga* ('aeon'), another war would be fought between the good and the evil and Arjuna would be born again to destroy evil. In the *Srimad Bhagavad Gita*, Sri Krishna declares that he will descend to the mortal world whenever evil forces become powerful and upset the cosmic balance that sustains the creation and that he will protect the virtuous and annihilate the sinners. The Alakshmi story is not part of this paradigm, which is an important reason why it deserves attention.

The story is this: the great deluge took place and the essence of things got assimilated into the supreme god Narayana, and the residue existed in the form of dirt and mud. In due course, calm returned and process of creation started again. Brahma first created *dharma*, so dirt and mud remained excluded from the creation. No one spared a thought for it. It was then born as Alakshmi, the daughter of Varuna, the god of water. Then the great churning of the ocean took place, and Lakshmi, the beautiful goddess of prosperity, emerged from the ocean. Her father, Varuna, married her to Vishnu. The elder sister remained unmarried. No one would marry the ugly, quarrelsome, jealous Alakshmi. Later at Lakshmi's entreaties Vishnu got her married to a renowned sage but she found the atmosphere of the ashram extremely stifling. Being the embodiment of negatives, she could not live with whatever was holy and whoever was virtuous. The sage took her to the forest under a false pretext and abandoned her there. When she realised what had happened, she cried aloud piteously and her cries reverberated through the entire creation. At Lakshmi's request, Vishnu invited her back to his abode, the ever blissful Vaikuntha, but she refused to go there saying that she would only suffer there, seeing the prosperity and the happiness of her younger sister Lakshmi. She requested Vishnu to find her a place congenial to her nature. The Supreme One told her to reside in places where there is quarrel, dishonesty, ugliness and unhappiness. He also said that once a week she would receive worship with him under the sacred peepal tree, where her sage-husband had abandoned her.

The significance of this story is that it does not eliminate Alakshmi but accommodates her. Vishnu found her request for a suitable place entirely reasonable and empathised with her on her rejection of Vaikuntha. He gave her legitimacy by sharing with her the worship offered to him. Acceptance of the negative aspect as part of reality and working out a way of living with it is celebrated in this story. Alakshmi could not be faulted for being what she was—ugly and jealous and quarrelsome; she did not choose to be so. Created out of mud and dirt, negativity was part of her essential nature. Jagannatha Dasa in his *Bhagavata* had articulated the same vision about two hundred years before *Kartika Mahatyma* was composed; the snake Kaliya told Krishna that he was not to blame for his wickedness because he was born as a snake and that was not because of his choice: *sarparejatakalu mote/swabhavachadibikemante* ['you gave me the birth of a snake/how can I give up my (snake-like) nature?']. Mahadeva Dasa's narrative strongly suggests that the best moral response to the negative is to find a way of accommodating it, knowing that the consequence could be extremely unwelcome and even catastrophic in future.

In mainstream Odia culture, Alakshmi has the same place as in traditional Indian culture. In Sanskrit, she is often referred to as 'Lakshmi's elder sister', as though the utterance of the word that names her is capable of bringing unhappiness to a family. In Odia, alakshmi is almost an abuse; one insults a woman by calling her 'alakshmi'. The word semantically related to this word, and apparently derived from it, namely, *alakshani*, is far more frequently used in contexts of gossip, backbiting and quarrel. It literally means 'the one with negative attributes', the superimposed meaning being 'the one who brings bad luck'. In sum, Mahadeva Das's Alakshmi lives today in Odia language as an abusive term.

Balarama Dasa's *Lakshmi Purana* has often been regarded as a narrative of protest against caste-based discrimination. Goddess Lakshmi is asked to leave the Big Temple by Jagannath and his elder brother Lord Balabhadra because she had accepted worship in a low-caste woman's house. She leaves and later, when Jagannath requests her to return home, she makes him promise that there would be no caste consideration while partaking of *mahaprasad*, the food that she cooks for him. A brahmin and a low-caste person would receive *mahaprasad* from each other's hands. Balabhadra assures her that she could visit anyone's house and accept worship, be it a brahmin's or a low-caste person's. What has not always been appreciated is that it also articulates a protest against denial of space to the homemaker.

Lakshmi Purana can be viewed as an important text of lived culture. It defines what constitutes a moral life and accordingly constructs a code of conduct for day-to-day living. Since it is about Odia lived culture, a characterisation of which has received neglect in scholarly writing in on the subject, some details of it are in order here. It is important to note that it articulates the code and questions a very important part of it at the same time, a matter to which we will soon return.

Incidentally, today this code would be rejected as sexist, which is not unexpected because a code is only a product of a certain socio-cultural milieu. The code under reference is more about what the virtuous woman must do than what the virtuous man must, and it is more concerned with the married woman than the unmarried girl. A married woman must do and must not do certain things on certain specific days and both men and women must not do certain things on all days. The code specifies the 'don'ts' a good deal more than the 'dos'. It is not surprising because this is the most economical way of listing, since a list of constraints about what to eat, what not to, and similar things, would always be shorter than that of recommendations.

The directives in *Lakshmi Purana* which, to repeat, characterise lived culture, are about physical and mental well-being: about food and food related pollution, cleanliness, family duties, and respect for tradition. On Thursdays, which is Goddess Lakshmi's day, women must not take non-vegetarian food, meat cooked in bottle gourd, things roasted in fire, and leftover or burnt food. They must not fry raw rice, neither must they beat children. One must not eat rice with curd at night, and on Thursday, *amavasya* and *sankranti* nights, one must not have food at all. One must not eat facing the south or the west, nor must one eat sitting on the floor without something to sit on.

Not washing one's face in the morning, not washing one's face after eating food, not washing one's hair on Thursday, having food without washing one's feet, and applying oil to the body after bath are among the forbidden. Not combing and tying hair in the evening is forbidden, as is sleeping on a crumpled bed. Sexual discipline is an important part of the code; on certain days, sex is forbidden and it is forbidden outside of the wedlock. Women must treat the guest with respect and must light the sacred lamp in the evening, they must respect tradition and observe traditional practices. And a woman must not be quarrelsome, lazy, unpleasant and bold.

Let us now examine how *Lakshmi Purana* questions the code. The most important part of it concerns the way a woman must relate to her husband. For her nothing is more important than serving her husband. No matter what religious acts she performs—going on pilgrimage, observing *bratas*, performing *tapas* ('meditation'), worshipping gods and goddesses—she acquires no religious merit if her husband is displeased with her. Her husband's joys and sorrows must be hers, and she must always obey her husband, and be pleasing in her dealings with him, and never get irritated with him. Goddess Lakshmi does not herself abide by the code. She curses her spouse and starves Him and Balabhadra for twelve years. This flagrant violation of the code is not condemned in the text; on the contrary, it is acclaimed.

Coming to the story of Rai, called *Rai-Damodara Katha*, it has a distinctly oral flavor to it (Patnaik, Arabinda 2012: 308–09). It has not been analysed and discussed in scholarly literature so far. Even an authentic text is not available now. Here goddess Lakshmi is portrayed as even more accommodative than in *Kartika Mahatmya*. It is one thing for a woman to be helpful and accommodating towards one's sister, however unpleasant and disgraceful she may be; it is quite another to be kind and indulgent towards one's co-wife. The normal relationship between the co-wives is captured in this Odia proverb: *ghaitapachakemaru, sautunirandaheu* ('let the husband die/ the co-wife becomes a widow'). The co-wife in question here is Rai, the Odia girl, who was eldest daughter of the head-priest of Puri temple in some unrecorded distant past. She is totally unrelated to Radha of Vaishnavite conception. Rai's consort was Jagannath himself. With 'Vishnu-isation' or 'Krishna-isation' of Jagannath, legends emerged in which he acquired wives. Rai was deified after her wedding. Pleased with her devotion to her, goddess Lakshmi granted her the boon that she would be worshipped with Jagannath for twenty-five days. This legend is celebrated in a ritual in Jagannath temple in Puri. From the first day of the month of *Kartika*, for twenty-five days, Rai-Damodara puja is held in the temple. The story of Rai is purely an Odia story in that it has no ancestry in classical Indian puranic literature. And this is a narrative of accommodation which characterises Jagannath culture and for many, by extension, Odia culture.

As for the supernatural beings about whom many tales exist, here we consider only *Babana bhuta* ('ghost named Babana'). There are two *Babana bhutas* in the traditional tales in Odia; one occurs in *Sarala Mahabharata* and the other exists purely in the orality. There is no tale about it. In the *Sarala Mahabharata*, there is an episode, which shows the damning consequences of enjoying the property that belongs to others as well. *Babana bhuta* occurs in this episode. Babana is a very powerful and malevolent ghost and because of his greed, he ends up being imprisoned by a tantric. The other *Babana bhuta*, with whom we are concerned here, is associated with Rath yatra ('chariot festival') in Puri. There is no published story of this ghost, not even in the form of a bazar booklet, to the best of our knowledge. During the twelve-day festival, the Gundicha temple becomes the abode of the deities for a week. When they leave this temple, it is *Babana bhuta* who keeps watch over the temple. When the deities are there, he quietly perches himself on the top of a wall of the compound. Before they partake of the *mahaprasad* in the precincts of the Gundicha temple, devotees set aside a bit of the sacred food on a small leaf for him. Unlike ordinary ghosts, he has no unfulfilled human desires, no interest in the world of the humans and does not interfere with them in any way. This story shows how Jagannath worship and Jagannath narrative are both inclusive—gods, humans and other lower existences, all have a place there. For some Odias at least, this attitude of inclusiveness is part of not merely Jagannath culture, but of Odia culture.

III

Culture changes, as does language. Sometimes a culture or a language changes on account of its contact with other cultures or languages, especially those which are highly valued by the community concerned. Language change and culture change have both been recognised as important subjects for study. Such a study can suffer, quite obviously, because of lack of reliable diachronic data. Consider the case of three Odia particles in this regard. The particle *je* was used in the sixteenth century as relative clause marker and also as an emphasiser, setting aside its other uses for the present; it is now being used as a reported speech marker as well. This may be due to the contact of Odia with English we provide no justification for this remark because that would take us far afield. Similarly, the particle *ki* was used as a question marker in the fifteenth century; it is now being used as an alternative reported speech marker. This could be because of the influence of Hindi. The particle *boli* was used as a reason clause marker (there were other uses also) in the twelfth century; it is used now as a reported speech marker as well, which may not be due to language contact, at least directly. Intuitively speaking, the change in each case could not have taken place suddenly; it must have happened over time but there is no diachronic data, as of now, that captures the process of this change. Similarly, going by *Sarala Mahabharata*, 'Babana', in the fifteenth century, was used as a proper noun; it was the name of a malignant ghost. Now it is used as a common noun referring to a good-for-nothing person with an unkempt appearance. The change in the category and the meaning of this term—bleaching of its malignant meaning and acquisition of its good-for-nothing sense, among others—cannot again be a one-time occurrence. But as of now, here is no diachronic data that informs us about the process of this change. The process of change is important in itself and it is even more so as it can lead to an insightful and comprehensive theory of language change.

Cultural practices change likewise when a culture comes in contact with another culture. Contact with Islam in Odisha gave rise to Satya Pir puja, as mentioned earlier. These days in some middle-class urban Odia families, on a birthday, puja is offered to Goddess Shasthi in the morning and the cake is cut in the evening. But not all changes are due to contact. The following feature of Jagannath culture, concerning the partaking of *mahaprasad* may be one such. 'Throughout the whole of caste-ridden India', says Chatterji, '...Puri is the only place caste is thrown to the winds under the aegis of Lord Jagannath' (1966: 70). He was surely referring to *mahaprasadsevana* ('partaking of *mahaprasad*'). As mentioned earlier, people would partake of it without any caste-based inhibitions. It is extremely unlikely that this was the practice from the very beginning because it is totally un-brahminical. Now, almost next to nothing is known about the origin of this practice and the nature of resistance that it must have faced from the priests in the beginning and subsequently as well and the way it withstood that pressure till it became the norm.

Diachronic data about change in practices belonging to lived culture is difficult to get; it often does not get recorded because the elite tend to view such practices of day-to-day life as rather trivial and as such, unworthy of serious attention. If we want to understand lived culture and construct interesting theories of it, we need to document change carefully and exhaustively.

For instance, the culture of *mahaprasadsevana* ('partaking of *mahaprasad*'), which is part of Odia lived culture is undergoing a change now under the pressure of modernisation. We cannot predict with confidence what form it will take, say, fifty years from now. We are witness to the change taking place at present and are best placed to capture it.

Rejection of caste is not the only feature of *mahaprasadsevana*. There are other non-spectacular features. One must sit cross-legged on the floor and have the sacred food from a leaf plate or a banana leaf. In the compound of the Jagannath temple in Puri, there is a small area, called 'Ananda Bazaar' ('market of divine delight'). People partake of *mahaprasad* there sitting on the floor. No one violates this tradition. Nowadays, it is difficult, even on normal days (when there is no special puja), to find a place in Ananda Bazaar to partake of *mahaprasad*. The space is inadequate for today's requirements, and is always overcrowded. With thousands of devotees partaking of the sacred food there, and in the lack of regular and efficient cleaning system, the place is hardly ever clean. Things get much worse when it rains. Besides, one can hardly have *mahaprasad* in peace, because urchins hover around asking for a portion of it. Tradition allows one to approach anyone, who may be entirely unknown, for *mahaprasad* and the latter is obliged to give him some from his own leaf as there is no concept of *aintha* ('leftover and contaminated food') with respect to this extremely sacred food. One is tradition-bound not to treat the person as a beggar.

For reasons of hygiene, avoidance of harassment of the kind mentioned above and physical comfort, urbanites these days prefer to buy *mahaprasad* at Ananda Bazaar and take it home. At home, too, they are expected to observe the same constraints: at the very least, they have to sit on the floor, without any *asana* ('seat') and use leaf plates and cups or banana leaf, etc. Besides, they must not eat cooked food prepared at home along with *mahaprasad*. But these days all these restrictions are not strictly observed, even in many Puri homes. Some, who are not advanced in age or physically disadvantaged, sit on a chair, while having *mahaprasad*. Others still sit on the floor but on some *asana*, be it a mat or a carpet or even a newspaper, so as to protect their clothes, and they eat from a plate, or sometimes from a special plate set aside for sacred food. Leaf plates and cups and banana leaves are not always easily available.

About half a century ago, in Puri, *mahaprasad* was routinely served in marriage receptions. There were certain disadvantages in this arrangement. Sometimes for reasons beyond the control of the host, *mahaprasad* would arrive late, sometimes at midnight or even later. This certainly did not happen very often but there was no knowing in advance on which day it might. Guests would return home hungry or wait till midnight, hungry. But no one would complain. Tradition does not allow one to comment on the quality of the sacred food in either negative or positive terms: a certain item is a little overcooked, another a little undercooked, the third being poor in taste, and the fourth, great in taste. If one is unhappy with the quality of *mahaprasad* served, they could partake of it a little and leave the rest on the leaf.

These days at weddings and receptions on non-religious occasions, both *mahaprasad* and 'party food', with a number of non-vegetarian items are served. The former is served in a small enclosure and very few, usually the elderly, opt for it. People's lifestyle has changed and with that their beliefs, values and their meaning. Practices which are difficult to follow or are not in consonance with the spirit of the day fade into history. Sometimes there remains a residue. It is through that residue, that enclosure where only a very few wedding guests go for *mahaprasad*, that we connect with our past, with our severely endangered culture.

IV

This section, with examples from Odia culture, deals with the matter of the preservation of culture and the role of the members of the cultural community in this regard. As their world changes, they adopt new practices, new world views and new narratives. The old texts and practices fade into the past. Many *vachanas* ('wise sayings'), idioms and proverbs, which have gone out of use, are unintelligible today to the younger generations of Odias. For instance, the proverb *asamayare gadhapaadhariba* ('holding the feet of a donkey in difficult times') is unintelligible to most today. Many may vaguely infer the sense from the literal meaning of the expression, but they would not be able to understand its full meaning and significance because they do not know the context of this expression, which is an episode in *Sarala Mahabharata*. As their full meaning is lost, people tend to dismiss the relevant entities as mere superstitions or silly burdens of the past. *Dahukas* ('ritual charioteers') no more call upon devotees to pull the chariots during Ratha yatra uttering the traditional *bolis* or couplets. With their tantric meaning lost for long in Odisha, which was once an important seat of tantra, these *bolis* came to be considered vulgar. People no more engage in some traditional linguistic activities; as a result, *kandana* ('the bride's songs of sorrow as she leaves for her husband's house'), riddles, naming game and tongue-twisters have disappeared. Palanquin bearers no more sing their songs as they no longer carry the bride in the palanquin to her husband's house and the grandmother or the mother does not sing traditional lullabies any more to make the child sleep. The community has lost its bridal songs and cradle songs. These brought out the creative potential in the unpretentious common man. The younger generation in Odisha no longer responds to the *bhajans* ('devotional songs') of Sala Bega or are aware of the legend of Manika *gauduni* ('Manika, the milk woman'), the story of Dasia Bauri or the expression *saradhabali*. Norms of acceptable behaviour, including linguistic behaviour, in public are not the same as what they were even two or three decades ago. For example, in India, it is now common for an elderly person to be addressed by his first name by a much younger person in Hindi or English language interviews on television. For this to become the norm in Odia language interviews is perhaps merely a matter of time. This address behaviour mimics contemporary American culture, which according to Robin Lakoff (2006), is changing from a culture of respect to one of 'camaraderie'.

There are some interesting parallels between language and culture. Both change and the notions of 'endangerment', 'preservation' and 'revitalization' (Crystal 2000; Hale 1992) apply meaningfully to both. If the preservation of an endangered language is important, then the preservation of culture, which in part is the knowledge repertoire of a community, is equally so. Just as a language can be preserved through documentation, so too can culture. In fact, myths, folktales, proverbs etc.—which are carriers of culture—are in some loose sense, a kind of documentation of it. But in the changed intellectual milieu, these cannot be the preferred mode of recording; this can be done in the form of 'knowledge-(based) discourse'.

Culture can be preserved through other means as well, for example, in the observance of cultural practices. In the public domain, *pala* ('a form of performance for the dissemination of puranic literature to the accompaniment of music'), *daskathia* ('a form of performance similar to *pala*'), performances such as *ramalila* ('deeds of Rama') etc., all of which have to compete with television shows on similar or comparable themes, need to be supported by the society so that these are performed in villages and small towns. In the home domain certain observances must continue or be revived, as the case may be. For instance, cooking traditional food at home, especially on festival days, would also be a desirable step in this direction. On particular festival days, specific foods are traditionally prepared. During the month of Kartika, a simple, special kind of vegetable-mixed dal, called *habisadali*, is traditionally prepared, and the vegetables used in it are purely local. Preparing it at home even for one or two days during the last five days of the month of Kartika, which are considered to be particularly holy, can inform the younger generation to a part of their tradition. The home domain is the best place for the preservation of this aspect of culture.

In sum, the paper distinguishes between aspirational and lived culture and explicates the latter in some detail. It maintains that culture is not a homogeneous concept and also that it must be conceptualised at the collective level, where it is an abstraction and at an individual level, where it is the specific manifestation of it, which could be an idea or artefact or observance. On the basis of an analysis of four narratives and a cultural practice, the paper maintains that inclusiveness is an important characteristic of Odia culture. It observes that the concepts of endangerment and preservation apply to both language and culture and ends with some suggestions for the preservation of a culture at the public and the home domains.

References

Chatterji, Suniti Kumar. (1966). *The People, Language and Culture of Orissa*. Bhubaneswar: Odisha Sahitya Akademi.

Crystal, David. (2000). *Language Death*. Cambridge: Cambridge University Press.

Dasa, Mahadeva. *Kartika Mahatmya*. Cuttack: Dharmagrantha Store.

Hale, Ken. (1992). 'Endangered languages: Endangered languages and the safeguarding of diversity'. *Language*, 68/1, 1–42.

Lakoff, Robin. (2006). 'Civility and its discontents: Or, getting in your face'. In. R. Lakoff, and S. Ide (eds), *Broadening the Horizon of Linguistic Politeness*. Amsterdam/Philadelphia: John Benjamins, 23–43.

Mishra, Ramachandra. (2004). In Balarama Dasa's *Sri Mahalakshmi Purana*. Cuttack: SB Publications.

Mohanty, Artaballava. (1973). *Sarala Mahabharata*. Bhubaneswar: Department of Culture, Government of Orissa.

Patnaik, Arabinda. (2012). *Odishare Lokadharmara Parampara*. Cuttack: Kanchan.

Patnaik, B. N. (2013). 'The story of Alakshmi'. http://saralamahabharat.blogspot.com/2013/12/the-story-of-alakshmi.html. Last accessed on 12.07.2021.

____ (2011a). 'Lakshmi Purana: An analysis'. In P. K. Palit (ed.), *Religion and Literature: Indian Perspectives*. New Delhi: Kaveri Books, 79–83.

____ (2011b). 'On *Brata kathaa* as discourse of power: A study of Sarala's *Nityaani Gurubaara Kathaa*'. In O.N. Koul (ed.), *Indo-Aryan Linguistics*. Mysore: Central Institute of Indian Languages, 213–18.

4

Language, Violence and Power*

Tariq Rahman

Abstract

Language is connected in several indirect ways with power. Those who have more power, as corporate entities or individuals, can increase their gratification both in tangible and intangible ways. The decrease, or restriction, in obtaining gratifications is violence.

As language creates discourses and makes it possible to control nature and society, it makes it possible for the human species to dominate and colonise the earth, thus creating a very real danger of the world coming to an end through poisoning or environmental disaster. Language also helps human elites to create myths which justify their rule and power. At the micro level, language encodes ways of honouring and insulting people; gender and class discrimination and so on.

---

* Originally published as 'Language, Violence and Power: A Theoretical Approach', in *Politics of Language*, edited by Neelam Hussain, Samiya Mumtaz, and Samina Choonara, Lahore: Simorgh Publication, 2005, pp. 197–206. Copyright © Simorgh Women's Resource and Publication Centre. With thanks to Simorgh Publications for permission to reprint this essay.

> In short, it is only the possession of language which makes human beings a violent species which has, above all, to justify its violence.

Introduction

There is a connection between language and violence. At the most obvious level all of us have experienced it when someone has scolded us, shouted at us or used ego-shattering invectives. But this is not where verbal violence begins and ends. Indeed, there are so many connections, albeit indirect and subtle ones, that it is difficult to catalogue and analyse all of them. This paper attempts to analyse some of them, though, of course, this would only be a crude beginning.

Definition of Terms

For the purpose of this paper, language refers to 'sounds coming out of the human mouth which ordinarily can, and generally do, convey meaning'. Violence is 'that activity which diminishes pleasure or increases pain or both'. Since I have used the hedonistic calculus of pleasure and pain while defining power in my book *Language and Politics in Pakistan* (1996), let me refer to it so as to clarify the meaning of violence further. My previous definition of power is as follows:

> Power is that which enables one to impose one's will directly or indirectly over others or resist the imposition of other people's will. The consequence of the exercise of power would be to increase the tangible or intangible means of gratification of its possessor (p. 8).

Later, while teasing out the implications of the concept, I said: 'it is a capability, a quality analogous to potential energy in physics, it cannot exist without a system to support it' (Rahman 2002: 39).

This system, even in primitive societies, is dependent upon ideas which cannot be transmitted, except in some very simple cases, without words. That is where language comes in; but first let us look at the uses of language.

Language and Its Uses

First, language conveys meaning. This creates systems of ideas—the way one interprets the world—and determines what power relations are considered legal and legitimate and what are not. Secondly, language conveys attitudes and emotions such as love, hatred, contempt, reverence, etc. Thirdly, language is an attribute of identity. In this role it conveys social class, educational status, ethnic identity, religious identity, gender identifications and so on. These are the broad category of the uses. Let us see how they relate to power and, because of it, to violence.

The Networks of Meaning and Violence

We create our social reality. This means that our social worlds do not exist as fixed and given facts. They are facts because we believe they are facts. When a human child is born, he or she is told to believe in familial relationships. Thus, while the real feelings for siblings may be those of competition and rivalry, the child is made to convert them into love and solidarity. Then the child is told about the extended kinship system, the tribe, the ethnic group, the nation, the religious community and so on. All these are constructed or imagined communities and language, as Benedict Anderson (1983) argues in the case of the nation, is used in different ways to imagine them.

Part of our social reality is the hierarchical order, i.e. who is greater or more valuable or better than the other. This hierarchical order is violent towards most of us because only a few can be at the top, but we legitimise it and reinforce it by accepting its validity. All this is done through language. If we did not have language, the basis of power would have been physical force which would have created individual violence but not systems of power creating and sustaining violence. Perhaps men would still have dominated women because the latter are physically weaker than men. However, philosophies of patriarchy would not have existed. We would have had fights as animals do but not wars. So, domination would have existed as it does among animals but not as a legalised system. As we know, animal studies suggest that this domination seldom results in actual murder or brutalisation. Indeed, argues Konrad Lorenz, aggression 'is really an essential part of the life-preserving organization of instincts' (1963: 39). Other well-known forms of domination, such as that of kings over their subjects, feudal lords over serfs, factory owners over labourers, one group of people over another, human over nature and animal species—these could not have been possible. All these forms of domination, which are violent in their nature towards those who are dominated, are products of ideologies: the theory of the rights of kings; the theory of aristocrats being naturally fitted to rule over others; racism; social Darwinism; patriarchy; nationalism etc. These ideologies justify domination and the resulting violence, both to those who dominate and those who are dominated. But for language, such ideologies could not have been constructed, let alone preserved, disseminated through the educational apparatus and justified by the clergy, the educationists, the intellectuals and the bureaucracy.

Violence is done to those who are made to believe they are inferior. This restricts their possibilities of obtaining gratification, i.e. they possess less power. The more readily and fully they believe in their lowly status, the better it is for those who dominate them. This is how Plato justifies the creations of such an ideology in *The Republic:*

> Citizens, we shall say to them in our tale, you are brothers, yet God has framed you differently. Some of you have the power to command, and in the composition of these he has mingled gold, wherefore also they have the greatest honour; others he has made of silver, to be auxiliaries; others again who are to be husbandmen and craftsmen he has composed of brass and iron; and species will generally be preserved in the children (380 BC: 269–70).

It is only through language that ideologies of this kind make it possible to perpetuate violence over slaves, the working classes (who are taught to know their place), over women (who are taught to accept patriarchy) and over the peoples of Africa and Asia (racism, Orientalism, social Darwinism, etc.).

Moreover, it is only because of language that an extension of memory is possible. This is essential for creating science and management—indeed, all forms of knowledge. However, one singles out science because it makes the human species much more powerful than any other species known in history. Because of science, we have grown in numbers till we threaten to crowd out many other species. Because of it we have changed the face of the earth, threatening the ecosystem itself. And, of course, because of it we have the capacity to blow up a large part of humanity, poison even a larger part and bring about climatic changes which may threaten life as we know it. That is why Ashis Nandy and others call science intrinsically 'violent' (Nandy 1988).

Domains of Power and Language

Ideas expressed through language make it possible for us to have a society at all. All our institutions—the religious order, the coercive apparatus, the justice apparatus, administration, commerce, education etc.—function because we have language. Indeed, as society got more complex, it got more organised and the Weberian bureaucracy, legalistic and rational, was created. This bureaucracy relied increasingly on documentation and paperwork and had a role in developing the standardised, print languages we have today (Fisher 1986). The result is that the modern state makes print language the major source of power. One cannot enter the white collar market without being able to manipulate the written word. In Pakistan, as I have argued elsewhere, the language of prestige and power is English. After it, comes Urdu, and in Sindh some jobs are available to those who know only Sindhi (though everybody does study Urdu in school even there). The other languages are not used in the domains of power in Pakistan and, hence, are not languages of power (Rahman 2000).

Violence consists in making language the device for closing the ranks of the elite, i.e. 'elite closure' as Carol Myers-Scotton calls it

(1993). The ruling elites of South Asia have always practised this kind of violence. First, Sanskrit was an elite preserve denied to the masses. In this society, the masses were not only denied prestige and lucrative jobs open to the brahmins—the preservers of Sanskrit—but could even be punished for trying to partake of the treasure of Sanskrit. The Mughals rationed out Persian, again necessary for jobs as well as honour, to a small, mostly Muslim, elite. Then the British rationed out English to the Indian elite, denying it to the masses because it would have been too costly to teach everyone quality English (Rahman 1996). This is what is done in Pakistan today. The state's declared policy is that the vernacular languages of the country should be the medium of instruction in schools, i.e. public funds should only be spent on implementing and adhering to a single policy uniformly for all citizens (teaching them through Urdu and Sindhi). However, the real policy is to support English-medium schooling through funding cadet colleges and schools run by the armed forces, bureaucratic organisations (railways, customs etc.) and welfare foundations of the forces (Fauji Foundation, Shaheen Foundation and Bahria Foundation).

Verbal Violence and Languages

Our emotions and attitudes are also connected with power and one expresses them through language. Such attitudes are expressed through tone, pitch, vocabulary etc. which is much more often used than any other weapon. Arab tribal wars, it is said, used to begin with poets reciting poems bragging about the military virtues of their tribes and threatening the adversaries. This, indeed, is the ritual of a street fight in which words precede blows. Family quarrels use tone and pitch even before words of an offensive nature and may not proceed to physical violence at all. What is interesting is that the words of offence refer to shortcomings in the adversary (stupidity, cowardice, greed, stinginess, servility, mendacity and so on); the supposed stigma of belonging to an inferior group identity (black, slave, coloured etc.); and, above all, sexual availability and threats of sexual aggression.

In Pakistan, verbal violence—the aim of which is to crush the opponent's ego and cause pain—is related to lack of power, stigma and sex. Not surprisingly, the sexual invectives are semantically connected with 'taking away' (*lena*) and 'beating' (*marna*). Moreover, the most sacred non-sexual relationships between brother and sister, son and mother are rendered sexual as part of the insult and, of course, the aggressor states intentions of wanting to violate the females of the adversary (mother, sister, wife etc.).

The language of insult, then, is the language of power. It points out the weaknesses of the adversary (stupid, slave etc.); it threatens to commit violence upon him or her (kicking, breaking teeth, limbs, beating etc.); and it threatens to sexually violate his female kins (sisters, mothers etc.). In all such cases, the abuser pretends to be more powerful while the adversary is made out to be weaker.

Language, Identity and Violence

We have multiple identities and these can change, especially in times of great social mobility and transformation. Our socio-economic class is expressed through a number of attributes—clothes, where one lives, the vehicle one drives, one's friends—and language is one of them. In English, for instance, the educated middle classes and the upper classes speak a standardised variety of English called RP (Received Pronunciation) or Oxbridge. In Pakistan, English is spoken by the urban, professional upper classes, Urdu by the urban middle classes and the indigenous languages by the rural and urban lower classes. Thus, not knowing using a posh accent or knowing a language of prestige (such as English in South Asia) gives one a stigmatised identity. The system which allows this to happen is violent in nature though, of course, individuals are not responsible for the violence in question.

Social roles and the hierarchical nature of society is also reflected by forms of address, use of honorifics (titles etc.) and the pronouns of power of solidarity [*tu* and *vu* forms as Brown and Gilman (1960) explain in their seminal article]. Pakistani society is overtly hierarchical, so non-reciprocal forms of address and use of pronouns is observed. For instance, the more powerful (employers, feudal superiors, grown-ups) say *tu* (*toon*, *tum*, *ta* etc.) to the less powerful (servants, serfs, soldiers, clerks, children) and receive the *vu* form (*tusi*, *aap*, *taso* etc.). Superiors can use the name of their inferiors without honorifics (*sahib*, *sahiba*, *janab* etc.), while the latter cannot. Such usages are violent because they openly proclaim the inferiority or lack of power and commensurate status of the inferiors. What would appear to be just and non-violent would be reciprocal usage of forms of address, honorific and pronouns (Rahman 1999).

However, some highly Westernised people in Pakistan have begun to violate our indigenous norms of politeness by adopting Western norms of linguistic usage. Thus, they do not use the mutual name + honorific (e.g., *Doctor Sahib*, *Benazir Sahiba* etc.) but insist on using only the first name of a person without his or her consent. This position comes from power because those who use the first name without any sensitivity to the feelings of the addressee belong to positions of authority and generally belong to the Westernised elite which is the pioneer of fashionable usage in the upper and upper-middle classes. This kind of pseudo-egalitarian usage of linguistic forms is as violent as the non-reciprocal usage which generally prevails in Pakistani society.

Moreover, while the use of all titles is violent in so far as they are indicators of inequality, the retention of some titles while discarding others is equally violent. At the moment, academic titles (Doctor, Professor), which are earned, are discarded. However, royal titles, aristocratic titles, ecclesiastical titles, military titles and even bureaucratic titles are retained. One could argue that if society is to retain any role models at all, then maybe academic excellence should determine which these models should be followed. As such, academic titles should be the last to be discarded and not the first as they are in Western culture and, increasingly, in our own.

Language is especially useful as a symbol of ethnic identity. Indeed, in Pakistan, Bengali ethnicity was expressed initially (in 1948 and 1952) through Bengali. Sindhi is the major symbol of Sindhi identity, and Urdu speakers, who regard Urdu as the symbol of their identity, clashed with Sindhi speakers in 1970 and 1972 over the status of Sindhi and, in reality, over the power which each community would enjoy in Sindh. In the North-West Frontier Province (NWFP), the Pashtun ethnic groups have regarded Pashto as a symbol of their identity, while in Balochistan Balochi, Brahvi and Pashto are symbols of the group identities of these three groups. Language-based ethnic identities are constructed, even when the languages themselves might have existed for a long time, in modern conditions when the state distributes goods and services, and groups must consolidate their power in order to obtain their just share of them (Rahman 1996).

The usual pattern is that the dominant group at the centre deprives other groups of power. This pattern of violence is opposed by constructing a group identity, often using language as a symbol. Sometimes the dominated group becomes overtly violent resorting to acts of linguistic, cultural and militant chauvinism. In the end, either the pattern of the distribution of power changes—such as the creation of the Irish Free Republic which used the Gaelic Irish language as a symbol of identity and that of Bangladesh mentioned earlier—or the challenging group is crushed. In most cases a compromise is reached as in Canada (both French and English are used) and Belgium (French and Flemish are official languages), reflecting the new power equation. In all cases, violence begets violence and a new pattern of perpetuating violence is evolved.

Gender Identity and Language

It is through language that patriarchy is expressed. There are many ways of doing it: through absence, marking, feminisation.

In the mode of 'absence', women are not mentioned or are mentioned as honorary men. In Punjabi, women are given honorary masculine pronouns.

O Jande ne

not

O Jandi e

In the marked case, the male is the normal and the female is the marked case, as in English doctor, professor, general, mankind etc. are assumed to be male and if they are female then that is either specified or understood to be the exception or 'marked' case. The feminist movement's efforts for eliminating androcentric language is changing this. However, corresponding changes in social reality lag behind.

The third case is common in the language of poetry, love, beauty and so on. Women themselves created a Women's Language (WL) that reflected their dependence on men's power and emphasised their 'delicacy' (*nazakat*) and 'beauty' (*husn*). The language of the Urdu and Persian *ghazal* is a special case in which the pronouns are masculine but are appropriated for erotic, amorous and mystic purposes. The language of *Rekhti*, *Sarapa Sakhan*, *Hazal*, *Vasokht* and the *Masnawi* are feminine in reference to female characters and boys.

Literary Texts and Power

Literary texts uphold the system of the distribution of power. Love stories—*Heer Ranjha* etc.—are about transcending the world. Punjabi texts do have women as the lover and God as the beloved. But women are not liberated by these. They are shelved and encapsulated. Society co-opted, contained and defanged these texts. Medieval Persian texts that were taught to Indian Muslims were androcentric and mysterious, i.e. they were written from the male point of view. In *Bahar i Danish*, *Alf Laila val Lail*, *Gulistan* and *Bostan* etc., one sees women's sexuality as a threat to society. Love, or erotic love, afflicts both men and women but for men it is a form of abnormality not related to societal norms in as central a way as it is for women. Women have to be controlled. This control is to be exercised by men. Likewise, the working classes are to be controlled and despised.

Literature is mysterious in that cause and effect are not connected. The feudal lord (or landowning despot) cannot be understood. He is arbitrary. Human beings too are subjected to mysterious power, unknowable forces, which cannot be understood. All we can do is to pray for salvation hereafter and safety here. Thus, our pre-modern texts—chapbooks on magic, mysterious versions of folk Islam etc.—are based on this enchantment. This is changing as modernist values, brought by colonial masters, are rational and sequential. But aspects of colonial modernity too are anti-human and anti-feminist. It too is androcentric because the nation is a power-oriented, militaristic enterprise. Women in Pakistani textbooks are, therefore, absent or only comforters or those who reconcile themselves to the consequences of violence.

Conclusion

This paper shows that language is connected—directly or indirectly—with the maintenance of ideas, discourse systems and perceptions which create and perpetuate violence. The paper has focussed on different functions of language and linked them with power and, hence, with violence towards these who are denied power or cannot obtain it. This does not mean that there are no other aspects of language and it must be emphasised that pleasure, which language can create, is one of the consequences of power and has, therefore, been dealt with without being specifically mentioned. What have been ignored are the aesthetic, affective and such other aspects of language which relate only indirectly to power and violence. This exclusion is the result of focussing on the theme of this paper—the relationship between language, power and violence.

References

Anderson, Benedict. (1983). *Imagined Communities: Reflections on the Origin and Spread of Nationalism*, Revised edn, 1991. London: Verso.

Brown, Roger, and Albert Gilman. (1960). 'The pronouns of power and solidarity'. In T. A. Sebeok (ed.), *Style in Language*. Cambridge, MA: MIT University Press, 253–76.

Fisher, John H. (1986). 'European chancelleries and the rise of standard written language'. *Proceedings of the Illinois Medieval Association*, 3, 1–33.

Lorenz, Konrad. (1963). *On Aggression.* London: Methuen and Co Ltd.

Myers-Scotton, Carol. (1993). 'Elite closure as a powerful language strategy: The African case'. *International Journal of the Sociology of Language*, 103, 149–64.

Nandy, Ashis (ed.). (1988). *Science, Hegemony and Violence: A Requiem for Modernity.* Delhi: Oxford University Press.

Plato. (380 BC). 'Dialogues of Plato'. In Justin D. Kaplan (ed.), *The Jowett Translations*. New York: Pocket Books, 1955.

Rahman, Tariq. (1996). *Language and Politics in Pakistan.* Karachi: Oxford University Press.

____ (1999). *Language, Ideology and Power*. Karachi: Oxford University Press.

____ (2000). 'The language of employment: The case of Pakistan'. *Journal of South Asian and Middle Eastern Studies*, 23/ 4, 62–87.

____ (2002). *Language, Ideology and Power: Language-Learning among the Muslims of Pakistan and North India*. Karachi: Oxford University Press.

5

Origin of Sinhala and Kālinga-Lanka Linguistic Affinities[1]

Sandagomi Coperahewa

Abstract

Kālinga-Sri Lanka relations are embedded in the history of the Sinhala language and people. Focussing on the origins of Sinhala and debates connected with the position of Sinhala among other Indo-Aryan languages, this paper aims to draw attention to one of the lesser known aspects of Kālinga-Lanka relations—linguistic affinities between eastern India and Sinhala. As South Asian languages, Odia (Oriya) and Sinhala belong to the Indo-Aryan subfamily of languages. The ascertainment of the place of Sinhala among the Modern Indo-Aryan has led to a controversy. It has long been disputed whether Sinhala originated as a Western or Eastern Indo-Aryan language. Scholars have argued for both Eastern and Western origins on linguistic and cultural-historical grounds (Geiger and

[1] This paper is based on a talk delivered at the seminar on *Kālinga-Lanka: Reviving Old Linkages and Exploring New Opportunities* [6–7 November 2015, Utkal University, Bhubaneswar, India. I am thankful to the Kālinga-Lanka Foundation for their support.]

Jayatilaka 1935, Geiger 1938, De Silva 1979). This seems to have partly, based on the interpretation of a legend known as the 'Vijayan legend' as preserved in the Sri Lankan Pali chronicles. According to island's epic tradition, Vijaya, an Indian prince in the sixth century BC was the founder of the race of people that came to be called Sinhala ('Sinhalese' in English)—the people of the lion race. The original homeland of the Prince Vijaya is known to be Simhapura, of which the exact location has not been identified. There are conflicting views and statements with regard to the particular region which was the home of Vijaya. However, some of the people in Sri Lanka considered Kālinga, ancient Orissa to be their original homeland. So far no comprehensive study of the subject has appeared and there is a need for further research on Kālinga-Lanka linguistic affinities. This paper suggests that it is time to take stock of all historical as well as linguistic data available on this controversy for further research and analysis as a step to explore the eastern Indian Kālinga connection in the history of Sinhala.

INTRODUCTION

Kālinga was an early republic in central-east India that comprised north-eastern parts of the modern state of Andhra Pradesh, most of the modern state of Odisha and a portion of the states of Chhattisgarh and Madhya Pradesh. From early times there seems to have been political, religious, and social connect between the people of ancient Kālinga and Lanka. According to *Mahāvamsa*, the great chronicle of Sri Lanka, an Indian prince called Vijaya and his followers inhabited and settled down in Sri Lanka in the sixth century BC. It is generally accepted that Vijaya, the son of Simhabahu, was the founder of Sinhalese race, and that the Sinhala language was introduced into the island by him and his followers. The original home of Prince Vijaya is known to be Simhapura, of which the exact location has not been identified. There are conflicting views and statements with regard to the particular region which was the home of Vijaya. However, some of the people in Sri Lanka regarded Kālinga, ancient Orissa to be their original homeland. In addition to historical links with Kālinga, the Sinhalese speak and write an Indo-Aryan language based on Sanskrit which is also the source of many Indian languages like Hindi, Marathi, Odia and Bengali. According to these legends, Kālinga-Sri Lanka relations are linked with the origin of Sinhala language and the history of the Sinhalese people. It has long been disputed whether Sinhala originated as an eastern dialect of India or a western dialect. Focussing on the origins of Sinhala and debates connected with the position of Sinhala among other Indo-Aryan languages, this paper aims to draw attention towards one of the lesser known aspects of Kālinga-Lanka relations—the linguistic affinities between eastern India (Kālinga) and Sinhala.

Sinhala and Other Indo-Aryan Languages

Languages are assigned to language families on the basis of a method adopted by historical linguists. Indo-Aryan languages constitute a subfamily within the larger family of Indo-European languages. Today, most of the Indo-Aryan languages are found in the Indian subcontinent, which consists of India, Pakistan, Bangladesh and Nepal. Outside the subcontinent they are found in Sri Lanka and the Maldives (Disanayaka 1994). Sinhalese, known natively as Sinhala (සිංහල; *singhala*), is the language spoken by the Sinhalese people, who constitute 74 per cent of the island's population. It is now generally accepted that Sinhala is a member of the Indo-Aryan subfamily of languages. As an Indo-Aryan language, Sinhala has its roots in classical Indian languages but is spoken nowhere else in the region. Thus, it is related to such Indian languages as Hindi, Bengali, Gujarati, Marathi, Punjabi, Odia and Kashmiri. A survey of sound correspondences between these languages and Sinhala prove that Sinhala is a member of the Indo-Aryan family of languages (Disanayaka 2012: 300–01).

Sanskrit	Bengali	Odia	Gujarati	Sinhala	English
danta	*dā̃t*	*dānta*	*dānta*	*dat*	tooth
agni	*agni*	*agni*	*āg*	*gini*	fire
putra	*put*	*putu*	*pūt*	*put*	son
sapta	*sāt*	*sāta*	*sāt*	*sat*	seven
ēka	*ek*	*ēka*	*ek*	*ek*	one
karṇa	*kān*	*kāna*	*kāna*	*kan*	ear

Sinhala developed in a way different from the other Indo-Aryan languages because of the geographic separation from its Indo-Aryan sister languages. As an island language, Sinhala has a number of features that make it especially interesting to the scholar of South Asian languages and the linguistic history of South Asia. The Sinhala language remained isolated and separated from the other Indo-Aryan languages by the broad belt of Dravidian languages that occupied south India. It occupies a special position among the languages of South Asia because of its close affinities with two of the major linguistic families of the Indian subcontinent—Indo-Aryan and Dravidian. Once it was accepted that Sinhala was an Indo-Aryan language, it left another question unresolved. Did the earliest speakers of Sinhala come from the east of India (Kālinga) or the west of India (Gujarat)? Whether Sinhala was, in its origin based on a western dialect of India or an eastern dialect, led to a long controversy.

The Vijayan Legend and Origin of Sinhala

Scholars have argued for both eastern and western origins of Sinhala on the basis of linguistic, cultural and historical reasons (Geiger 1938, De Silva 1979). This seems to have partly based on the interpretation of legend called the 'Vijayan legend' as preserved in the island's Pali chronicles referring to the Aryan colonisation of Sri Lanka. According to these Pali chronicles, *Mahavamsa* and *Dipavamsa*, an Indian prince called Vijaya and his followers settled down in Sri Lanka in the sixth century BC.[2] He was the founder of the race of people that came to be called *Sinhala* ('Sinhalese' in English)—the people of the lion race. The original homeland of the Prince Vijaya is known to be Simhapura. However, there is much debate on the identification of the exact location from which they originated. Different interpretations of this legend have been advanced by various scholars. Historians and linguists found it difficult to identify the exact homeland of Vijaya due to three main reasons (Disanayaka 2012: 294).

1. The composite character of the myth and legends narrated in the chronicles.
2. Place names that appear in these languages have been identified or interpreted by different scholars in different ways.[3]
3. The composite character of Vijaya's retinue.

If Vijaya was the founder of the Sinhala race, the history of the Sinhala language goes far back as the sixth century BC. There is no doubt, that Sinhala is an Indo-Aryan speech brought from the mainland by the first immigrants under Vijaya. It is said that Vijaya was accompanied by seven hundred men. The majority of them spoke one language and others spoke different languages. What was the language that the majority spoke? Most probably, the language of one of the following states:

1. Lāla
2. Vanga
3. Kālinga
4. Magadha

Because of this uncertainty, scholars have attempted to seek supporting evidence in the earliest available stratum of the language

[2] See chapter 9 of the *Dipavamsa* and chapter 6 of the *Mahavamsa* for this first Aryan migration into Sri Lanka.

[3] There are some geographical names, mentioned in the chronicles which point to eastern India (Vanga, Lāla, Simhapura, Magadha and Kālinga) (Geiger 1938, De Silva 1979).

(Geiger 1938, De Silva 1979). Fortunately, there are linguistic records of Sinhala from as far back as the third century BC. Attempts have been made by linguists to solve the problem of the original habitat of the Sinhalese, posed by the contradictions in the historical tradition by a comparative study of Sinhala with the Modern Indo-Aryan languages of north India (Geiger and Jayatilaka 1935, Siddhartha 1935, Sahidulla 1962). The main thrust of the controversy has been the identification and location of 'Lāla', the homeland of Vijaya. While scholars like H. W. Codrington, Wilhelm Geiger, and S. K. Chatterji, identify Lāla with Lāta in Gujarat and conclude that Vijaya and other early colonists to Sri Lanka came from western India, others like Reverend R. Siddhartha, M. Sahidulla and P. B. F. Wijeratne identify Lāla with Rādha in West Bengal and conclude that the first band of colonists to Lanka came from Eastern India (Geiger 1938, De Silva 1979, Karunatillake 2011). Various arguments and explanations are propounded by them in support of their individual theories, and they all admit some measure of historical truth underlying the tradition. But no conclusive result has been achieved by these linguistic investigations. However, these two conflicting views, which may be referred as 'Eastern and Western hypotheses' provide linguistic evidence on the similarities between old Sinhala and the languages of north India.

Kālinga Migrations and the 'Eastern Origin Hypothesis' of Sinhala

Proponents of the 'Eastern hypothesis', comparing old Sinhala with the language of the Asokan inscriptions, both of the eastern and western groups, point out that Sinhala agrees more with the East-Asokan dialects rather than that of the west and conclude that the base for Sinhala was an Eastern Indo-Aryan language. In his article titled 'The Indian Languages and Their Relation with the Sinhalese Language', Reverend R. Siddhartha says that 'if one studies Bengali and compares it with Sinhalese, one will surely say that Sinhalese is directly connected with Bengali; and again, if one would study Oriya and compare it with Sinhalese, he will say that the Sinhalese language is nothing but a modified form of Oriya' (Siddhartha 1935: 135). Endorsing the eastern origin view of Sinhala, Reverend Siddhartha further states:

> It must be said, however, that the identification of the home of Vijaya either with Lāla of the Eastern coast or with Lāta of the Western coast, would not make any difference as to the family of languages to which Sinhalese belongs. It will only change the branch, or the subdivision and no more ...If we accept the traditional Sinhalese view, we would have to put Sinhalese in the Eastern branch of the Indo-Aryan family of languages, and if we accept the new theory we would have to place it in the Western branch. For my part, I follow the scholars and historians of my own country, with good reasons, and take Lāla of the Eastern coast as the home of my ancestors, the Vijayan people.
>
> (pp. 136–37)

M. Sahidulla, who uses philological facts to prove that the ancestors of the Sinhalese people migrated from eastern India, sees affinities in old Sinhala with language of the eastern edicts of Asoka. He provides the following grammatical affinities which point to its eastern origin (Sahidulla 1962: 108–11).

1. Sinhala *api* 'we' (old, *āp*, *ap*) *topi*, *tepi* 'you'. They are derived from the Eastern Asokan *aphe*, *tuphe.* Geiger also admits that 'the immigrants who brought these forms, *api* etc. to Ceylon had come from the Kālinga country.
2. The Sinhala words for two and three show its eastern origin. Sinh. *De,* Bengali, Assamese, Odia, Nepali, *dui*<Eastern Asokan *duvei*<Skt. *dvei*; whereas Hindi, Panjabi *do*<Western Asokan *dvo*<Skt. *dvau*. Old Sinhala *tini* Modern Sinhala *tun* agrees with eastern vernaculars, e.g. Bengali, Nepali *tin* Assamese, Odia *tini* and disagrees with western, e.g. Gujarati *trin.*

One other argument in favour of the Eastern hypothesis that needs examination is the language of the early Sinhala inscriptions.

The earliest Brāhmī inscriptions of the island also reveal that immigrants from eastern India formed the foundation of the early settlements of Lanka. P. B. F. Wijeratne in his introduction to *The Phonology of the Sinhalese Inscriptions*, summarising the different views of scholars states that 'the early language shows that it must have originally belonged to some Eastern tract of India by its salient Eastern characteristics' (P. B. F. Wijeratne 1945: 587). D. J. Wijeratne also says in his *History of the Sinhalese Noun* that 'the earliest Sinhalese as recorded in the inscriptions of the third century BC shows unmistakable evidence that it was a Middle Indian dialect descended from Sanskrit, having affinities with the Eastern group of Middle Indian' (D. J. Wijeratne 1956: 2).

The main proponent of the Western hypothesis, Professor Wilhelm Geiger in his *Grammar of the Sinhalese Language* says that this connection of the Vijaya legends with eastern India is 'an invention of later date' and argues that 'the Western elements constitute the ancient portion of the language' (Geiger 1938: xi). Geiger and Jayatilaka, the founder-editors of *A Dictionary of the Sinhalese Language* also state that 'whilst immigration from North-Western India happened but once, intercourse with Kālinga, Vanga and Magadha was continued more or less intensively through many centuries' (Geiger and Jayatilaka 1935: xvii). Commenting on this debate on Eastern and Western hypothesis of the origin of Sinhala, Geiger and Jayatilaka continue to say that:

> The base seems to be a Western dialect brought to the island by the first Aryan colonists. But this base overgrown with new elements imported into Ceylon at various times, probably already soon after the colonization, and from different parts of the continental India, chiefly from the East (Kālinga).
>
> (1935: xxiii–xxiv).

One fact is clear both from historical traditions as well from linguistic evidence. There had been, not once but many streams of immigrants to the island from different parts of India (mainly from the east and west), all contributing their share to the new language, that was to evolve as 'Sinhala' (Paranavitana 1959). Immediately after the death of Vijaya the chronicles speak of a lively intercourse between Lanka and the eastern provinces of India. King Vijaya's successor Panduvāsadeva came from Simhapura. In the latter part of the *Mahāvamsa* this town is mentioned as the capital of Kālinga (Paranavitana 1959). This account of the arrival of Panduvāsadeva affords evidence of the possibility of a second wave of colonisation, a hypothesis strengthened by the linguistic affinities between the Sinhala language in the early phase of its development and dialects of eastern India. Commenting on this second wave of colonisation Geiger says:

> The new immigrants spoke dialects of Eastern India, which, therefore, were different from that of the first settlers, and the mixture which thus took place in Ceylon becomes manifest by the composite character of the Sinhalese language. In spite of its north-western base there are phonological innovations which seem to point to the influence of Eastern dialects.
>
> (1938: 3)

Geiger further argues that 'it was in this later tradition that Vijaya's ancestry was connected with the royal family of Kālinga' (1938: 3).

There was a strong belief in medieval Sri Lanka that the location of Simhapura was Kālinga. During the Polonnaruwa period (twelfth century AD), the Kālinga king, Nissankamalla (1187–1196 AD) repeatedly mentioned that his origin was from Simhapura in Kālinga where Prince Vijaya was said to have arrived from. He held the view that Kālingas alone had the rightful claim to the throne (Liyanagamage 1968: 49, Manatunga 2014). The Kālinga dynasty attained the kingship of Lanka and there were many familial ties between the royal families of the two countries.

As a result of these subsequent migrations, the Sinhala language rapidly went through numerous changes and modifications, some of which seem to be quite unique in the history of Indo-Aryan.Owing to the geographical isolation and peculiar development of the Sinhala language, it is extremely difficult and perhaps impossible to assign it a definite place among the Modern Indo-Aryan languages. As the Sinhala language sprang up from at least two different sources it exhibits a composite character (Geiger and Jayatilaka 1935).

According to Senarat Paranavitana—the eminent Sri Lankan archaeologist and historian—'the basis of this language was a Western Prakrit, the character of which has been profoundly modified by a superimposed linguistic stratum of Eastern origin' (Paranavitana 1970: 1221). This contradictory nature of evidence furnished by an examination of the literary tradition as well of the language has led historians and linguists to conclude that there had been a two-fold origin of the Sinhala language—Eastern and Western origin. This composite character of the Sinhala language appears to have been further increased by the influences exerted by the Dravidian languages spoken by the nearest neighbours of Sri Lanka.

CONCLUSION

From a linguistic point of view it is not possible to come to a certain and indubitable result concerning the question from which part of India the first colonists of Lanka came. It is true that in the chronicle tradition, Vijaya is connected with kingdoms in eastern India, Vanga (Bengal), Magadha and Kālinga. Sri Lanka's continued association with Kālinga, ancient Orissa is attested not only by the legends relating to foundation of the Sinhalese monarchy by Vijaya, the introduction of the Sacred Tooth Relic, and the presence of the Kālinga dynasty, but also by the linguistic contacts between Kālinga and Sri Lanka. As this discussion showed, the legacy of ancient Kalinga is deeply embedded in the history of the Sinhala language and people. So far no comprehensive study of the subject has appeared and there is a need for further research on this Kālinga-Lanka linguistic affinities. A comprehensive study of the linguistic affinities between the Sinhala language in the early phase of its development and the languages of eastern India (Odisha and Bengal) will provide another dimension to study Kālinga-Lanka relations from a linguistic point of view. It is time to take all historical as well as linguistic data available on this subject for further research and analysis as a step to explore the eastern Indian Kālinga connection in the linguistic history of Sinhala.

References

De Silva, M. W. S. (1979). *Sinhalese and Other Island Languages in South Asia*. Tübingen: Narr.

Disanayaka, J. B. (1994). *Sinhala – Unique Indo-Aryan Language*. Colombo: M. H. Publications.

—— (2012). *Encyclopedia of Sinhala Language and Culture*. Dehiwela: Sumitha.

Geiger, Wilhelm. (1938). *A Grammar of the Sinhalese Language*. Colombo: The Royal Asiatic Society Ceylon Branch.

Geiger, Wilhelm, and D. B. Jayatilaka. (1935). 'Sinhalese language and literature'. *A Dictionary of the Sinhalese Language*, I/I, xvii–xxxviii.

Karunatillake, W. S. (2011). 'The position of Sinhala among Indo-Aryan languages'. *Link*. Colombo: Godage, 2011. 225–30. [First appeared in the *Indian Journal of Linguistics* 1977].

Liyanagamage, Amaradasa. (1968). *The Decline of Polonnaruwa and the Rise of Dambadeniya*. Colombo: Department of Cultural Affairs.

Manatunga, Anura. (2014). 'Kalinga-Sri Lanka relations: Patronage to Buddhism by Kalinga king, Nissanka Malla (1187–1196 AD) of the Polonnaruva Kingdom'. In S. K. Patnaik (ed.), *Buddhism and Maritime Heritage of South East Asia: Odishan Perspective*. Delhi: Pratibha Prakashan, 69–75.

Paranavitana, Senarth. (1959). 'Aryan settlements: The Sinhalese'. *University of Ceylon History of Ceylon*, 1/1. Colombo: Ceylon University Press, 82–97.

—— (1970). 'The evolution of the Sinhalese language'. *Sri Sumangala Sabdakosaya*, Part II. Colombo: Anula Press, 1220–238.

Sahidulla, Muhammad. (1962). 'The origin of the Sinhalese language'. *Journal of the Royal Asiatic Society (Ceylon Branch*), New Series, VIII/ I, 108–17.

Siddhartha, Reverend R. (1935). 'The Indian languages and their relation with the Sinhalese language'. *Journal of the Royal Asiatic Society (Ceylon Branch)*, XXXIII/88, 123–52.

Wijeratne, D. J. (1956). *History of the Sinhalese Noun*. Colombo: University of Ceylon Press.

Wijeratne, P. B. F. (1945) 'Phonology of the Sinhalese inscriptions up to the end of the tenth century AD'. *Bulletin of the School of Oriental and African Studies, University of London*, 11/ 3, 580–94.

6

Two Less-Studied Chapters of Indology

Kirāta Jana and Āhira Jana

Suniti Kumar Pathak

ABSTRACT

Attention is invited to a publication, namely *The Cultural Heritage of India*, volume V (1978) published by the Ramakrishna Mission Institute of Culture, Calcutta (now Kolkata), edited by Suniti Kumar Chatterji. A brief survey of numerous dimensions of Indian literatures has been dealt with in its chapters. Since then, about half a century has elapsed. Meanwhile, the land and people have changed. Strikingly enough, Indianism in our country demands re-estimation in the present-day context, two chapters of Indology have not yet been adequately studied. Those are:

(i) The Kirāta jana (Indo-Mongoloid, Indo-Tibetans, Indo-Burmese) and the numerous Indian Austric groups among the Indian nationals. The Indian Constitution follows the British legacy in declaring them as 'Scheduled Tribes'.

(ii) The Āhira jana or Ābhīraka in Sanskrit, as recorded in the Mahabharata, the Ramayana and Vishnu Purana, are the cattle-rearing groups of mixed origin, known as *apabhraṣṭa* ('barbarians') in olden days. Their languages are regarded *Apabhraṃśa*. The Gujars of the Western Himalayas, particularly the cattle-rearing people of Himachal Pradesh, claim to be of Āhira descent.

In the growth of Indology, the ancient Āhira janas and the Kirāta janas contributed no less than what is claimed by others belonging to the mainstream.

This paper attempts to elaborate on the contributions of the above two groups in developing Indological studies since their appearance in *Bhāratavarṣa*.

JANA IN INDOLOGY

Indology, a compound word in English, refers to a wholesome study of the peoples of *Bhāratavarṣa* (India). India had been known to the Greeks with reference to the Indus River and peoples therein. Alexander's march to the Indus River belt was historical. Prior to that, Ionian Greeks around the Caspian Sea had shown interest in the Indian people. The geomorphic structure of India is peninsular, with numerous inhabitants dwelling in this land since the hoary olden days. Thereby, the peninsular inhabitants had not been as whites as the Greeks had been, on account of topographic variations. Even today the Dokpa group in Ladakh is a claimant of a mobile pastoral group (*'brsog pa* in Tibetan). They claim to be descendants of the immigrated Aryans in the Indus belt. They reside on the upper Indus belt formed as a result of the Indus flowing through the gorges of the Upper Himalayas. They claim to be the earlier settlers of the region whereas the Budi group of people entered the area as conquerors and possess specific body features distinct from them. They however display the Gesar Saga (*Ge-sara Sgrungs*) in melodious presentations no less efficiently than the Buddhist Bod groups there. Thus, *jana* in the context of Indology definitely refers to a particular group of humans with a distinct identity from other human groups residing in this vast country.

Indology generally deals with communication of culture traits among numerous inhabitants of India that includes the current Afghanistan, i.e. *Gāndhāra* with reference to the Mahābhārata, and lower *Sindhu* (Indus) belt in Pakistan, upto the Kaccha Strait in the west and also Bharat and Bangladesh. The present study deals with the people prior to the above geographical division happened. Indological investigations by Christian Westerners had started since the middle of the seventeenth century. Abraham Roger wrote the *Open Door to the Hidden Heathendom* (1651) and that may be presumed as one of the first printed specimens of Indological research. Johan Hanxdolan composed the *Grammatica Granthamma Seu Sanscerdemica* (1699); these books aroused the curiosity of the Europeans, who were eager to know about the pecularities of the multiple groups of human communities in the Orient. Thereafter, Indians too began to research about India and her people since the mid-nineteenth century. Among them, Bhau Daje, Bhagwanlal Indraji and Rajendralal Mitra deserve mention as pioneer investigators.

Octopronged Culture Traits among Humans

Indology covers octopronged Universal Culture Traits followed by the people of India with a range of variation. In addition, multifold groups of Indian inhabitants, *jana*(s) are yet to be studied in this respect. Those universal traits are:

1. **Material traits for livelihood**: It refers to sustenance, clothing, and shelter. Innumerable paraphernalia related to these traits speak about their standards of a particular group among humans depending on ecological variations.
2. **Institutional social traits**: Such traits are encompassing enough to generate a particular group-culture, negotiating with social relationships, like marriage, kinship, law of inheritance, funerals. They depend on economic disparities and social status of various groups.
3. **Communication/media traits**: Each human being has speech and language that determines how they communicate. With the help of speech and language, humans created literature in multiple ways.
4. **Mental/rational and spiritual traits**: Faiths, beliefs, religions with institutional management, scriptures, prayers

with devotional attitude are universal among humans, despite their variations.

5. **Aesthetic traits**: Beginning with symbolic diagrams, various art forms have come into existence either in application or in performances like dance, songs etc.
6. **Mythological and traditional traits**: Humans have a unique treasure namely memory, unlike most other animate beings. Every human group commonly experiences its past in the myths and traditions, and tends to preserve them either in writings or in designs and images.
7. **Inquisitive traits**: It indicates the ever growing eagerness of humans for knowing their own surroundings.
8. **Warring traits**: Perpetual conflicts and wars among various groups have resulted in endless struggles for existence, and discovering strategies thereof, becomes inevitable.

Indological Coverage of Culture Traits

Indology, studied so far by the Eastern and the Western Indologists has been equally octopronged. As regards the subject matter, the people who are in the mainstream of culture growth, have been focussed excessively in the studies. Indians, who are distributed into two broad categories, namely *śiṣṭajana*—the mainstream elite group, and *a sura* ('non-god')—the neglected rest, do not present any exception. The śiṣṭajana groups received more attention in demonstrations of the above octopronged culture traits than the rest. The groups identified as a-sura have been ignored in the literature in many respects on account of their 'wild' livelihood, while the śiṣṭajana groups themselves claimed superiority among all. Indianism occasionally overlooks the rest as they have been portrayed since the age of early scriptural evidences in the four Vedas. This indicates a dark chapter in Indology.

Resultantly, a wider section among the people of peninsular India has been omitted. Despite occasional references of Kirāta in the Vedic texts so far available now, the Kirāta jana have been less studied.

Interestingly Śukrāchārya took the opposite side in order to combat against the *sura*(s). In a few instances, the non-Vedic groups of people had been referred to but with inadequate descriptions. In the second half of the first millennium AD, Bharavi composed *Kirātārjunīya* in order to praise Draupadi's political experience in supersession to others, and also Shaivite liberal approach by the embodiment of a Kirāta hillman. By then the Śaiva cult among the five major cults became strong enough than the Brahmanic Vedic superiority among *deva*(s).

Non-Brahmanic Folds and Indianism

Indianism, however, is not limited to the Vedas, though the Veda-oriented Brahmana leadership became a strong social force in the *Smārta* ('a Hindu philosophical tradition') culture-scape of peninsular India. The Dravidians took leadership in spite of the Brahamanic girdles since the entrance of sage Agastya of the late Brahmana *Śrauta* fold. Vedic culture broadly descended into a separate fold after the compositions of the *Gṛhya Sūtra* ('rules for the house-holders') in parallel to *Śrauta Sūtra* ('rules for the fire-ritualists') by the first millennium BC.

The Ramayana presents an important *vrātya* evidence of Vedic culture expanding southwards up to Sri Lanka, but fails to cope with the Dramila culture led by the Naga(s), Shavara(s) and others. The old Dramila scriptures referring to Dramila-Veda was challenged by *Dramila Vidyā* in promulgation of the Naga cult.

On the other hand, the linga worship of the Shaivites could forward alternative socio-economic programmes and rituals conforming to the downtrodden. Alwars from the Malaya hill regions are engaged in *Dāsa-bhakti* and *Nṛsiṃha* manifestation of the *Vaiṣṇavas* on one hand, and on the other, *Śrīpadmanābham* among *aiśvarya bhakti* are practiced too.

Besides them, Jaina Digambara and Shvetambara flourished. Later on, Buddhism spread through *Odivisha* (Odisha) and *Andhraka* (present Andhra Pradesh). The above narrative shows that the mental, rational and spiritual traits of human culture-spectra could gear Indianism well beyond the Vedic trends ventured earlier. Thereby, the scenario of indology with its several culture traits became chequered, despite the entrance of Vedic, better to say Brahmana, rituals in some instances.

Nevertheless, the people belonging to the hill tracts of the Himalayas never received adequate attention. Even the occasional pilgrimage up to Lake Manasarovara on the Kailash mountain by the few like Adinath among the Jainas, and some Shaiva practitioners were not fruitful in this regard. Resultantly, the contribution of the Kirāta jana of the Himalayan hill tracts was not quite acceptable to the major sections of the mainstream descending from the *sanātana dharma* ('eternal order') holders and the Smārta groups.

Indology Claims a Sumtotal

In the past, India could not be unified as a single state because of multiple reasons. Ashoka in the pre-Christian period and Akbar in the Mughal period attempted to integrate the people as one nation, but neither of them was successful. Disintegration among the people of India stands against the mission to make Indians a 'nation'.

Professor Suniti Kumar Chatterji addressed the lacuna in the nation-making process in his works by focussing on the existence and contribution of the people marginalised in the mainstream records. He introduced a new horizon of Indology in his research paper entitled 'Adivasi languages and literature of India' (1957). There he refers to the indigenous people under two broad heads, namely, the speakers of Sino-Tibetan and those of the Austric group of languages. In spite of various languages as their respective 'culture traits of communication', these have been regarded as 'backward tribes'. As a linguist, he dealt with the details of the Indo-Mongoloid, Indo-Tibetan, Indo-Burmese and the Austric languages along with their respective literary works.

Furthermore, his *Kirāta-jana-kṛiti* (1951/1974) deals extensively with their indigenous identity, different from those who belong to the mainstream. These indigenous groups of Indian nationals have not been adequately introduced in Indology for millenniums. Chatterji writes (p. 660) in his learned assessment—'The original Sino-Tibetan had its *nīdas* or areas of characterisation, the head waters of the Hwang Ho or Yellow River to the northwest of China. Here, the original Sino-Tibetan speech, the ultimate source of Chinese (Ancient Chinese and its various modern forms), Tibetan and Burmese, and possibly the Siamese had taken its form at least 3000 years before the birth of Christ. Their languages namely Chinese, Burmese, Siamese and Tibetan have advanced literatures.'

Besides them, a large number of backward Adivasi Austroloid groups in the Indian peninsula and the Mon Khmer (pre-Aryan and pre-Dravidian) settlers in South India had to flee to the nearby Nicobar isles under the pressure of the dominant groups who were greater in number. Thus Andaman and Nicobar come under the periphery of Indian nationals. Indianism never excludes them, but the conductors of the mainstream do not pay heed to them.

Similar is the case of the Āhira jana, who were engaged in cattle-rearing throughout the year. During the summer they prefer to go to hill tracts for grazing their cattle. In the winter they usually come down where green fodder suffices. Here hill tracts do not always refer to the upper Himalayas; they also refer to those in the Tarai belts inclusive of the river valleys adjacent to the highlands of North-western India since olden times.

Similar trends of transhumance in groups had occurred in the cultural account of human migrations such as the movement of the earlier Dravidians from the Mediterranean coast areas in West Asia and that of the Aryans into this peninsular India. In respect of North India, Professor Chatterji (1974) in *Kirāta-jana-kṛiti* dealt with their language affinity, including those of Manipur and upper Assam. In addition, the cultural contributions to Indianism is not only restricted to communication traits like the literary compositions; games, dances, musical instruments, and presentation of art too claim their space in the realm of Indianism. All these together come under what is called 'Indology'.

Melody, Indology and Indianism

An interesting feature of Indian culture is love for melody. All groups among the people of the peninsular India have melodious oral traditions, each distinct from that of others. The written traditions of melodious presentations enrich their communication traits. Through the melodious presentations, 'Indianism' builds a tone of unity in diversity. Indology and Indianism thereby become 'one' in melodious songs throughout the history of the people.

The Indo-Mongoloids claim their groups' identity as *ama hor* ('basic Mongolian'). They gave priority to *cando* ('the moon') and also to *siricando* ('the Sun') in the sky. They do emphasise on *moncate rar*, the oral speech, than *moncate kutsu*, the writing. The understanding of oral speech is stronger than that from written documents. Even oral promise or verbal agreement, i.e. *moncate kulsu*, is sufficient for all sorts of social negotiations, instructional agreements, and monetary transactions, which is why the written scripts are almost untraceable among them.

It may not be irrelevant to add that the venture of introducing written language among the different branches of Austroloids since the availability of translation of the Holy Bible in various regional spoken languages have now become very significant.

Professor Suniti Kumar Chatterji identifies the wide area in the North-east Assam as the Bodo area, excluding Bhutan and the Balipara Frontier areas, prior to the formation of the North-East Frontier Area (NEFA), the present-day Arunachal Pradesh.

Āhira Jana(s) in India

About the identity of Āhira jana vis-à-vis Ābhīra jana, a note of disowning by the elite śiṣṭajana may be noticed. Āhira groups had been engaged in the task of rearing cattle. Patañjali, the author of *Mahābhāṣya*, the great commentary of Pāṇini's Sanskrit grammatical aphoristic treatise in eight chapters, the *Aṣṭādhyāyī*, rightly pointed out that one Sanskritised word might have many distorted forms. Instances cited by Patañjali in respect of a Sanskrit word *go* 'cow' are—(i) *gavi* (ii) *goni* (iii) *gopatalika* (Chowkhamba edition). Prior to Patañjali, no direct reference about the animal husbandry groups were traceable. Ashokan inscriptions too had been inscribed in regional expressions with no mention of the community. According to the author of *Mahābhāṣya*, such ignoble expressions had been spoken by the low-professional groups. Those were the cattle-rearing groups among the low-borns.

The latest trends among the Himalayan vanjars, shepherds, cattle-rearing groups of the Himalayan Eastern Sector, Middle sector and Western sector have not yet been taken into account since India is constituted in such a way that these groups do not belong to the mainstream of Indian people. Attention to them is still due, as they too belong to the Indian nation. In Indological studies by the Indians, their literary contributions have been overlooked. A few travellers and tourists occasionally came across them in their Himalayan travels. However, few specimens have been studied so far by scholars like Vidyasagar Negi.

Thus the cattle-rearing communities with no knowledge of the Aryan four-folds in social living had their speeches indigene in multiple forms. In that respect, the author of *Mahābhāṣya* had been appropriately faithful to note them as *Apabhraṃśa*, the downcast speech of cowherd-rearing peoples in pluralities. Āhira jana had an alternative Ābhīra jana.

Classical Apabhraṃśa in Indology

In the course of spreading the aesthetic traits of Indian people, Apabhraṃśa have played an excellent role, as Bharata the author of *Nātyaśāstra* had shown (second century AD), as seen into the socio-aesthetic impact of Apabhraṃśa songs on the elite śiṣṭa group. Thereby the Āhira jana, otherwise Ābhīra jana became a part of the Indological scenario. The impact of Apabhraṃśa in communications through literatures excelled in Saurashtra, Maharashtra and Shurasena (*Śaurasena*; Mathura area) regions of the north-western

Bhāratavarṣa. The case of eastern Bhārat is chequered in contrast. Despite that, the songsters like Āhira jana lagged behind with no recognition in Indology.

The speakers of multi-traits of Apabhraṃśa remained neglected, with no identity, until Bharata appeared. Patañjali in his writing severely criticised Apabhraṃśa, as already mentioned. Despite that, the vast literary compositions from Bharatamuni (second century AD) to Candradhara Dhoyi (twelfth century AD) speak about Apabhraṃśa literature of the ancient period. Those specimens, though had been acceptable to the śiṣṭajana(s) partially, hardly included the cattle-rearing groups.

The Āhira jana of the olden days had been given a space in the mainstream as mentioned above. But traits of the pastoral livelihood among the Gujars in Kumaon, Garhwal, Himachal Pradesh and Kashmir up to the Gilgit region have not been covered adequately. In the last six decades, very few among them were able to settle in recognised societies. But their contributions in settlements of these regions are not negligible, just as their communication traits in Indological coverages through melody of pastoral songs are no less worthy. In this respect, adequate quests are awaiting indologists. These people are not only Indian 'nationals'; they also provide 'Indianism' with the least contaminations in the material traits and the institutional traits of universal culture patterns.

Kirāta Jana(s) in India

Any group of human beings is generally identified by their distinctive physical features and speech. The *Linguistic Survey of India* (1898–1928, henceforth LSI) by George Abraham Grierson determined the plurality of speeches among the inhabitants of peninsular India. Prior to that, Sten Konow under the guidance of G. A. Grierson took the initiative in 1903–04 in this respect, as the LSI volume 3 preserves. In the second half of the nineteenth century, European Scholars like W. W. Hunter prepared *A Comparative Dictionary of (Non-Aryan) Languages of India and High Asia* (1868), thereby establishing the pluralities amongst the Indian speakers. Thereafter, Brian Houghton Hodgson's *Essays on Languages and Religions of Nepal and Tibet* (1874) was followed by his complete survey published in *Miscellaneous Essays Relating to Indian Subjects* (1880). All these ventures confirmed that Indians had been distinct in 'pluralistic culture formats' among the human world.

The Kirāta people in the peninsular India claimed specific identity from members of the white raced Indo-European inhabitants of Caucasus, and from those of the black-skinned woolly-haired people. They belong to an anthropomorphic type of the yellow-skinned straight-haired people. Since their settlement in the Indian Himalayan regions from hoary olden days, those people are broadly known as the Indo-Mongoloid people. In the Indian distinction, those are known as Kirāta jana as was determined by Professor Suniti Kumar Chatterji in his *Kirāta-jana-kṛiti* (1951).

Demographically, they are broadly known as Bodo, arising out of bod; *bod yulskad* been used as the local name for the vast land of snow, *gangs yul* (pronounced as *kanyul*), later popularly known as Tibet. The change in name involves a morpho-phonic disorder in pronunciation by Eastern travellers since the middle of the second millennium AD as *to bod>tobot>tho-bot>Tibet* (the literary term *stod bod* in writing becomes *to bod* in pronunciation). Presumably, Bodo people are those who originated from the Bod community.

In this regard, Sumpa khan po (sum pa mkhan po), otherwise named yese paljor (ye shes dpal 'byor), in his history of Tibet named *Pag samjon zang* (dpag bsam ljon bzang), refers to the migration of peoples in the vast Himalayan land of snow i.e., gangs yul. After the great mountain had sprung out of the sea, the hill tract had been vacant, barren, and full of snow. In course of time, people were blocked in that vast land of snow from different quarters. As a result, the vast land of snow was known as bod yul, divided into two parts—the high bod (s*tad bod*) and the low bod (*smad bod*). Since there had been no checkpost and the actual line of control had been a barbed wire or a tin plank, communities in groups used to move to and fro. Thus, many highlanders preferred to settle down in the mid-Himalayas and lesser Himalayas in course of time.

According to Professor Suniti Kumar Chatterji the four main 'language-culture' groups of India, namely, the Aryan, the Dravidian, the Sino-Tibetan and the Austric, can be labelled respectively as the Ārya, Drāmiḍa or Drāviḍa, Kirāta and Niṣāda.

In *Kirāta-jana-kṛti*, he laid emphasis on the contributions of Sino-Tibetan culture, especially of the Eastern North-East India referring to the Bodo inhabitants. Through the passage of time, multiple groups of Kirāta held multiple nomenclatures with reference to their separate ethnographic identity, as has already been determined by scholars. During the last several centuries or so, their group identity became varied, ethnically and linguistically. Despite that, the Kirāta jana in the Indian civilisation have contributed no less than those by the Āryan, the Drāvida or Drāmida, the Niṣāda, and the Austric groups belonging to the peninsular India.

Kirāta-jana-kṛti is devoted to the Bodo people spread through Nepal, Cooch Bihar, and they lived in Lohit and Brahmaputra River valleys. Balipara Frontier Division and Sadiya Frontier Division were restricted to Indians when the studies on Kirāta people were done by the author. Since India became a sovereign Republic there is now a wider scope for accounting for the large number of Kirāta people in the lesser Himalayan regions. In this respect, Edward Tuite Dalton may be regarded as the pioneer in compiling a descriptive ethnology of Bengal (1872). Prior to him, several learned articles were published in the *Journal of the Asiatic Society of Bengal* by authors like Brown, Hodgson, Mason Robinson and Steward who had forwarded a broad notice on the Indo-Mongoloid and Sino-Tibetan vocabularies spoken by separate communities of these peoples, such as, (in alphabetical order) Abor, Ahom, Angami, Arung Empeo, Biate (Old Kuki), Bodo* (Mech?), Bod (Tibetan), Burmese*, Bhota Chutiya, Dhimal, Dophla/Dafla, Garo, Karren (red), Hruso, Karen (yellow), Koceh/Kouch/Koch/Panikoech, Kuki*/Kuki chin/ Kumi/Northern Khami or Meithei, Mech (Bodo)*, Lao, Lepcha/ Rong, Limbu, Manipuri (Meothei)*, Mikir, Miri, Mithan, Muru, Murmi, Rong (Lepcha), Sho, Siamese/Tai, Talung/Taleng, Tengima (Angami), Thado (Kuki?) etc. The names marked with asterisk are recorded in *Kirāta-jana-kṛti*.

G. H. Daman in his article published in the *Journal of the Asiatic Society of Bengal* (1880, New Series: 228–58) recorded more communities like Aiton, Anal, Andro, Banpara, Dimasa (belonging to Kachari hills), Kutcha, Hallam (helma?), Kabui, Kwoirang, Lhota, Lushei, Phadang, Maitrai Rabha, Rengima, Sema/Soma, Tableng.

Besides them, Kirāta jana historically may be traced to before the lifetime of the Shakyaputra Gautama, the Buddha.

In this line, several research studies have been published in the *Journal of Bihar Research Society*, Patna, such as,

(i) Robert Shafer suggested ethnic connections of the Lepchas with some Nagas in Nagaland (volume 36, 1950) and presented classification of some languages of the Himalayas.
(ii) Also his classification of the Northernmost Naga languages in the said Journal (Patna, volume 39, 1953: 225–64).

The Nagas have thereby been included among the Indo-Mongoloids, a group distinct from the Tibeto-Mongoloid Bod (Bhota) people. The Nagas, despite their separate spoken tongues, are known as 'Nagamese' speakers (Census, 1931). They are regarded as Tibeto-Burman group belonging to the Tibeto-Burman group of speakers.

Among the other Indo-Mongoloids of North-East India, particularly in Assam, the Empeos, Hoirao, and Kabuis of the Mikir hills are regarded distinct from the Naga(s) and the Bodo(s) referred to above. The Austric-speaking Khasis preserve their distinct identity despite being the descendants of the ancient Mon-khmer group, the pre-Dravidian and pre-Aryan inhabitants of the ancient peninsular India.

A major group in Assam is known as Ahom, Aham or Asam belonging to the ancient Han-Dai or Siamese-Chinese group. As a result, a wide cultural fusion has occurred among the Kirāta janas.

Dalton did not pay attention to the spread of Indo-Mongoloid and Tibeto-Mongoloid culture extension in Nepal. Professor Suniti Kumar Chatterji took care of that extension carefully since the Mallas had come to power and also the Kochs. In developing 'Indianism' since about a millennium before Christ, *Kirāta-jana-kṛiti* depicts a colourful illustration of the contributions of the Kirāta groups in multiple *gana* to the language diversities of the land.

REFERENCES

Abhayankar, K. V., and J. M. Shukla. (eds). (1986). *Patanjali's Vyakarana Mahabhasya*, volumes 1–3. Poona: Bhandarkar Oriental Research Institute.

Cappeller, Carl. (1912). *Bharavi's Poem Kiratarjuniya: Or Arjuna's Combat with the Kirata*. Cambridge, MA: Harvard University.

Chatterji, Suniti Kumar. (1974). *Kirāta-jana-kṛiti, The Indo-Mongoloids: Their Contribution to the History and Culture of India*. Calcutta: The Asiatic Society (First published by The Royal Asiatic Society of Bengal, Calcutta, in 1951).

_____ (1978). 'Adivasi languages and literature of India'. *The Cultural Heritage of India*, volume 5. Calcutta: The Ramakrishna Mission: Institute of Culture, 659–76.

_____ (ed.). (1978). *The Cultural Heritage of India*, volume 5. Calcutta: The Ramakrishna Mission: Institute of Culture.

Dalton, E. T. (1872). *Descriptive Ethnology of Bengal*. Calcutta: Office of the Superintendent of Government Printing.

Daman, G. H. (1880). 'Notes on the locality and population of the tribes dwelling between the Brahmaputra and Ningthi rivers'. *Journal of the Royal Asiatic Society of Great Britain & Ireland*, 12/ 2, 228–58.

Grierson, G. A. (1994). *Linguistic Survey of India*. Delhi: Low price publications.

Hanxdolan, J. (1699). *Grammatica Granthamma Seu Sanscerdemica*.

Hodgson, B. H. (1874/1828). *Essays on the Languages, Literature, and Religion of Nepal and Tibet: Geography, Ethnology, and Commerce of those Countries*. London: Trübner and Co.

_____ (1880). *Miscellaneous Essays Relating to Indian Subjects*. London: Trübner and Co.

Hunter, W. W. (1868). *A Comparative Dictionary of the Languages of India and High Asia*. London: Trübner and Co.

Muni, B., and M. A. Śāstrī. (1971). *Natyashastra*. Varanasi: Banaras Hindu University.

Negi, V. (2007). *Pashcimottar Himalay ke Aranyak-bhed-paalak: Kinnaur ke Sandarbha men Saamaajik – Saamaskritik Adhyayan*. Sarnath, Varanasi: Central Institute of Higher Tibetan Studies.

Oldenberg, H., and F. M. Müller. (1989). *The Gṛihya-Sūtras: Rules of Vedic Domestic Ceremonies*. Delhi: Motilal Banarsidass.

Roger, A. (1691). *Open Door to the Hidden Heathendom.* Leiden.

Shafer, R. (1954). *Classification of the Northernmost Naga Languages.* Reprinted from the *Journal of the Bihar Research Society, etc.* Patna: Shantilal Jain.

Valmiki and M. Venkataswami. (1915). *The Ramayan of Valmiki* (Library of Alexandria edition, volume 1). R. T. Hotchkin Griffith (ed.), Library of Alexandria.

PART III

Essays in Modern Linguistics

7

A Comparative Note on the Bangla Particle *to* and the German Particle *doch*[*]

Josef Bayer

Abstract

The Bangla discourse particle *to* and the German discourse particle *doch* share a number of syntactic and semantic properties. Their phonetic similarity suggests a remote historical relation. While the historical connection will only be mentioned and must remain for the specialists in Indo-European reconstruction, this study will highlight points of convergence between the two languages with respect to these particles along a series of concrete test cases.

In this note, I would like to draw the attention to a number of parallels that can be found between the Bangla particle *to* and the German particle *doch*. Although appearing in very distant Indo-European

[*] First published in *Making Worlds Accessible: Essays in Honor of Angelika Kratzer*, edited by Rajesh Bhatt, Ilaria Frana and Paula Menéndez-Benito, 2020. https://scholarworks.umass.edu/ak_festsite_schrift/1/

languages, the parallels are surprising. Both elements have their roots in Indo-European (IE). Perhaps they have a common ancestor, perhaps not. But even if not, the comparison could still prove to be interesting for reasons of their similar function in grammar and discourse.

The article is organised as follows: After a note on their respective etymologies in section 1, section 2 will start with a dichotomy of morphological autonomy and boundedness that can be found in *to* but not in *doch*. Section 3 will present the semantic core of the particles under consideration. Section 4 turns to shared properties in regard to information structure. Section 5 considers restrictions with respect to sentence mood. Section 6 takes a look at their distribution in embedded clauses and island effects. Conclusions appear in Section 7.

ETYMOLOGY[1]

The recent history of German *doch* is well-documented. The modern conjunctive adverb *doch* relates to Old High German *thoh*, *thō*, Middle High German *doch*, Old Saxon *thŏ̄h*, Dutch *toch*, Old English *þēah*, Modern English *though*, Old Norse *þō* and Gothic *þauh*. The word is originally composed of two parts. Its first part is said to be related to Old Indic *tú*, *tū́* which had an adversative meaning and has, according to certain researchers, developed out of the IE second person singular **tŭ̄-*; alternatively, a development out of the pronominal stem **te-*, **to-* is considered (see Kluge 2011: 208, Lühr 1976: 77–79). The second part relates to the Gothic strengthening particle *-uh*, *-h* ('and'); see also Latin *que*, which derives from Indo-European **k̯ue-*.

It is less clear where exactly *to* in modern Indo-Aryan (e.g., in Bangla and Hindi) comes from. According to Sen (1971), it comes from *tad-u*, which is a *tadbhava* and originates from the Sanskrit *tad* followed by *u*, *tad* being the third person neuter pronoun while *u* is a widely used particle. Montaut (2016) locates the etymology

[1] I will throughout represent the examples in the transcription found in the source texts.

of Hindi *to* in an ancient pronominal basis (Sanskrit *ta-*) referring to third person ('that', 'he'), which is still used as such in certain Indo-Aryan languages such as Marathi (to 'he'). According to Dunkel (2014, volume II, 776f.), the oldest function of IE **tó* was prosecutive, sequential, continuative; the adversative form **tú* should be considered to be an ancient Aryan innovation.

Free versus Clitic Usage

Whatever the etymological status of Bangla *to* is, it is interesting to see that both interpretations that Dunkel refers to can be found in the modern language. The non-adversative, sequential interpretation can be found in Bangla examples in which to start the sentence.

(1)

to tumi	dilli	jabe	na	bole	Thik	korecho!
TO you	Delhi	go.fut.2	not	COMP	right	make.pst.2

'So you have decided you will not be going to Delhi!'

A related usage appears also in final position as in (2) or as a standalone as in (3).

(2)

ritar	dilipke	bhalo lage	na,	to?
Rita.gen	Dilip.obj	like.3	not	TO?

'Rita doesn't like Dilip, so what?'

(3) **A:**

baire	khub	briSTi	hocche
outside	much	rain	occur.3

'It's heavily raining outside.'

B: to?

TO

'So what?'

The same holds for Hindi, as the following examples from Montaut (2016) show:

(4) **A:**

to	kyâ	huâ?
TO	what	be.aor

'And then, what happened?'

B: to?
TO
'And then?'

In these cases, *to* should not be confused with an interrogative element as the translation may suggest. It simply means '(and) then'. The interrogative impact follows only in a second step, namely by rising intonation and the challenge of the preceding proposition. 'Rita doesn't like Dilip, so what?' The conversational implicature of this sequencing is question-like ('so what?', 'who cares?' etc.) but *to* as such has no interrogative impact.

In all these cases, *to* is a free-standing temporal adverb. It fulfills the criteria for what is understood as a 'discourse marker' (Schiffrin 1988). It is outside the clause, and it links the clause to the discourse.

Things change when we consider the usage of *to* as an enclitic element, or what Dasgupta (1984, 1987) calls an 'anchor'.[2]

(5) a. dilip to kal aSbe
Dilip TO tomorrow come.fut.3
'Dilip will come tomorrow, won't he?'
b. dilip kal to aSbe
c. dilip kal aSbe to

We see a variety of options. The common denominator is that *to* as a weak clitic-like anchor needs a phonological host to its immediate left which it can lean on. As Dasgupta (1987) shows, *to* in the sense of an anchor can never occur in initial position. There is good evidence that the material to the left of *to* must be a major syntactic constituent. In (5a), this constituent is the subject, in (5b) it is the adverb, and in (5c) it is the entire clause.

The discourse marker/ clause linker *to* and the clitic *to* can obviously not be identified semantically. In its free appearance, *to* is simply a temporal adverb meaning 'then'. As a clitic it communicates

[2] The difference between a free form of *to* and an enclitic form of *to* has also been described for Hindi in Lakshmi Bai (1977).

that the speaker takes the hearer to believe that the proposition p is true and conveys the additional expectation that the hearer should acknowledge that p is true.[3] Thus, clitic *to* triggers a reading according to which the addressee is reminded that p holds. Almost certainly, the clitic *to* lacks interrogativity in the same way that the clause linker *to* does. Emphasis of the truth of p gives rise to potential adversativity.

Adversativity is the core semantic ingredient of German *doch*. Maybe the clearest case is its use as an answering particle. A negative statement like (6) is not corrected with *nein* ('no') but with *doch*.

(6) **A:** Du bist heute nicht in die Uni gegangen.
you are today not in the university gone
'You didn't go to the university today.'

B: Doch / * Nein
DOCH NO
'No, I DID (go to the university).'

Doch signals rejection of the previous proposition. It comes across as adversative because it is in fact the focalisation of the truth of the proposition that has been denied in a previous speech act.[4] Something similar is found when *doch* appears as a clause linker.

(7) Klaus ist intelligent, doch er ist unmotiviert
Klaus is intelligent DOCH he is unmotivated
'Klaus is intelligent {but/however} he is unmotivated.'

The second clause does not challenge the truth of the former as such but challenges one aspect of it, here the positive properties of

---

[3] Working on *to* in Hindi, Lakshmi Bai (1977) came to a similar conclusion. According to her, the conjunctive *to* in Hindi must be distinguished from what she calls the 'emphatic' *to*. The former is a sentence-external discourse marker/ clause linker, while the second is a sentence-internal clitic element that attaches to major subconstituents of the clause.

[4] Thus, it would be worthwhile to explore to what extent there is a use of *doch* that relates it to the familiar notion of 'verum' focus, i.e. focussing the truth value.

Klaus. One can be both intelligent and unmotivated, but the latter property may hamper one's general success. Various authors have suggested that *doch* p corrects a salient q that entails p; see Abraham (1991), Doherty (1987), Grosz (2014), Karagjosova (2004), Ormelius-Sandblom (1997) and others.

Interestingly, we find in German *doch* also in a role that resembles *to* in its function as an anchor. It is a central property of German discourse particles that they have a clause-medial fixed position from which they cannot be moved to the front or to the end of the clause.[5] *Doch* is such a particle. Imagine the following discourse (stress signalled by capitals):

(8) **A:** Ich fahre morgen ans Meer.
I go tomorrow to.the sea
'I'll go to the sea tomorrow.'

B: Aber du musst doch ARbeiten!
but you must DOCH work
'But don't you have to work!?'

Here, B reminds A of something that A is supposed to know, namely that he or she has to go to work and therefore most likely cannot take a day off at the sea. One can observe that an adversative clause linker, namely *aber* ('but'), introduces B's utterance. Thus, *doch* cannot be identified with *aber*. It must by all means make an additional semantic contribution. It functions as a reminder that p [=A must go to work] is true and should be known to A. This is compatible with adversativity as already expressed by *aber*, but it adds a presupposition about the assumed mental state of the addressee. Interestingly, in this function, *doch* must remain in a fixed pre-VP position, and it must find a focussed element in its scope, which in (8) is *arbeiten*. The alternative in (9a) lacks the 'reminder'-meaning of the discourse particle. Notice that (9a) is fully grammatical but only with *doch* interpreted as an adversative clause

[5] See Thurmair (1989) among various others.

linker. The reminder—components is definitely missing here. (9b) is downright ungrammatical.

(9) a. Doch du musst ARbeiten!
b. *Aber du musst ARbeiten doch!

In its role as a discourse particle, *doch* is a functional element on (9a) par with negation and other grammatical elements. Although it is not a clitic like Bangla *to*, it is not a phrasal element either. Various researchers have argued that it is a functional head.[6]

SEMANTICS

As already indicated in Section 2, *to* and *doch* are semantically similar. We can distinguish the usage as a clause linker from the usage as a discourse particle. Obviously, both hang together as is especially clear in German *doch*.

Clause Linker

As a clause linker, the function of *doch* is like the logical connective Λ, enriched with the property that the simultaneous truth of the propositions p and q that are linked with Λ is unexpected, unusual etc.[7] This is the source of adversativity. In Bangla, one would use the connective *kintu* but not *to*.

(10) dilip iSkule jay {kintu/*to} Sipra baRite thake
Dilip school.loc go.3 but/then Sipra home.loc stay.3
'Dilip goes to school but Sipra stays at home.'

[6] See Bayer (2018) and other works mentioned there.

[7] This is the reason why weakly contrastable properties give rise to awkward interpretations as seen in *??Mary is tall but intelligent*, *??2+2=4 but 4-1=3.*

Discourse Particle

In their usage as discourse particles, *doch* and *to* are quite similar. The clause linker meaning of *doch* reappears in its use as a discourse particle. Karagjosova (2004: 183) suggests that in *doch* (p) the speaker's belief is that p is explicit but inactive common knowledge. To the extent that p is situationally relevant, this amounts to the implicature that the speaker has reason to believe that the hearer has 'forgotten' p and needs to be 'reminded' of it.

The Bangla clitic particle *to* has much in common with these characteristics. Again, the speaker assumes that p is known to the hearer, and that there is reason to believe that p is not in the hearer's focus of attention; *to* is then actually a signal to the hearer to acknowledge p and react in a way that is consistent with subscribing to the truth of p. This must be the reason why sentences with *to* are often interpreted as quasi interrogatives. The addressee is expected to show that he or she acknowledges the truth of p. (5c), *dilip kal aSbe to*—is then interpreted in such a way that the speaker claims that p holds (p = Dilip will come tomorrow), that he assumes that the hearer already knows that p but that it is worthwhile to ask him to acknowledge that the truth of p should continue to be assumed. Of course, this brings the speech act quite close to the interrogative speech act that involves the enclitic interrogative particle *ki*. (11a) shows an explicit polar question; (11b) shows that the particle *ki* maybe missing. The latter is possible if the question is a main clause with rising intonation.[8]

[8] Some researchers may assume that (11b) is equipped with a zero interrogative particle. I would hesitate to accept such a conclusion. One could, in the same way, argue that *dilip kal aSbe* is a *to* sentence with a zero particle corresponding to *to*. In my view it is more reasonable to assume that (11b) is syntactically a declarative clause that is pronounced with interrogative intonation as in English *You are married?* The declarative form is underspecified and as such receptive to specifications by intonation.

(11) a. dilip kal aSbe ki?
Dilip tomorrow come.fut.3 Q
'Will Dilip come tomorrow?'
b. dilip kal aSbe? [with rising intonation]

Information Structure

When *to* is used as a discourse particle, it can be found in different places as has been shown in (5). In (5a), *dilip to kal aSbe*, the speaker wants the hearer to confirm that it is Dilip who will come tomorrow. In (5b), *dilip kal to aSbe*, the speaker wants the hearer to confirm that it is tomorrow that Dilip will come. The most straightforward syntactic solution says that *to* is a functional head. Functional heads do not float around in the clause. They hold a fixed position in the grid of other such positions in clause structure. Functional heads may give rise to a specifier position. Constituents which match the respective head in feature structure can move to its specifier position; -*to* can attract elements if they qualify (a) as constituents in Bangla, and (b) are drawn from a set of semantic competitors, say, Dilip in comparison with Hiren or Projit or Mukul, or tomorrow in comparison with next week or next month or next year. (5c) would then be the neutral form in which the entire proposition has been moved to the specifier of *to*. In this case, the speaker assumes that p is common ground between himself and the hearer, and that it is worth reminding the hearer of p.[9] We see that, due to its clitic nature, *to* is able to express different pragmatically relevant focalisations.

The German particle *doch* seems to be a functional head but it is not a clitic; our assumption is that *doch* is generated in a pre-VP position and that VP-internal constituents may move out of the scope of *doch*.

[9] This is in a much-abbreviated form of what Bayer, Dasgupta, Mukhopadhyay, and Ghosh (2014) have suggested.

(12) a. Damals hat doch [dein Bruder] [dem Professor]
then has DOCH your brother.nom the Professor.dat
[seine Dissertation] gezeigt.
his dissertation.acc shown

'In those days, your brother showed his dissertation to the professor, didn't he?

b. Damals hat [dein Bruder] doch __ dem Professor seine Dissertation gezeigt.

c. Damals hat [dein Bruder] [dem Professor] doch __ __ seine Dissertation gezeigt.

d. Damals hat [dein Bruder] [dem Professor] [seine Dissertation] doch __ __ __ gezeigt.

Given that VP is the natural place for focal information and that German allows reordering of arguments (known as 'scrambling'), different options emerge as to which constituent is highlighted by *doch*. In (12a), it is the entire proposition SHOW (x, y, z). Here the speaker invites the hearer for confirmation that this proposition is true. Once the subject has been scrambled out of VP, as in (12b), the proposition remains what it is; however, now confirmation is asked for showing the professor his dissertation; the subject is outside the focus domain. In (12d) we see that *doch* can scope over a VP all of whose arguments have been evacuated; only the verb remains. Here the speaker asks for confirmation about the predicate 'show' in comparison with competitors such as 'send' or 'take away' etc. We see that despite their syntactic differences, *to* and *doch* achieve very similar pragmatic effects by seemingly contrary means: While *to* attracts focal elements to its left, *doch* uses scrambling of non-focal so-called 'old information' elements in order to narrow down the domain in which it associates with a focal constituent.

Mood

Given what we have seen so far, it may not be too surprising to see that Bangla *to* and German *doch* attend to the same core restrictions on sentence mood. Both appear in declarative and imperative clauses, and they are strictly impossible in questions. Consider imperatives.

(13) a. edike eSo to
this.direction come.2 TO
'Please come here!'
b. Komm doch her!
come.2 DOCH here (=toward the speaker)
'Please come here!'

In both cases, the use of the particle turns the imperative into a friendly invitation. The semantics is not as straightforward as in declaratives. Nevertheless, it may be possible to argue that the particle's adversative potential adds to the speech act in such a way that the speaker invites the hearer to make the underlying proposition true, and that he/she should do so in spite of reasons that may suggest otherwise.

Karagjosova (2004: 169), who offers a formal speech-act theoretic account of *doch*, speaks of a *contrast between desire and reality*. The speaker's positive attitude seems to be the result of an enhanced effort to invite the addressee to act in the sense of making the underlying proposition true.

To the extent that verb-less or nonfinite fragments of speech exist and are interpreted as imperatives, both Bangla and German show that their respective particles cannot be used in such constructions.[10] For German, see Gärtner (2017).

(14) a. matha uMcu!
head up
'Keep your head up!'
b. *matha-to uMcu!
c. *matha uMcu-to!

[10] As Jogamaya Bayer points out to me (p.c.), since Bangla is a zero copula language, (14a,b) can be interpreted as declarative sentences, in which case *to* does have a place.

(15) a. Kopf hoch!
head up
'Keep your head up!'

b. *Kopf doch hoch!

(16) a. Alles aussteigen!
all out.step
'Get all off (the vehicle)!'

b. *Alles doch aussteigen!

Obviously, fragmentary imperatives of this sort lack functional vocabulary; if in their usage as discourse particle both Bangla *to* and German *doch* are a proper part of the respective language's functional vocabulary, these facts would follow straightforwardly.[11]

Interrogative sentences exclude *to/doch* in both languages.

(17) Polar question

a. tui ki aSbi? / tui aSbi ki?
you Q come.2 / you come.2 Q
'Will you come?'

b. *tui ki aSbi to? / *tui aSbi to ki? / *tui aSbi ki to

(18) a. tui kObe aSbi?
you when come.2
'When will you come?'

b. *tui-to kObe aSbi? / *tui kObe aSbi-to?

[11] Gärtner (2017) shows that the picture is less than fully homogeneous. DiPs like *mal*, derived from *einmal* 'once', and *denn*, related to 'then', may appear in fragments.

i. Alle mal herhören!
all MAL here.hear.inf
'Everyone listen to me!'

ii. Wozu denn hingehen?
wherefore DENN there.go.inf
'Why go there?'

(19) Polar question

a. Wirst du kommen?
   will.2 you come
   'Will you come?'

b. *Wirst du doch kommen?

(20) Constituent question

a. Wann kommst du?
   when come.2 you
   'When will you come?'

b. *Wann kommst du doch?

Given that both particles have roughly the same semantic function, the ban of interrogatives is expected. Since the speaker desires information from the hearer, the true answer cannot be common ground between the interlocutors. As a consequence, the speaker cannot felicitously ask the hearer for confirmation of the underlying proposition.[12]

Let me finally return to the question of whether the Bangla discourse particle *to*, which we have seen is incompatible with interrogative mood, may itself be a question particle. As such, *to*

---

[12] Notice that not all *wh*-clauses are alike. There are, for example, *wh*-exclamatives of the style *What a shame!*, *How beautiful!* or *How good your son can already swim!* Here the proposition p = P(x), e.g., x can swim, is presupposed, and the new contribution is roughly that the speaker exclaims that property P holds to a surprising degree. German exclamatives of that kind permit *doch*.

(i) Wie gut dein Sohn doch schon schwimmen kann!
    how good your son DOCH already swim can

With *doch*, the speaker reminds the hearer of the fact that his son is, for his young age, a very good swimmer. Interestingly, corresponding *wh*-exclamatives in Bangla like *tomar meye ki Sundor nacche!* ('How beautifully your daughter is dancing!') do not permit *to*, as pointed out to me by Probal Dasgupta and Jogamaya Bayer. I have no explanation for this discrepancy.

would be a competitor of *ki*. Intuitions appear to be a bit unreliable. As I said before, *to* sentences are often pronounced with the rising intonation that is typical for questions. Without doubt, *to* sentences can also be 'answered' by acknowledging or denying that p holds. Therefore, it is advisable to employ more formal testing. Such formal testing is provided by the use of negative polarity items (NPIs). We know that some NPIs are not only licensed by negation but also by interrogativity. As seen in (21), one such NPI is Bangla *ekTu-o* ('little-even').

(21) dilip ki **ekTu-o** Sahajjo koreche?
Dilip KI little-even help do.past.3
'Did Dilip help at all?'

The question is whether the use of *to* provides a relevant NPI-licenser as well. If *to* is related to *ki* in the sense that it is also a source of interrogative force, it should. The result of my little research revealed that examples such as (22) are deviant.[13]

[13] Probal Dasgupta (p.c.) informs me that in Bangla NPIs may also be licensed by bare interrogative intonation. Unlike in various languages in which the NPI must be licensed by an overt lexeme or by a change in word order as is the case in inversion, (i) seems to be an option in Bangla.

(i) dilip **ekTu-o** Sahajjo koreche?

If so, *to* may be added to such an interrogative clause in the sense of a tag. (ii), in fact, is possible if intoned with dripping sarcasm and 'not p' is strongly implicated.

(ii) ora rakar almari theke EkTa-o gOena curi
they Raka's cupboard from one-even ornament steal
korte parbe to?
will be.able.FUT3 TO
'I bet they won't be able to steal a single ornament from Raka's cupboard!'

This analysis would not be available if *to* appears in clause-medial position. Importantly, the designated interrogative marker *ki* gives a licence to the NPI from a clause-medial position as well. Thus, the relevant difference between *ki* and *to* remains.

(22) *dilip to **ekTu-o** Sahajjo koreche?
Dilip TO little-even help do.past.3

In German questions, one can use the NPI *überhaupt* ('at all') among others as seen in (23a); non-inversion (alias failure of movement to C) as in (23b) leaves the NPI in limbo.

(23) a. Hast du überhaupt das Licht ausgeschaltet?
have you at.all the light off.switched
'Have you switched off the light at all?'
b. *Du hast überhaupt das Licht ausgeschaltet
you have at.all the light off.switched

When we consider the particle *doch*, one could argue that it turns a declarative sentence into a request, which would make it indistinguishably similar to an interrogative. (24) would be a typical check-question for which an affirmative answer is strongly expected.[14]

(24) Du hast doch das Licht ausgeschaltet?
you have DOCH the light off.switched
'Have you switched off the light? I hope you have.'

In spite of this pragmatic nearness to real questions, such speech acts must not be confused with real questions. They can never licence an NPI. (25) is as deviant as a pure declarative such as (23b).

(25) *Du hast doch überhaupt das Licht ausgeschaltet?
you have DOCH at.all the light off.switched

Thus, to the extent that our comparison between Bangla *to* and German *doch* looks promising so far, the failure of NPI-licensing by *to* seems to converge with this result from German.

Islandhood

Particles like Bangla *to* and German *doch* are classical root clause phenomena. The reason must be that they tap into the epistemic

[14] See Karagjosova (2004: 175ff).

system of the speaker and his/ her evaluation of the common ground with the addressee. Thus, it is not sufficient for them to be hosted in a proposition; they must be hosted in a speech act that is formally typed according to the mood system of the language. Bangla is a good example for this generalisation. According to the joint research with my colleague Probal Dasgupta, the discourse particles of Bangla can hardly ever be found in embedded clauses (clausal complements, relative clauses, adjunct clauses). Normally, if a particle like *to* is located in such an 'island', it cannot reach the domain of the root clause, which according to standard assumptions is privileged in being in possession of the grammatical layer in which illocutionary force is implemented.[15]

The situation in German is less clear. There are various particles that can arise in bona fide islands; *ja* (lit. 'yes') is a notorious example.[16] The situation with *doch* is clearer. It can arise in attributive but not in restrictive relative clauses; see (26a). The former is something like separate ('parenthetical') speech acts; the latter is not. *Doch* cannot arise in clausal complements unless they are in the scope of verbs of speaking and thus count as reported speech; this is seen in (26b).

(26) a. Klaus/*jeder, [der doch gerade in Indien ist],
Klaus/everyone who DOCH right.now in India is
hat angerufen
has called
'Klaus/everyone who is right now in India has called.'

b. Jeder sagt /*glaubt, [dass die Regierung doch
everyone says /believes that the government DOCH
versagt hat].
failed has
'Everyone says/believes that the government has failed.'

[15] For influential early work, see Hooper, and Thompson (1973).

[16] Extensive work by Yvonne Viesel has explored the use of *ja*. See Viesel (2017) and her ongoing dissertation work.

Islandhood holds for most adjunct sentences. There is, however, an exception: reason clauses. Reason clauses that are initiated with *weil* in German and with *karon* in Bangla are certainly embedded clauses. But both of them can host the respective particles under discussion.

(27) Max geht jetzt ins Bett, [weil er doch morgen
Max goes now in.the bed because he DOCH tomorrow
eincn anstrengenden Tag hat]
a strenuous day have
'Max goes to bed now because he will have a strenuous day tomorrow.'

(28) a. dilip aj khub SOkale uTheche [karon
Dilip today very early rise.past.3 because
o to SOhor-e EkTa mEla dekhte jabe]
he TO city.loc one.cl fair see go.fut.3
'Dilip got up early today because he will go to see a fair in the city.'

b. dilip aj khub SOkale utheche [karon o aj SOhore EkTa mEla dekhte jabe to]

According to Frey (2012), reason clauses belong to a class of what he calls 'Peripheral Adverbial Clauses' (PACs). These clauses show signs of 'non-integration'. Unlike integrated adverbial clauses, PACs seem to have their own illocutionary force. Since they are nevertheless dependent clauses, their force depends on and is in the responsibility of the speaker who utters the root clause. For detailed discussion see Haegeman (2012). It would be worth exploring to what extent Bangla *to* is licit in other clause types that have been subsumed under the PAC-generalisation, and to what extent other tests concerning the theoretical isolation of PACs could be applied to Bangla. Following this line of research would, however, be beyond the scope of the present contribution.

Conclusion

The comparative exploration of the particles *to* and *doch* in Bangla and German, respectively, reveales a surprising convergence in terms of their syntactic and semantic/pragmatic properties. This convergence may be due to linguistic universality or to large-scale parametric properties. If so, we would expect to find more languages, and in particular also genetically unrelated languages, with similar lexical elements in the service of similar functions and distributions. Given that little attention has so far been paid to 'little words' with 'fuzzy meaning', such findings could indeed be possible. The other expectation would be that the two elements under discussion emerge in a more narrow sense from a common Indo-European ancestral language. Their phonetic similarity and the few historical records we have access to, suggest that this possibility exists. If so, it would be worthwhile to explore more deeply whether the features that are shared by Bangla *to* and German *doch* could indeed have survived in a history of 2000 years or so.

Acknowledgments

Thanks to Jogamaya Bayer for sharing her intuitions about Bangla, to Heinrich Hettrich, Rosemarie Lühr and Paul Kiparsky for useful historical information and especially to Probal Dasgupta for joint research and discussions of Bangla grammar, as well as to Sibansu Mukhopadhyay for compiling a corpus of Bangla sentences with *to*.

References

Abraham, Werner. (1991). 'Discourse particles in German: How does their illocutive force come about?' In W. Abraham (ed.), *Discourse Particles*. Amsterdam: John Benjamins, 203–52.

Bayer, Josef. (2018). 'Criterial freezing in the syntax of particles'. In J. Hartmann, M. Jäger, A. Kehl, A. Konietzko, and S. Winkler (eds), *Freezing: Theoretical Approaches and Empirical Domains.* Berlin and Boston: Mouton de Gruyter, 225–63.

Bayer, Josef, Probal Dasgupta, Sibansu Mukhopadhyay, and Rajat Ghosh. (2014). 'Functional structure and the Bangla discourse particle *to*'. Talk at SALA 30, Hyderabad, 06-08 February 2014.

Dasgupta, Probal. (1984). 'Bangla emphasizers and anchors'. *Indian Linguistics*, 45, 102–17.

____ (1987). 'Sentence particles in Bangla'. In E. Bashir, M. Deshpande, and P. Hook (eds), *Selected Papers from SALA 7*. Distributed by Indiana University Linguistics Club, 49–75.

Doherty, Monika. (1987). *Epistemic Meaning*. Berlin: Springer.

Dunkel, George E. (2014). *Lexikon der indogermanischen Partikeln und Pronominalstämmen*, 2 volumes. Heidelberg: Winter.

Frey, Werner. (2012). 'On two types of adverbial clauses allowing root-phenomena'. In L. Aelbrecht, L. Haegeman, and R. Nye (eds), *Main Clause Phenomena: New Horizons*. Amsterdam: John Benjamins, 405–30.

Gärtner, Hans-Martin. (2017). 'Root infinitivals and modal particles: An interim report'. In J. Bayer, and V. Struckmeier (eds), *The Formal Syntax and Semantics of Discourse Particles*. Berlin and Boston: Mouton de Gruyter, 115–43.

Grosz, Patrick. (2014). 'German *doch*: An element that triggers a contrast presupposition'. *Proceedings from the Annual Meeting of the Chicago Linguistic Society*, 163–77.

Haegeman, Liliane. (2012). *Adverbial Clauses, Main Clause Phenomena, and Composition of the Left Periphery*. Oxford: Oxford University Press.

Hooper, Joan, and Sandra Thompson. (1973). 'On the applicability of root transformations'. *Linguistic Inquiry*, 4, 465–97.

Karagjosova, Elena. (2004). *The Meaning and Function of German Modal Particles*. PhD Thesis, Universität des Saarlandes.

Kluge, Friedrich. (2011). *Etymologisches Wörterbuch der deutschen Sprache*. Berlin: Mouton de Gruyter.

Lakshmi Bai, B. (1977). 'Syntax and semantics of the particle *to* in Hindi'. *Osmania Papers in Linguistics*, 3, 64–75.

Lühr, Rosemarie. (1976). 'Die Wörter für "oder" in den germanischen Sprachen'. *Münchener Studien zur Sprachwissenschaft*, 34, 77–94.

Montaut, Annie. (2016). 'The discourse particle *to* and word ordering in Hindi: From grammar to discourse'. In M. Fernandez-Vest, M. Jocelyne, and R. D. Van Valin (eds), *Information Structuring in Spoken Languages from a Cross-linguistic Perspective.* Berlin: Mouton de Gruyter, 263–82.

Ormelius-Sandblom, Elisabet. (1997). *Die Modalpartikeln ja, doch und schon. Zu ihrer Syntax, Semantik und Pragmatik*. Stockholm: Almqvist & Wiksell International.

Schiffrin, Deborah. (1988). *Discourse Markers.* Cambridge: Cambridge University Press.

Sen, Sukumar. (1971). *An Etymological Dictionary of Bengali: c. 1000–1800 AD*, 2 volumes. Calcutta: Eastern.

Thurmair, Maria. (1989). *Modalpartikeln und ihre Kombinationen.* Tübingen: Niemeyer.

Viesel, Yvonne. (2017). 'Discourse particles "embedded": German *ja* in adjectival phrases'. In J. Bayer, and V. Struckmeier (eds), *The Formal Syntax and Semantics of Discourse Particles.* Berlin and Boston: Mouton de Gruyter, 173–202.

8

Splitting and Recombining Abstract Lexical Levels in Contact Phenomena

Carol Myers-Scotton

Abstract

This contribution argues that the mechanism behind many innovations in the structure of language contact phenomena is the possibility to split abstract levels of lexical features from one language and combine them with the levels in another language. The mechanism involved is a feature of the Abstract Level model, a model that identifies three levels of abstract lexical structure that underlie all linguistic elements (Myers-Scotton 2002, Myers-Scotton 2006, Myers-Scotton, and Jake 2001). Examples of such hybrid forms from creole development and codeswitching illustrate data that show such hybrid forms. In creoles, content morphemes from the lexifier language can be reanalysed to serve as grammatical elements and be combined with syntactic features from the substrate language. In codeswitching, nonfinite verb forms from one language undergo reanalysis in some language pairs so that they can appear with finite language inflections from the other participating language, which is called the Matrix Language under the Matrix Language Frame (MLF) model (Myers-Scotton 1993a, 1976 *inter alia*).

Introduction

There are many examples in the contact linguistic literature of one language impinging in various ways on the structure of another in bilingual speech, not just as elements that are borrowed and used across languages, more or less as they are used in the donor language (e.g., French sauté > English). However, this contribution is about some of the cases of words that have been restructured in some way, not just borrowed. While many have been often documented, such reconfigured elements have a basis in the abstract nature of language production that has hardly been considered. The goal here is to consider this abstract foundation for some types of linguistic outcome. The premise here is that there is a certain flexibility in language production at the pre-linguistic level; it points to a mechanism explaining the possibility of certain innovations that occur under some language contact conditions and specifically when bilinguals are conversing. The evidence of flexibility is that elements from one language can take on new morpho-syntactic functions in the grammatical frame of another language. That is, the results are hybrid elements based on abstract features from more than one language.

It is generally recognised that certain social conditions promote such linguistic developments. One condition is the milieu in which creole languages develop. In brief, when creole languages have developed, it has generally been in a plantation-type situation in which workers are required to work together and otherwise live together with others who do not share the same first language. They do share some limited exposure to a prestige language spoken by overseers. These speakers may develop a common language with features from the variety of language sources in the community. As an example of how elements in one language can be reanalysed when a creole is formed, consider the English phrase *by and by* which retains its phonological form in Tok Pisin varieties, the main creole spoken on Papua New Guinea, but its meaning and its lexical category have changed. Thus, *bai n' bai* generally becomes the verbal marker of future tense. In the variety of Tok Pisin spoken on the island New Ireland (part of Papua New Guinea) it is reduced to *bai* as in *baiemi go long situa* 'He will go to the store' (Jenkins 2000: 138). Also, note that *bai* occurs in sentence-initial position; this is where the irrealis marker (*vo*) occurs in Tibak, the main first language on New Ireland, to mark non-past times. In some varieties of Tok Pisin, *bai* has moved to a position immediately before the verb (where future markers occur in English).

Another social condition that may coincide with the development of a different type of hybrid element is conversational codeswitching. If bilingual speakers employ two or more languages very frequently in a codeswitching pattern in social situations that do not call for monolingual or more formal discourse, certain hybrid verbs occur in the codeswitching (CS) involving some language pairs. That is, some CS patterns may show a nonfinite verb form from one of the languages, but it occurs with the verbal inflections of the other participating language, not those inflections of its own. For example, in Swahili-English CS, in an informal conversation in Nairobi (Myers-Scotton 2015) the English verb form *apply* occurs in the Swahili-framed clause, *u-ki-apply kama leo* 'if you apply for example today...' (u=2S; -ki- = conditional).

The theoretical basis for producing such innovative linguistic constructions is contained in the Abstract Level Model, developed by Carol Myers-Scotton and Janice Jake (2001), and first discussed in detail in Myers-Scotton (2002). The basic premise of the model is not new, that there are several or more different levels in the abstract nature of any lexical element. What the Abstract Level Model brings to the discussion of abstract levels is the premise—especially when speakers are bilingual—that the possibility exists to split abstract levels from one linguistic variety and combine them with levels from another language or variety. The Abstract Level Model identifies three levels of abstract structure: lexical-conceptual structure, predicate-argument structure, and morphological realisation patterns.

Lexical-conceptual structure refers to the semantics and pragmatics in an element that is directly elected early in the production process (at the conceptual level of production). This is the level at which the abstract lemmas that underlie content morphemes (e.g., nouns and verbs) are directly activated by the speaker's intentions regarding communicating messages. In addition, those morphemes that are called 'early' system morphemes under the 4-M model are indirectly activated by their content morpheme heads. Examples include determiners, plural markers, and satellites in compound verbs. Both content morphemes and early system morphemes can be described as conceptually-activated.

In contrast, the morphemes that become fully salient at the abstract level of predicate-argument structure are called structurally-assigned. Predicate-argument structure refers to the level that contains language-specific directions for morpho-syntactic structure. Such structure includes the abstract features that underlie the surface-level morphemes that indicate relationships among elements in the clause. That is, these morphemes are assigned or activated through a syntactic relationship, not a conceptual relationship. Under the 4-M model, these morphemes are called late system morphemes (also called 'outsiders' because they actually occur outside the positions in the clause of the morphemes that initiate them). The clearest example of an outsider system morpheme is the morpheme that shows subject-verb agreement on the verb in many languages—not on the subject which calls it. Another type of late system morpheme (called 'bridges') occurs between phrases in a clause, making up a larger constituent, often of two noun phrases. Thus in English, *of* in *book of John* is a bridge. The complementisers that join together two clauses are also bridges. The third level in the model is the level of morphological realisation patterns. The patterns that actually occur vary from one language to another. For example, German is a language that marks case on object pronouns. Some German verbs require that their objects must be marked with accusative case (e.g., *mich* 'me'), but others mark 'me' as an object with dative case (e.g., *sie stand mirbei* 'she stood by me'). Another example of morphological realisation patterns is the position of the verb in a clause; in some languages, such as Hindi, the verb is in final position.

The three levels of the Abstract Level Model underlie all surface-level elements in languages. What is relevant about these levels in this contribution is that these levels can be split at the abstract level, with the result that new surface level words and affixes may develop a process that occurs within a language as well as cross-linguistically.

For example, in English, a new noun now in frequent use, is selfie. It was coined to refer to the photo that a person can produce by applying the photo feature on a cell/mobile phone to himself or herself. Selfie is a noun, but it obviously builds on the pronominal form, self. Thus, we can say that the predicate-argument structure of the original lexical category of self has been changed to a nominal category.

The argument developed here is that reconfigurations of abstract structure at abstract levels also is the mechanism that accounts for new uses of existing words in the bilingual speech that characterises language contact phenomena. As will become clear, in contact phenomena, only conceptually-assigned elements (content morphemes and early system morphemes), not the structurally-assigned system morphemes of the 4-M model, are available to participate in such developments. That is, conceptual material can be reanalysed to serve the roles of structurally-assigned elements. Identifying the mechanism responsible for such changes as the possibility to split and recombine abstract levels across languages offers an explanation of such innovations that other descriptive terms such as 'transfer' or 'interference' or even 'creolisation' do not.

CREOLE DEVELOPMENT

Creole languages interest linguists for a number of ways that seem to be different or similar to other naturally occurring languages or contact phenomena; whatever the case, the evidence discussed here indicates that the mechanism behind modifying lexical elements through splitting and recombining abstract material across languages is a major factor distinguishing creoles. In contrast, many creolists have been more interested in the nature of the syntactic frame of a given creole, especially in its relation to the first languages of the actual creators of the creole (called substrate languages). Others focus on the similarities across creoles and argue for an origin relating to typological features or language universals. Still others concentrate on the background in which creoles developed, especially the ethnic groups involved, and therefore they focus on the likely substrate languages that could contribute to the structure of a given creole. Beyond recognising that lexifiers are the major source of the creole lexicon, less attention is paid to their role. Lexifiers (also called superstrates) are those languages spoken by the owners/ overseers of the plantations and businesses where creoles developed for communication purposes. Many lexifier elements in creoles, if derived from lexifiers, retain some of their phonological features, especially content morphemes do this. Creoles often have names reflecting the lexifier. Yet, such names do not mean these 'new' creole elements are intelligible to speakers of the lexifier. That they are generally non-intelligible indicates their levels of abstract lexical structure have been modified in some way.

Myers-Scotton and Jake (2009 *inter alia*) and most recently in Jake and Myers-Scotton (2016) have argued that the only lexifier forms that are available to the creators of a creole are morphemes that are directly or indirectly elected at the level of lexical-conceptual structure; these include those morphemes that are called content morphemes and early system morphemes under the 4-M model. They satisfy two requirements: (1) they carry semantic meaning, and (2) the context adds procedural meaning or various implications to a proposition. They are the morphemes that undergo reconfiguration and serve in the slots for what would be structurally-assigned elements, as illustrated below.

In referring to lexifier contributions to creoles, creolists regularly mention grammaticalisation. Grammaticalisation is generally recognised as a process at a cognitive level; however, its usual definition is more descriptive than explanatory: it is defined as the process that changes a content word into a so-called function word or a grammatical affix. That is, grammaticalisation is the term often employed to describe the stimulus or source of the changes that occur in a variety whose speakers are in contact with a more socially or politically dominant variety (Heine and Kuteva 2005; Matras 2009). For a recent study of creole complements that also refers to grammaticalisation, see Migge and Winford (2013). Especially in relation to creoles, in addition to referring to grammaticalisation, such terms as 'reanalysis' have been used.

However, naming the process of changes in a language in a contact situation as grammaticalisation or reanalysis does not explain what is involved to effect the change. Rather, a hypothesis about the mechanism behind such change is needed. Again, the argument here is that the splitting and recombining of abstract levels of lexical structure across languages is that mechanism. Examples follow illustrating how splitting and recombining operates in creoles. Example (1) illustrates how a compound adverbial phrase in English, *close to*, which can be locative in its original English meaning, or can be used metaphorical to imply 'near completion', is employed as an adverb meaning 'almost' in the Tok Pisin variety spoken on New Ireland.

(1) Tok Pisin

Em	i	klostu pinis
3S	PRED M	almost finish

'He's almost finished.'

(Jenkins 2000: 132)

In another example (2) from Tok Pisin, the English verb *belong* is employed in the position of an associative bridge system morpheme, meaning 'of'. That is, the lexical category of belong is changed (it is no longer a verb), and its predicate-argument structure is modified even though it retains most of its semantics. Note that *bilong* is a content morpheme that serves as a structurally-assigned morpheme. Reconfigured content morphemes for what are called bridge or outsider late system morpheme under the 4-M model are a hallmark of creoles.

(2) Tok Pisin

... pes	bilong	olgeta man
face	belong	PL/all man

'... face of everyone/of every person.'

(Jenkins 2000: 133)

In a well-known example from Hawaiian Creole-English, the English verb, *get*, is bleached of its lexical category as a verb and it takes on several different features of predicate-argument structure; which feature is salient depends on its syntactic position. In initial position it is a place holder or dummy element for existentiality, but it also can function to convey the type of 'possession' conveyed by *have*, as it does in the second clause (in 3). English *get* can also serve in Hawaiian Creole as a complementiser. In many creoles, complementisers are a form that retains much of its original lexical-conceptual structure, but it is reanalysed as a complementiser; it loses its abstract status as a verb or a preposition. Such complementisers are common; for example, *taki* is derived from English *talk* and *sey* [English *say*] and *fo* [English *for*] are also examples. See (3) for an example of *say* reanalysed as a complementiser.

(3) Nigerian Pidgin-English

À tí	(sé) yù	gó	Káno
I think	(say) you	go	Kano

'I think (present) (that) you went (past) to Kano.'

(Faraclas 1988: 183)

In example (4), a well-known example from Hawaiian Creole-English, the English verb *get* is bleached of its lexical category as a verb and it takes on several different features of predicate-argument structure (which may reflect a substrate). Which feature is salient depends on its syntactic position. In initial position, it is a dummy element for existentiality, but it can also function to convey the type of 'possession' conveyed by *have* in English, as it does in the second clause. It can also serve as a complementiser, but not in this example.

(4) Hawaiian Creole-English

Get	wan wahine	shi	get	wan	data
Existential	one woman	COMP	have	one	daughter

'There is a woman who has a daughter.'

(Bickerton 1981: 87)

In example (5) a French prepositional adverb *après* 'after' is reconfigured as a marker of future tense. This is a classic example of grammaticalisation; the mechanism at work keeps the partial semantics of *après* and strips its role in the French level of predicate-argument structure (i.e., it loses its lexical category as an adverb), while keeping its place in French morphological realisation patterns (i.e., its syntactic position).

(5) Haitian Creole

Mari	ap	manjekrab	le
Mary	IMPERF/FUT	eat crab	DET

'Mary is eating the crab.'

(Lefebvre 1993: 240)

Another example (6) shows how the nominal status of a French content morpheme is neutralised to become a reflexive pronoun in Mauritian Creole.

(6) Mauritian Creole

Mo	va	touye	mo	lékorps	(French *le corps*)
1S	FUT	kill	1S	body	(French *se tuer*)

'I am going to kill myself'

(Corne 1988: 88)

Under the Abstract Level Model, grammaticalisation can refer to the process that results in splittings and recombinations that produce an element based on the lexifier's lexical-conceptual level, but with new material especially at the abstract level of predicate-argument structure, possibly from substrate languages or perhaps universal principles. Certainly, the abstract level of predicate-argument structure is modified if an element's lexical category changes. The abstract material added may be derived from substrate material or from other sources, such as universal principles.

In addition, lexifier elements can undergo less radical changes; they can retain their original three levels of abstract structure but can modify the semantic or pragmatic aspects of their original lexical-conceptual structure. A term that can cover both classical grammaticalisation and less radical semantic/ predicate changes is 'reconfiguration, employed earlier' (Myers-Scotton 2001, 2002: 283). Reconfiguration is more comprehensive than other terms; it is also more transparent than grammaticalisation, even though it still implies cognitive realignments. It also can cover simple realignments of morphemes, such as *lazah* 'money' (French *l'argent*) or *dewil* 'some oil' (French *de huile*) cited for Mauritian Creole in Baker (1972).

Reconfiguration of Embedded Language Verbs in Codeswitching

Another contact phenomenon that shows splitting and combining of abstract levels of lexical structure, but one that refers specifically to inflected verbs, is found in some codeswitching corpora. Following the Matrix Language Frame (MLF) model, the term 'Matrix Language' (ML) refers to the language that supplies the grammatical frame of a bilingual clause in codeswitching (CS), while the term 'Embedded Language' (EL) refers to the other language(s) involved. EL languages typically supply nouns (content morphemes) in CS as well as full phrases, such as prepositional phrases, but within a grammatical frame from the ML.

In CS, the expected/unmarked verb that occurs in the grammatical frame set by the ML is a finite ML verb inflected with ML verbal affixes. However, in some corpora, EL nonfinite verb forms occur instead, along with ML verb affixes. The premise to explain these occurrences is that these EL forms are accepted by the ML frame because they convey the speaker's intentions. Further, they differ from EL finite verbs, which do not occur. The specifications of the Abstract Level Model suggest that EL nonfinite verb forms, such as infinitives, differ from finite verbs in their relation to their levels of abstract lexical structure, particular in regard to the level of predicate-argument structure. This leads to the hypothesis that ML finite verb frames in codeswitching can accommodate such EL nonfinite verb forms, but not EL finite verb forms; the rationale is that nonfinite forms do not require interaction at the level of the Formulator that EL finite verb forms would require to appear in an inflected verbal frame. EL finite verbs carry directions to become salient that would conflict with similar directions in the ML frame (Myers-Scotton and Jake 2014, 2016).

The following examples illustrate EL nonfinite verb forms in an ML frame. Such examples as *wa-na-vyo-behave* 'how they behave' in (7) are possible in some pairs of languages when their speakers are engaged in CS. To date, these examples have been found in corpora that include various African languages, but languages that are typologically diverse. Examples come readily from CS in which a Bantu language is the ML, but also from West Africa when Ewe is the ML (see example 8).

(7) Swahili-English CS

U-ki-kaa	huko	Baringo ...	u-na-anz-a	
2S-CONDIT-live-FV	there	Baringo	2S-NONPST-FV	begin

ku-behave	kama	wa-na-vyo-behave
INF-behave	as	3PL NONPST-MANNER-behave

'If you live there [in] Baringo...you begin to behave as they behave.'

(Myers-Scotton 1993: 103)

(8) Ewe-English

Mo	ná-ná	be the poor	ná-express	*f*	view
3PL	give-HABIT	that the poor	SUBJ-express	POSS	view

'They won't allow that the poor [should] express their view.'

(Amuzu 2010: 270)

Explaining such examples depends on two suppositions: first, generally EL nonfinite verbs can be elected as fully salient at the level of lexical-conceptual structure because they only carry features having to do with the semantics and pragmatics that satisfy the speaker's intended message. Their main role is carrying semantics and, in monolingual data, they are only syntactically relevant in infinitive phrases. That is, other abstract features that are part of finite verbs are not salient in nonfinite verbs. Finite verbs must interact with the Formulator to produce larger constituents that may involve agreement checking or case assignment. Second, not all elements that are identified as verbs cross-linguistically have the same set of abstract features. When EL nonfinite verbs do appear with ML verbal inflections, it may be because they are sufficiently congruent with the ML frame at abstract levels in certain corpora, in ways as yet not understood.

In general, whatever their nature, very few EL verbs appear in CS corpora compared with ML verbs. Those that do appear fall in three groups—firstly, the most common are those that occur as infinitives in light verb constructions ('do' verb constructions). That is, an ML light verb that stands for 'do' or a related meaning receives all the necessary ML inflections that the clause requires. It is followed by a nonfinite form that is the complement of the 'do' verb. Of course, such constructions are common in Indian languages, but are also well known in many other language groups. For example, in Turkish-Dutch CS, a likely pattern for this construction is that the Turkish verb for 'do' (*yap*) receives ML inflections and is preceded by a Dutch infinitive. In Chichewa, a Bantu language spoken in Malawi, the nonfinite infinitive *ku-chita* 'to do' appears in such constructions. Secondly, in a number of other cases, nonfinite verbs do appear in ML frames, but only if they receive an ML 'verbaliser' as an affix that seems to neutralise the verb forms' EL origin. For example, if Finnish is the EL, the Finnish verb receives the affix *-at* and then it can appear in an ML frame and is inflected with ML verbal affixes. Finally, as analysed here, some nonfinite verbs appear fully inflected with ML inflections, as shown in (7) and (8). For another example, see (9) in which the French infinitive *soumettre* is inflected with Chiluba affixes for finite verbs.

(9) Chiluba-French

...Je-n-ai-pas	oublié	problème	u-mu-wu-vw-a
1S-NEG-have NEG	forget	problem	2S-OBJ-COP-FV

m-n-soumettre
2S-CL9.OBJ-submit

'... I haven't forgotten the problem [that] you submitted to me.'

(Kamwangamalu 1987: 169)

In some language pairs, it is not the infinitive but the present participle from the EL that receives ML inflections. This is the case in Acholi-English CS (i.e. *gi-emphasising* 'they emphasise ...'). All verbs in Acholi mark aspect, and the present participle rather than the infinitive conveys aspect.

In sum, the very occurrence of nonfinite EL verbs in ML frames in CS with no other structures to increase the acceptability implies that some splitting and recombining of levels of abstract lexical structure is involved. That is, the EL is active at the level of lexical-conceptual structure when an EL verb form is selected as the underlying lemma that best satisfies the speaker's intentions. But it is the ML that integrates it into the levels of predicate-argument structure and morphological realisation patterns. All of this seems to occur with no obvious additional effort than those expended to inflect an ML verb with ML inflections. That such complex verb forms do occur, offers strong validation for the Abstract Level Model.

Conclusion

This contribution has shown how the Abstract Level Model offers an explanation for the structural nature of much of the lexical content in clauses in creole languages and the acceptability of EL nonfinite verbs into ML verbal frames. Regarding creoles, examples illustrate how lexifier content morphemes are reconfigured, through a splitting and combining of the levels that underlie morphemes at the abstract level. Through this process, content morphemes are reconfigured to satisfy the roles that structurally-assigned morphemes carry in other naturally occurring languages. The same model offers a more tentative explanation for the occurrence of nonfinite EL verbs in bilingual clauses in CS. The premise is that the nature of these nonfinite verbs at the levels of abstract lexical structure sufficiently satisfy the requirements of the ML frame so that they receive ML verbal affixes in well-formed bilingual clauses. This possibility depends on the structure of nonfinite verbs: they basically are directly elected at the level of lexical-conceptual structure and therefore do not require further saliency regarding predicate-argument structure at the level of predicate-argument structure.

ABBREVIATIONS

1S	first person singular
2S	second person singular
3S	third person singular
3PL	third person plural
CL9	Bantu class 9
CONDIT	conditional
COMP	complementiser
COP	copula
DET	determiner
FUT	future
FV	final vowel (verb form)
HABIT	habitual
IMPERF	imperfect
ING	infinitive
NEG	negative
NONPST	non-past
OBJ	object
PL	Plural
POSS	possessive
PRED M	predicate marker
SUBJ	subjunctive

REFERENCES

Amuzu, Evershed. (2010). *Composite Codeswitching in West Africa: The Case of Ewe-English Codeswitching*. Saarbrucken: Lambert Academic Publishing.

Baker, Philip. (1972). *Creole*. London: C. Hurst & Co.

Bickerton, Derek. (1981). *The Roots of Language*. Ann Arbor, MI: Karoma Publishers.

Corne, Chris. (1988). 'Mauritian creole reflexives'. *Journal of Pidgin and Creole Languages*, 3/1, 69–94.

Faraclas, Nicholas. (1988). 'Nigerian Pidgin and the languages of southern Nigeria'. *Journal of Pidgin and Creole Languages*, 3/2, 177–98.

Heine, Bernd, and Tania Kuteva. (2005). *Language Contact and Grammatical Change*. Cambridge: Cambridge University Press.

Jake, Janice, and Carol Myers-Scotton. (2016). 'Cognitive structure and context: Lexifier grammatical forms in creole development'. Paper presented at annual meeting, Society for Pidgin and Creole Linguistics. Washington, D.C., January.

Jenkins, Rebecca Sue. (2000). 'Language contact and composite structures in New Ireland, Papua New Guinea'. Unpublished PhD Dissertation. Columbia, SC: University of South Carolina Linguistics Program.

Kamwangamalu, Nkonko. (1987). 'French/vernacular code-mixing in Zaire: Implications for syntactic constraints'. In B. Need, E. Schiller, and A. Bosch (eds), *Papers from the 23rd Annual Meeting of the Chicago Linguistic Society*. Chicago, IL: Chicago Linguistic Society, 166–80.

Lefebvre, Claire. (1993). 'Relexification and syntactic analysis in Haitian Creole: Methodological aspects of a research program'. In S. Mufwene (ed.), *Africanisms in Afro-American Language Varieties*. Athens, GA: University of Georgia Press, 254–79.

Matras, Yaron. (2009). *Language Contact*. Cambridge: Cambridge University Press.

Migge, Bettina, and Donald Winford. (2013). 'Fact-type complements on Gbe and the Surinamese Creoles'. *Lingua*, 129, 9–31.

Myers-Scotton, Carol. (1976). 'Strategies of neutrality: Language choice in uncertain situations'. *Language*, 52/4, 919–41.

____ (1993a). *Duelling Languages: Grammatical Structure in Codeswitching*, 2nd edn, 1997. Oxford: Oxford University Press.

____ (1993b). *Social Motivations for Codeswitching: Evidence from Africa*. Oxford: Oxford University Press.

____ (2001). 'Implications of abstract grammatical structure: Two targets in creole formation'. *Journal of Pidgin and Creole Languages*, 16, 217–73.

Myers-Scotton, Carol. (2002). *Contact Linguistics, Bilingual Encounters and Grammatical Outcomes*. Oxford: Oxford University Press.

——— (2006). *Multiple Voices: An Introduction to Bilingualism*. Malden, MA: Blackwell/ Wiley.

——— (2015). Unpublished New Nairobi Corpus.

Myers-Scotton, Carol, and Janice Jake. (2001). 'Explaining aspects of codeswitching and their implications'. In Janet Nicole (ed.), *One Mind, Two Languages: Bilingual Language Processing*. Oxford: Blackwell, 84–116.

——— (2009). 'Sources of inflection: Testing the Creole System Morpheme hypothesis'. Paper presented at annual meeting, Society for Pidgin and Creole Linguistics. San Francisco, January.

——— (2014). 'Nonfinite verbs and negotiating bilingualism in codeswitching: Implications for a language production model'. *Bilingualism, Language and Cognition*, 17/3, 511–25.

——— (2016). 'Revisiting the 4-M model: Codeswitching and morpheme election at the abstract level'. *International Journal of Bilingualism*. Available online. DOI: 10.1177/1367006915626588. Last date of accession: 12.07.2021.

9

Translation Theory as an Ever-Emerging Phenomena

Udaya Narayana Singh

Abstract

The paper contributes to the Theory of Indeterminacy to understand the complex act of translation. It begins with issue of stability or certainty of the concept of 'Signs' in human language, and its Saussurean conceptualisation. If in spoken language, 'Signs' are open to multiple interpretations, and are hence indeterminate, the written mode of communication does not make it easier either. It discusses the Derridean argument if all writing has the property of communicability, transmitability, decipherability, iterability for every possible user, and what its consequence could be in understanding the nature of translation. It also expresses the discomfort with the Theory of Iterability which may be applicable to 'ordinary' communication and writing but not to literary texts that need to be translated. Its rejection is also necessary as it cannot handle polysemy or contextually driven interpretations. It is also pointed out that each speaker's use of an expression may carry unseen individual values that are neither assessable, nor discernible. While what determinist linguistics does to our understanding of this complexity is purely in the interest of the progression of the Science of Linguistics, it may be difficult for translation specialists to completely abandon the issue of indeterminacy in translation, it is argued.

Ever since Ferdinand de Saussure tried to freeze the meaning of linguistic signs as a stable entity 'which does not change arbitrarily, or at a given individual's whim' mainly because 'It is shared...by all the members of a given linguistic community at a historical moment, although it can change over time' (Sim 2001: 295), the theory of language and meaning proceeded in a certain direction. However, in the postmodern thinking, Sign is an unstable and fractured entity which can never capture the 'full' meaning of words as in Derrida's description about which Gayatri Chakravorty Spivak's comments (namely, signs are 'half not there and half not that') question their stability because they are open to wide range of interpretation, mainly drawn from its past use. The point to note is that the Signs or Symbols in 'Communication' or 'Spoken Discourse' conform to a tradition of language use, and they echo their past use when a given meaning is derived thereof. As against this, in all 'written' forms of language use, the matter gets complicated according to Derrida (1972/1988) because of a series of 'absenses'—the physical absence of the writer, the undefined role of the reader, and the possible absence of the communicative intent itself (Madsen 2014). He further elaborates when he argues:

> In order for my[1] 'written communication' to retain its function as writing, i.e. its readability, it must remain readable despite the absolute disappearance of any receiver, determined in general. My communication must be repeatable—iterable—in the absolute absence of the receiver or of any empirically determinable collectivity of receivers. Such iterability (*iter*, again, probably comes from *itara*, 'other' in Sanskrit, and everything that follows can be read as the working out of the logic that ties repetition to alterity) structures the mark of writing itself, no matter what particular type of writing is involved (whether pictographical, hieroglyphic, ideographic,

[1] Derrida, Jacques. (1972/1988), 19–20.

> phonetic, alphabetic, to cite the old categories). A writing that is not structurally readable—iterable—beyond the death of the addressee, would not be writing...This implies that there is no such thing as a code—Organon of iterability—which could be structurally secret. The possibility of repeating and thus of identifying the marks is implicit in every code, making it into a network [*une grille*] that is communicable, transmittable, decipherable, iterable for a third, and hence for every possible user in general. To be what it is, all writing must, therefore, be capable of functioning in the radical absence of every empirically determined receiver in general.

A determinacy theory of translation would therefore emerge from this belief that a large portion of what we write is double-bound by Social Convention on the one hand, and Grammatical (lexical) Convention on the other, and the best proof is that writing is iterable, and so is re-writing of the same text in another form (or call it another language). But what about the 'rupture' between the words as signs and thought as meaning that Derrida points out? Etienne Condillac (1714–1780) and his treatise 'Essay on the Origin of Human Knowledge' which Derrida refers to in detail, argues that it is the characteristics of writing that continues to cause effects even after the writer departs. However, that is true of the great speeches as well in an electronic age, because like written texts, such oral texts are also available in public space more often than not. Condillac thought that man discovered the new symbolic system of coding or writing because the idea was to perpetuate those thoughts and make them known to persons who were absent. To that extent, his ideas suited Derrida's theory.

However, I feel very uncomfortable with the Iterability Theory as it makes a few assumptions that may be true of 'ordinary' communication and writing but not applicable to literary texts. For instance, appeal to consciousness or intended meaning will have to be dismissed if this position is to be believed. Secondly, it must divorce itself from all hermeneutics to mean fixed and predictable things always. Thirdly, the contextual variation of interpretation of a given text differently will have no place here. Fourthly, Polysemy or Polysemics with which we are all so familiar in poetic texts (or even in densely-composed certain prose texts) will have to be sacrificed. Lastly, the notion of ambiguity with which authors often like to play as they write must have no place in this approach. If one says that 'Writing' breaks away from its 'Context(s)' of production once it is written would mean that newer contexts in which it is to be read or used will determine its meaning—and its readers or users or receivers would then assign it meaning which may or may not match with what the author-scripter may have intended. That may ultimately take us to the position that argues in favour of death of the author once a text is scripted.

In this context, we may recall how Derrida once asked in his 1985 essay, 'Des Tours de Babel' ('How do you translate a signature?')—meaning thereby that there are 'moment(s) of impossibility invested in all translations' (Pym 2008: 248). But given our experience with multilingual authors, we do know that they are in fact perfectly capable of coming up with signatures in different languages, except that each one of them perhaps obeys the spelling conventions of (hand-)written languages in use at that point of time besides the individual's decision as to how their signatures would look like. A mere reproduction of signature in one language in another may not work. In modern-day communication technologies, dubbing an actor's voice in another language and with another (perhaps, near-equivalent) voices, or super-imposing a voice onto someone's enactment on screen may be common phenomenon in films and digital media but they suffer from the same problem of equivalence and (inter-semiotic) transferences. Finding a one-to-one match would always seem to be a futile task.

This would take us back to the example of 'Jungle linguist' used by Willard Van Orman Quine, the philosopher, who described the methodology of finding equivalent glosses during the field linguistics work on unknown languages as purely speculative with a lot of uncertainty and indeterminacy. The judgement of such scholars in associating a hitherto unheard-of set of noise (phonetically transcribed) with an object which her informant may point out to as open-ended. Similarly, in translation of a text, numerous interpretations are possible, and that no amount of questioning or debating as to which one was the closest will ever produce any certainty. Added to that, there is this possibility that each speaker's use of the word carries unseen individual values that are not assessable nor discernible. Thus, in translation, it seems the indeterminacy will never completely go away. One could recall Even-Zohar in this context who commented in the following manner:

> How many times we have been tortured by the clichés of the uninitiated, veteran or novice, that translation is never equal to the original, that languages differ from one another, that culture is 'also' involved with the translation procedures. That when a translation is 'exact' it tends to be 'literal' and hence loses the 'spirit' of the original, that the 'meaning' of a text means both 'content' and 'style' and so on.
>
> (1981: 1)

He further claimed that when we talk of functioning of verbal sign systems, the dynamic and heterogeneous positions were gaining ground these days, as against the age-old a-historical concept of system (structure), as isolated from the other semiotic co-systems—analysed in terms of homogeneity. The consequence of this is the realisation that all linguistic phenomena, including texts, could be analysed in terms of more than one theory, each one of which may have some merit. It is a different matter that Noam Chomsky (1980: 14/16) would describe this as 'True and (=but) uninteresting'. What we notice is that in the sciences as well as in literary criticism, divergence of theories and evidence has been the common trend. What is important is that this problem of finding equivalences is true not only across languages, but also within each language.

One can understand the problems faced by Saussure or Chomsky who had to make assumptions that language systems achieve some degree of staticity at a given moment because otherwise one could not build theories and explanations. Whether it was *la langue* as against the divergent and slippery *parole*, or the deep or logical (underlying) structure, a determinist linguistics was necessary for the progress of this science. Pym takes us back to Plato and his Cratylus where we find Hermogenes trying to establish that words were 'arbitrary labels' encoded in human language, whereas Cratylus tries to argue—on the basis of etymology and onomatopoeia that name-givers in human societies would use names of entities to reveal their characteristics or properties just as painters use different colours and lines to depict and assign contours and shapes of described entities on the canvas. Once again, multiple choices or options of naming the same objects would show that matters of language are arbitrary (and indeterminate). If Cratylus were to be believed, synonyms, ambiguities and equivalences or near-equivalences could never be found in language.

Further, each language imposes its own (arbitrary) categories and conceptualisations on naming and understanding an object. If Germans see 'Death' as in the masculine, and the Russians describe her as a woman, whereas 'Sin' is feminine in German and masculine in Russian, this clearly shows the futility of a deterministic position. This 'world view' theory of Humboldt, Sapir and Whorf as well as Roman Jakobson was shown as the modern version of Cratylistic determinism, as 'for Cratylus, the nature of the thing determines its correct name; for linguistic relativism, the nature of the language system determines perception of the thing. Either way, there is a strong deterministic link between expression and referent...' (Pym 2008: 7). That form and content in painting seem inseparable, the same thing is echoed in ancient Indian saying '*Vāgarthāvivasampṛktauvāgarthampratipatyaye...*' where form and meaning seem intertwined in similar fashion. For the followers of T. S. Eliot, meaning begins its journey from the time the text gets its form. But Benedetto Croce (1902: 73) uses 'similarity' or 'approximation' (distinguished from the impossible identity we call 'equivalence') as a 'family likeness' to describe 'relative possibility of translation'. Others like Heidegger would, of course, differ and give more preference to the productive conflict of differences between the source and target texts because words of a language convey, hold and communicate knowledge within their own social and linguistic system. In that sense, translations hand down legacy to the new generation or new societies as providing with interpretations of the previous (=source) text or the past in a modern diction. In his essay on 'The Task of the Translator' (1923/1977), Walter Benjamin would argue that all current languages are imperfect parts of the perfect language, 'fragments of a broken vessel', and that translating would thus be the piecing together of those fragments, a constant search for the lost true language.

In fact, all these theories and arguments based on which they are proposed, sound good but none of them seriously challenge the notion of indeterminacy and the social practice of translation. The question is if translations could be based on the realisation that perfect equivalences are a myth, and yet are able to demonstrate that the two texts—the Source and the Target do talk about the same thing. One position could be like what Pym describes as the 'Illumination Theory' of Augustine of Hippo (Aurelius Augustinus, 354–430 AD) who talks about ideas appearing as 'traces' or 'vestiges' (*vestigia*), erupting in one's mind like a rapid illumination, tucking our thoughts in its secret places as it were, and words and expressions in whatever language we speak will come out later. What is communicated here is anterior to language, and thus potentially available to all in some language-neutral format. That is why meaning is actively created from what readers bring to the text. Secondly, the formulation used by John Locke would be different in the sense that it gives more emphasis on the Social Consensus—particularly useful when we discover that two or more translations of the same text are all good and reliable translations—even though different from each other. This position then helps us in dealing with indeterminacy. Thirdly, Constructivism or Social Constructivism vis-à-vis Translation (cf. Donald Kiraly 2000), as opposed to the transmissionist paradigm of encoding and decoding, says that since knowledge could be moved from one passive receptacle to another, like water being dished out into buckets, translation would allow some knowledge to go from one text into another (where language acts as a 'conduit' making it possible for meaning to flow as if through a tube from one language to another). Translation as a kind of transmission is at the base of the way many translators are trained. Translators would thus actively construct the text they produce, just as students actively participate in their learning process. Students have to find their own illumination, and while doing group work, they must get together to talk about what they are doing. This is also the way, translations could happen.

From the perspective of indeterminacy, there can be no absolute rule for deciding between different Translation Theories. One could always claim that 'the translation has to have the same cultural function as the source,', but that cannot be universally true. Not only are there many cases in which translations are more determined by the form of the source as in lip synchronisation in film dubbing, but different people will see the source 'function' as being different things. Even here, most of the translator's decisions cannot be called wholly 'right' or wholly 'wrong'.

There is no end to these ongoing debates about the nature of human language and translation, and theoretical positions do emerge like waves from time to time in all ages. My purpose here was to demonstrate that we have not been able to resolve some of our most fundamental notions about language structure and function, or textual form and interpretations, and hence Translation Theory seems to be an endless process using all kinds of metaphors. I had pointed this out in my Plenary talk titled 'Translating the World: Asian Perspectives on Translation' at the First World Congress on Translation in Paris on April 14, 2017. For example, we use the metaphor of 'governance' in finding out which text will rule—SLT (Source Language Text) or TLT (Target Language Text)? There is this metaphor of 'disease' in 'Uncontaminated' vs. 'Contaminated' texts, or metaphor of 'War' (or, is it one of 'Business'?) in Gains and Losses of translation. Similarly, metaphor of 'Inheritance' can be seen in the issue of whether 'translated texts' are to be described as 'Partly Inherited' and 'Partly Made-up'. The metaphor of 'Recursion' works in embeddedness of a literary text in the cultural 'CON-text,' and metaphor of 'Agency' is at work when we find 'Word' as an inseparable 'Agent' of cultural memory or as a 'Patient' of social history. The debate must go on.

References

Benjamin, Walter. (1923). 'The task of the translator'. An introduction to the translation of *Les fleurs du mal* by Baudelaire.

Chomsky, Noam. (1980). *Rules and Representations*. New York: Columbia University Press.

Croce, Benedetto. (1902). *L'Estetica come scienza dell'espressione e linguistica generale*. Commonly referred to as Aesthetic in English.

Derrida, Jacques. (1972/1988). 'Signature event context'. *Jacques Derrida, Limited Inc*. Evanston, IL: Northwestern University Press, 1–25.

____ (1985). 'Des Tours de Babel' (English and French versions). In J. F. Graham (ed.), *Difference in Translation*. Ithaca, NY: Cornell University Press, 165–207; 209–48.

Even-Zohar, Itamar. (1981). 'Translation theory today: A call for transfer theory'. *Poetics Today*, 2/4, 1–7 (Summer-Autumn number: Translation Theory and Inter-cultural Relations).

Kiraly, Donald. (2002). *A Social Constructivist Approach to Translation Education: Empowerment from Theory Practice*. Manchestor/ Northamoton: St. Jerome.

Madsen, Mathias Winther. (2014). 'Notebooks on language: Commentaries on literature about language, thought and action'. Retrieved from http://academiclogbook.blogspot.com/2014/03/ derrida-signature-event-context-1972.html. Last date of accession 12.07.2021.

Pym, Anthony. (2008). 'On indeterminacy in translation: A survey of Western theories'. Retrieved from http://citeseerx.ist.psu.edu/ viewdoc/download?doi=10.1.1.1083.2407&rep=rep1&type=pdf. Last date of accession 12.07.2021.

Sim, Stuart (ed.). (2001). *The Routledge Companion to Postmodernism*, 3rd edn, 2011. London and New York: Routledge.

10

Bengali Postlexical Rules

Lengthening and Shortening

Aditi Lahiri

Abstract

Bengali, i.e. Standard Colloquial Bengali (SCB), spoken in Calcutta was described in detail by Suniti Kumar Chatterji in his seminal work, *The Origin and Development of the Bengali Language*. In this chapter, we have put together a set of the most synchronically productive phonological rules, both allophonic as well as neutralising. These include feature-based processes as well as those related to quantity. Although consonantal quantity is contrastive (i.e. most consonantal phonemes have a geminate counterpart), vowel quantity is not, even though vowel lengthening does appear. The interaction of various processes suggest that the domains of these phonological rules can be restricted to the phonological word but may also go beyond it, and be constrained only by the phonological phrase.

Introduction

When a Calcuttan speaks of the Bengali language, he/she refers to what Suniti Kumar Chatterji described as the Standard

Colloquial Bengali or SCB. For ease and brevity, in this chapter we shall refer to SCB as simply 'Bengali'.[1] The phonological patterns of Bengali have been discussed in detail by Suniti Chatterji in his magnum opus, *The Origin and Development of the Bengali Language*, or ODBL (1926, reprinted 1975). Delving through the pages of these volumes, one encounters hidden gems. Sunitibabu's extremely informative account was both descriptive as well as historical. However, given the sheer volume of material, it is not always easy to extract the most productive phonological rules from the book. In this chapter, we have concentrated on a few of the recurrent processes in Bengali which affect both features as well as quantity, many of which are governed by prosodic contexts. Predominantly, the phonological processes (assimilations, dissimilations, deletions and lengthening) are lexical and neutralising, although purely allophonic rules also exist cutting across all word types.

Most segmental processes in Bengali are assimilatory in nature for both vowels and consonants. The only dissimilatory process is related to aspiration, which we will touch upon later. The theoretical analyses are given in terms of the phonological features developed under the *Featurally Underspecified Lexicon* (FUL: cf. Lahiri 2012, Lahiri and Reetz 2010). The feature tree is given under Figure 10.1. Two pairs of opposing features—CONSONANTAL/VOCALIC and SONORANT/ OBSTRUENT—are the major class features available in all

[1] One of the reasons for referring to the Calcutta speech as Bengali rather than Bangla is not linguistic but rather due to reasons of 'anglicisation' in the sense that many of our proper names when spoken in Bengali would be 'Chattopadhaya, Mukhopadhaya' etc., while the anglicised version as transliterated by the British were usually 'Chatterjee, Mukherjee' etc., or some similar variant. In our graduate days we were taught that one used 'Bangla' when speaking in Bengali but referred to the language as 'Bengali' when referring to it in English. The prejudice has remained. A second, more pertinent reason, is that Bangla is the official language of Bangladesh and although in essence they are the same, keeping aside arguments of dialect vs. language, the phonology can be rather different. Thus, we shall stick to 'Bengali'.

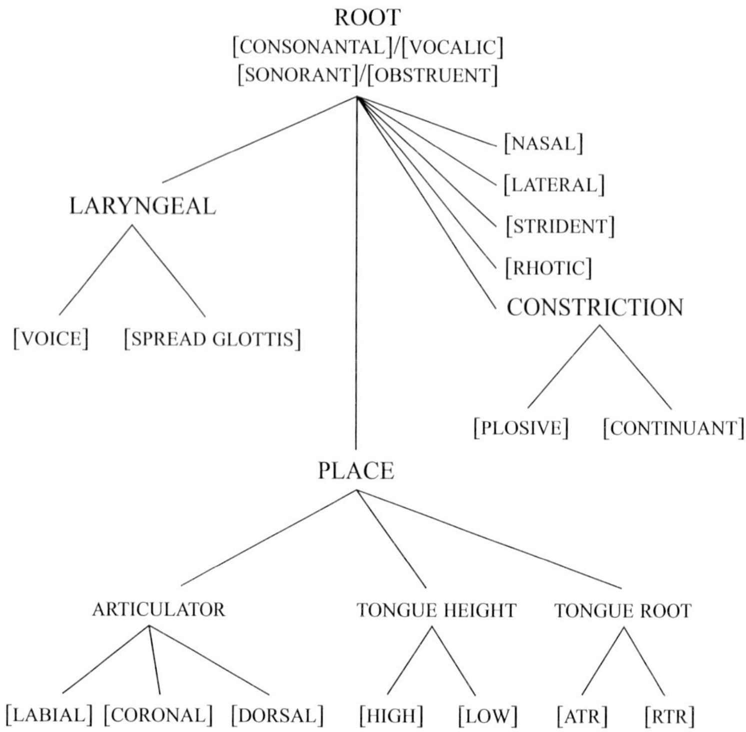

Figure 10.1: Feature tree for Bengali based on FUL

languages. All phonemes must be either CONSONANTAL or VOCALIC and SONORANT or OBSTRUENT. The members of each pair are conflicting—i.e. CONSONANTAL implies *not* VOCALIC and vice versa. All features are monovalent and, unlike Halle et al. (2000) and Clements (2001), there is no mixture of some binary features (e.g., [±back]) and some monovalent features (e.g., [dorsal]). A few additional points need to be noted. First, all features are monovalent, i.e. privative. Second, based on the seminal work of Jakobson, Fant and Halle (1952) (see also Clements 2001), place features are shared by consonants and vowels. Thus, front vowels such as /i e æ/ and dental, retroflex and palatoalveolar consonants are [CORONAL],while back vowels /u o ɔ/ and velars are [DORSAL]. Third, there are no dependent features such as the features [±anterior] or [±distributed] which occur in Clements (2001) or in *The Sound Patterns of English* (Chomsky and Halle 1968). As we shall see, distinctions between the various [CORONAL] obstruents are established via TONGUE HEIGHT and TONGUE ROOT features.

The Bengali obstruent and sonorant consonantal phonemes with their relevant contrastive features are given in Tables 10.1 and 10.2.

TABLE 10.1: Constrastive features for voiceless and voiced obstruents in Bengali

	p	t̪	ʈ	tʃ	k	pʰ	t̪ʰ	ʈʰ	tʃʰ	kʰ	ʃ
	b	d̪	ɖ	dʒ	g	bʰ	d̪ʰ	ɖʰ	dʒʰ	gʰ	
[OBSTRUENT]	✓	✓	✓	✓	✓	✓	✓	✓	✓	✓	✓
[STRIDENT]				✓					✓		✓
LARYNGEAL											
[SPREAD GLOTTIS]						✓	✓	✓	✓	✓	
[VOICE]	✓	✓	✓	✓	✓	✓	✓	✓	✓	✓	
CONSTRICTION											
[PLOSIVE]	✓	✓	✓	✓	✓	✓	✓	✓	✓	✓	
[CONTINUANT]											✓
ARTICULATORS											
[LABIAL]	✓					✓					
[CORONAL]		✓	✓	✓			✓	✓	✓		
[DORSAL]					✓					✓	
TONGUE HEIGHT											
[HIGH]			✓					✓			
[LOW]		✓					✓				

Table 10.2: Contrastive features for sonorant consonants in Bengali

	m	n̪	ŋ	l	r	ɽ
[CONSONANTAL]	✓	✓	✓	✓	✓	✓
[SONORANT]	✓	✓	✓	✓	✓	✓
[NASAL]	✓	✓	✓			
[LATERAL]				✓		
[RHOTIC]					✓	✓
ARTICULATORS						
[LABIAL]	✓					
[CORONAL]		✓		✓	✓	✓
[DORSAL]			✓			
TONGUE HEIGHT						
[HIGH]			✓			
[LOW]		✓				

Next we turn to the vowels. Here the phonological features may appear to be unexpected, given the phonetic shape of the vowels. However, lexical vowel harmony rules, particularly those applying on verbs (cf. Dan 1992, Lahiri 2000), support the fact that /ɔ/ is phonologically [LOW], patterning with /æ/.

Table 10.3: Root vowel morpho-phonological alternations in verbs

ROOT		3P PRES	1P PRES
/o/ ʃon-	hear	ʃon-e	ʃun-i
/e/ tʃen-	recognise	tʃen-e	tʃin-i
/ɔ/ kɔr-	do	kɔr-e	kor-i
/æ/ dækʰ-	see	dækʰ-e	dekʰ-i
/ɑ/ nɑtʃ-	dance	nɑtʃ-e	nɑtʃ-i

We will not discuss morpho-phonological alternations in this chapter. Suffice to know that given alternations as in Table 10.3, we can see that /ɔ/ patterns on a par with /æ/ in the simple tenses just as /o/ and /e/ behave in the same way, while /a/ remains constant (in the perfective tenses, /a/ alternates with /e/, but that is a different issue). Thus, in terms of height, /æ/ and /ɔ/ have to be the same, characterised here as [LOW].

TABLE 10.4: Vowels with their contrastive features in Bengali

	i ĩ	u ũ	e ẽ	o õ	ɔ ɔ̃	æ æ̃	ɑ ɑ̃
[VOCALIC]	✓	✓	✓	✓	✓	✓	✓
ARTICULATORS							
[LABIAL]		✓		✓	✓		
[CORONAL]	✓		✓			✓	
[DORSAL]		✓		✓	✓		✓
TONGUE HEIGHT							
[HIGH]	✓	✓					
[LOW]					✓	✓	✓

The nasal and oral vowels are listed together in Table 10.4, since the only difference is that the nasal vowels have the additional feature [NASAL].[2] Given these features, we can now turn to the most crucial productive phonological processes in Bengali. The first two are related to vowels, one which is purely allophonic (and changes quantity), while the second is neutralising.

VOWELS

Lengthening in a Monosyllabic Word

Vowel length is not contrastive in Bengali. Nevertheless, all vowels undergo monosyllabic lengthening as a part of a minimal word

[2] We have not listed the glides [w]/[o̯] and [j]/[e̯] here ([kʰɑo̯ɑ] < [kʰɑ - ɑ] 'eat-INFINITIVE') as in most instances these are used for hiatus. However, if they are to be considered as phonemes they would have the same features as the corresponding vowels without moras.

effect (cf. Dasgupta 1984, Lahiri and Fitzpatrick-Cole 1999). Furthermore, this lengthening is constrained within a prosodic word (see example 1).

(1) V → V: / —]$_{\omega}$

Unlike many European languages, this lengthening is insensitive to the feature specification of any following consonant. Thus, in English the vowel /æ/ would be lengthened before a voiced consonant leading to a surface contrast between *back* and *bad*, the latter with lengthening. Bengali vowels are always longer in a monosyllable and not perceptibly different in a voicing context.

Examples of vowel lengthening in different contexts are as follows.

(2) a. monosyllabic | monosyllabic with suffix | disyllabic
[kɑ:n] ear | [kɑn-er] ear-GENITIVE | [kɑnɑ] blind

b. different voicing context
[nɑ:k] nose [nɑk-i] nasal
[ro:g] illness [rog-i] ill person

The effect of the lengthening is also observed in monosyllabic open syllable words with and without suffixes as well as with a clitic. Emphatic clitics are added to a prosodic word and since the lengthening is within a word, the vowel is lengthened as we can see in the examples in (3) (cf. Fitzpatrick-Cole 1996, Lahiri and Fitzpatrick-Cole 1999).

(3) Monosyllabic open syllable words
a. [tʃɑ:]$_{\omega}$ want.IMPERATIVE.2nd P.COMMON / tea
b. [tʃɑ-i]$_{\omega}$> [tʃɑi]$_{\omega}$ want-PRES.1P
c. [[tʃɑ:]=i]$_{\omega}$ tea=also

In (3c) the vowel-lengthening rule makes the vowel /ɑ/ long, resulting in two syllables in the output while in (3b) the nucleus is a diphthong. Native speakers are extremely sensitive to this difference. Nevertheless, the language has no real vowel length contrast.

We now turn to feature-based assimilation rules.

Nasalisation

One of the most frequent processes is that of vowel nasalisation which affects all seven vowel phonemes. All vowels nasalise in the context of a following nasal consonant. The place of articulation of the nasal is not relevant. As far as we can tell, this process is:

(4) Vowel nasalisation
V → Ṽ / [NASAL] C

Nasalisation affects only word initial vowels, i.e. stressed vowels, and can occur in monomorphemic words as well as across morphemes. In (5) we provide very common examples across all the seven vowels. Each nasalised vowel is paired with an underlying nasal vowel.

(5) Monosyllabic words with productive vowel nasalisation and corresponding underlying nasal vowels.

a.	[kɑ̃n]	ear	[kɑ̃d̪ʰ]	shoulder
b.	[kʰũn]	murder	[kʰũt̪]	fault
c.	[ɖĩm]	egg	[gĩʈ]	knot
d.	[bæ̃ŋ]	frog	[bæ̃k]	bend
e.	[d̪ʰõn]	wealth	[tʃʰõ]	touch!
f.	[ʃɔ̃ŋ]	clown	[gɔ̃d̪]	glue
g.	[pẽn]	pen	[ʃẽk]	toast!

Nasalisation is not restricted to monomorphemic words, but can occur across morphemes: examples with monosyllabic words are listed in (6).

(6) Monosyllabic heteromorphemic words with nasalised vowels

kʰɑ-n	[kʰɑ̃n]	eat-2P.HONORIFIC.PRES
d̪i-n	[d̪ĩn]	give-2P.HONORIFIC.IMPERATIVE
d̪ʰo-n	[d̪ʰõn]	wash-2P.HONORIFIC.PRES
d̪æ-n	[d̪æ̃n]	give-2P.HONORIFIC.PRES

The examples in (6) can be homophonous with monomorphemic words such as [d̪ʰõn] 'wealth' or [d̪ĩn] 'day'. Underlying nasal vowels become indistinguishable from nasalised vowels when preceding a nasal consonant morpheme. We see this in (7). The underlying /õ/ when followed by the honorific /n/ suffix is pronounced as nasal. To the native ear, there is no distinction between the nasal vowel in a nasal phoneme context from an oral vowel in a similar context; i.e. the /õ/ from [tʃʰõ-n] and [d̪ʰõn] would be to all intents and purposes identical.

(7) Nasal and nasalised vowels

a.	tʃʰõ-	touch$_{\text{VERB}}$
b.	tʃʰõ-e	touch-3P.PRESENT
c.	tʃʰõ-b-en	touch-FUTURE-2P.HONORIFIC.PRES
d.	tʃʰõ-n	touch-2P.HONORIFIC.PRES

An early psycholinguistic experiment using gating revealed that the nasalisation, be it from the nasal or the nasalised vowel, appeared to access predominantly the lexical nasal vowel (Lahiri and Marslen-Wilson 1991). Thus, when listeners perceived [kɑ̃], they were prone to confidently assume that it was part of a word such as [kɑ̃dʰ] 'shoulder' rather than [kɑ̃n] 'ear'. On hearing the full coda consonant, of course, the listeners switched their choice from the nasal vowel to the nasalised vowel. We may then conclude that the nasalisation from the nasal consonant could be perceived, but was initially interpreted as a nasal vowel.

Consonants

Lengthening via Assimilation

We now turn to consonants. Unlike vowel lengthening, which is an allophonic rule, consonant lengthening is neutralising since Bengali has a full set of geminate consonants. The most productive rule of lengthening or gemination is related to [CORONAL] consonants. When the rhotics /r/ (or /ɽ/) is followed by a [CORONAL] obstruent (see Table 10.1), the obstruent becomes a geminate. This gemination can potentially apply within a word and across morphemes, but is constrained by a phonological phrase (cf. Hayes and Lahiri 1991).

(8) Rhotic assimilation and gemination

within a word

a. [pʰɔrʃɑ] > [pʰɔʃːɑ] fair skinned

b. [dordʒi] > [dodʒːi] tailor

across morphemes within a word

c. [kor-tʃʰ-e]>[kotʃʰːe] do-PROGRESSIVE-PRES.3P

d. [mɑr-t̪-o] >[mɑt̪ːo] beat-HABITUAL PAST-3P

compounds, complex predicates

e. [bɔɽ]$_{\omega}$ [d̪i]$_{\omega}$>[bɔd̪ːi]$_{\omega}$ elder sister

f. [mɑr] [dʰor] > [mɑd̪ʰːor] beat-and such

If, however, the first prosodic element carrying the rhotic immediately precedes a phrase boundary, the assimilation is blocked. This may happen if the word is focussed or if there is a clausal break forcing a phonological phrase break. Examples are given below.

(9) Rhotic assimilation blocked by a phonological phrase break

[ɑmi	ɑdʒ	[d̪id̪i-r	dæor-ke]$_{\phi}$	dekʰ-e-tʃʰ-i]
I	today	elder-sister -GEN	husband's younger brother-DAT	see-PERF-PROG-1P

a. No focus:

[d̪id̪i-r dæor-ke]$_{\phi}$> [d̪id̪idːæor-ke]

'Today I saw my elder sister's husband's younger brother.'

b. With focus:

[d̪id̪i-r]$_{\phi}$ [dæor-ke]$_{\phi}$> no gemination

'I saw my **elder sister's**$_{\text{FOCUS}}$ husband's younger brother (not anyone else's).'

Focus in Bengali is demarcated by the tune L* Hp, which means that the focussed element is demarcated by a phonological phrase boundary (Hayes and Lahiri 1991, Lahiri and Fitzpatrick-Cole 1999). Since the rhotic gemination is constrained to apply within a phrase, the /r/ is pronounced. A similar process constraint governs regressive voicing assimilation. Since Bengali allows all plosives to occur word-finally, the combinations are quite comprehensive. Again, we find that this rule is blocked as soon as the first prosodic word is at the end of a phrase. Furthermore, given the right sequence, the output could become a geminate. That is, if the two consonants share all features except voicing, then it could lead to a geminate.

(10) Voicing assimilation leading to gemination

a. rɑt̪ d̪in > rɑd̪:in night and day; 'daily'

b. pɑ̃tʃ dʒon > pɑ̃dʒ:on five people; 'five persons'

Assimilation across different place of articulation; no gemination

c. lok dʒon > logdʒon persons and people; 'many people'

d. mɑtʃʰ bʰɑt̪ > mɑdʒbʰɑt̪[3] fish and rice; 'a simple, but complete meal'

e. pɔt̪ʰ d̪ækʰ-ɑno > pɔd̪:ækʰɑno road see-CAUS.INF; 'showing the way to go'

Again, the same phrase-internal constraint holds, viz. if the first prosodic word is also the end of a phrase, the assimilation is blocked. Consider the examples in (11) in the two following contexts.

(11) Phrase break and voicing assimilation

a. mit̪ʰu ʃɑt̪ d̪in t̪ʰɑk-b-e > [ʃɑd̪:in]$_{\phi}$
Mithu seven days stay-FUT-3P
'Mithu will stay for seven days.'

b. mit̪ʰu ʃɑt̪ d̪in t̪ʰɑk-b-e, d̪u d̪in nɔe > [ʃɑt̪]$_{\phi}$ [d̪:in]
Mithu seven day stay-FUT-3P, two day not
'Mithu will stay for **seven** days, not two.'

[3] We turn to the issue of deaspiration in following section titled Deaspiration and Other Consequences.

Deaspiration and Other Consequences

Most of the phonological rules in Bengali are assimilatory. However, loss of aspiration is reminiscent of Grassmann's Law in Sanskrit and Greek where a sequence of two aspirated consonants were not tolerated. Nevertheless, it is difficult to say in Bengali whether the deaspiration is related to an Obligatory Contour Principle (OCP)-like effect or is simply coda-final. Again the deaspiration process, like the others above, is optional. Consider the following examples.

(12) Deaspiration

a. [bɑgʰ] > [bɑg]
'tiger'

b. [bɑgʰ]$_\phi$ [d̪ekʰ-l-ɑm]$_\phi$
tiger see-SIMPLE PAST-1P
'I saw a tiger.'

c. [[bɑgʰ] [d̪ækʰ-ɑ]]$_\phi$ [ʃɔhodʒ] [nɔe] > [bɑgd̪ækʰ-ɑ]
tiger see-INF easy not
'Tiger-viewing is not easy.'

This can obviously lead to homophones such as [kɑt̪ʰ] 'timber', 'wood', which will become identical with [kɑt̪] which is the imperative of the verb 'to cut'. As we have seen earlier, when there is an aspirated consonant followed by a voiced consonant, the voicing will spread but the aspiration can be lost—cf. [mɑtʃʰ] [d̪ʰɔr-ɑ] > [mɑdʒd̪ʰɔr-ɑ] fish catch-INF; 'to catch fish'. If there are two aspirated consonants, we have the same result, viz. that the first one is deaspirated; [kɑt̪ʰ][t̪ʰokrɑ] > [kɑt̪][t̪ʰokrɑ] > [kɑt̪ʰ:okrɑ] 'wood pecking' 'woodpecker'.

A further example is relevant to make a related point. Consider the following (one example repeated from above):

(13) Same place of articulation, but difference in voicing and aspiration

a. hɑt̪ d̪ʰɔr-ɑ > hɑd̪d̪ʰɔr-ɑ > [hɑd̪ʰ:ɔrɑ]
hand hold-INF
'to hold hands'

b. pɔt̪ʰ   d̪ækʰ-ɑ > pɔd̪ʰd̪ækʰ-ɑ > [pɔd̪ːækʰɑ]
   road   see-INF
   'to find the way'

Since the coda consonant is deaspirated and regressive voicing assimilation applies, the output of [t̪d̪ʰ] and [t̪ʰd̪] are [d̪ʰː] and [d̪ː] respectively.

Note that here, for (13a), we have given the intermediate output as [d̪d̪ʰ]. However, to all intents and purposes, this sequence is identical to that of [d̪ʰː]. There is no contrast beween sequences of [CCʰ] and [Cʰː], nor is there a contrast between [CʰC] and [Cː] when all other features of the C are the same (cf. (14)).

(14) Equal surface output

GEMINATES, GEMINATION AND FEATURE CONSTRAINTS

The obstruents listed in Table 10.1 can all occur word-initially but not word-medially or word-finally. Word-finally, neither /ɖ/ nor /ɖʰ/ occur. Word-medial /pʰ/ and /ɖʰ/ are not frequent although they do occur, such as [lɑpʰɑno] 'to jump' and [ɔɖʰel] 'plentiful'. Although /ɖ/ does not occur medially as a singleton, it does occur as a geminate. Indeed, all consonants occur medially as geminates, except /-pʰː-/ and /-ɖʰː-/. Given that a combination of deaspiration and voicing assimilation may potentially lead to phonemes which do not occur in the coda nor as geminates, do the same constraints occur in a derived environment? Consider the word [kɑʈʰ] 'wood' in assimilatory contexts.

(15) Gemination and contextual constraints

a. /ʈ^h + b/ > [ʈb], not *[ɖb]

[kɑʈ^h]$_\omega$ [beʈɑl]$_\omega$

wood cat

'squirrel'

with voicing assimilation ? *[[kɑɖ^h]$_\omega$[berɑl]$_\omega$]$_\omega$

after deaspiration ?* [[kɑɖ]$_\omega$[berɑl]$_\omega$]$_\omega$

BUT since*/ɖ^h/is not permitted word finally, the correct surface form is [kɑʈberɑl]

b. /ʈ^h + ɖ^h/ >[ʈɖ^h], not *[ɖ^h:]

[[kɑʈ^h]$_\omega$[ɖ^{h}ɑl]$_\omega$]$_\omega$

wood shield

'wooden shield'

Thus, as one may expect, the distributional constraints restrict the ouput of optional phonological rules.

Lengthening and Shortening in Bengali

In general, Bengali phonology shows lengthening of vowels and consonants, but not shortening. Vowel length is not contrastive, and consequently vowel shortening is not an issue. Nevertheless, as we have seen, a minimal word requirement enforces vowel lengthening in a monosyllabic word. Consonant length is contrastive, but the singleton-geminate distinction occurs only medially. In most languages, degemination is constrained by syllable structure and often occurs at word edge, as in Old English *cynn-es* 'kin-GEN', but *cynn* > *cyn* 'kin-NOM', or when a consonantal affix follows such as *cyss-an* 'kiss-INF' but *cyss-te* > *cyste* 'kiss-PAST'. Since geminates do not occur at word edges, degemination is not of any concern. Again, however, like vowel lengthening, consonant lengthening can occur via assimilation as seen in the previous sections. There is, however, one instance where degemination plays a role, and that occurs with a verbal affix consisting of only a geminate. This is the progressive suffix /tʃʰː/ to which we now turn.

Progressive /tʃʰː/ Suffix

In the following set of examples, we provide both the progressive as well as the future with suffix /b/ for comparison. We also give the present tense which has no special marking.

(16) Present (PRES 3P ORDINARY), future (FUTURE 3P ORDINARY) and progressive forms (PROGRESSIVE-3P ORDINARY) of verbs

a. Roots ending in consonants other than /r, ɽ/

root	**gloss**	PRESENT	FUTURE	PRESENT PROG.
/ʃon-/	hear	[ʃon-e]	[ʃun-b-e]	[ʃun-tʃʰ-e]
/ɖɑk-/	call	[ɖɑk-e]	[ɖɑk-b-e]	[ɖɑk-tʃʰ-e]
/d̪ækʰ-/	see	[d̪ækʰ-e]	[d̪ekʰ-b-e]	[d̪ekʰ-tʃʰ-e] > [d̪ektʃʰ-e]

b. Roots ending in /r, ɽ/ leading to assimilation and gemination

root	**gloss**	PRESENT	FUTURE	PRESENT PROG.
/pɔɽ-/	read	[pɔɽ-e]	[poɽ-b-e]	[poɽ-tʃʰ-e] > [potʃʰːe]
/mɑr-/	beat	[mɑr-e]	[mɑr-b-e]	[mɑr-tʃʰ-e] > [mɑtʃʰːe]

c. Roots ending in a vowel: CV

root	**gloss**	PRESENT	FUTURE	PRESENT PROG.
/kʰɑ-/	eat	[kʰɑ-e]	[kʰɑ-b-e]	[kʰɑ-tʃʰː-e]
/ʃo-/	lie down	[ʃo-e]	[ʃo-b-e]	[ʃu-tʃʰː-e]

The crucial point here is that the progressive form alternates between /tʃʰ/ and /tʃʰː/. If the verb root ends with a vowel, the progressive is a geminate, otherwise it is not. It is difficult to justify a gemination rule here; there is no reason why a consonantal suffix should geminate—none of the others do so: cf. [ʃu-t̪-o], [ʃu-l-o] 'lie down', HABITUAL PAST-3P.ORDINARY, SIMPLE PAST-3P with the corresponding forms for 'to hear', [ʃun-t̪-o], [ʃun-l-o]. However, we do find a difference between [ʃutʃʰːe] 'sleep-PROG.3P' and [ʃuntʃʰe] 'hear-PROG.3P'. There is a perfectly reasonable historical reason for the progressive suffix being a geminate. It originally comes from the auxiliary /ɑtʃʰ-/ 'to be'.

(17) Diachronic shift from early Bengali to the modern progressive

	CV-root /kʰɑ-/	to eat
	[kʰɑ - i] [ɑtʃʰ-e]	eat has
>	[[kʰɑi]=ɑtʃʰ-e]	cliticisation of the auxiliary
>	[kʰɑi-tʃʰ-e]	loss of initial vowel of auxiliary and clitic becomes suffix
>	[kʰɑ-tʃʰ:e]	loss of /i/ and compensatory lengthening

μ μ μ   μ μ μ
| | | | | |
kʰɑ i tʃʰe > kʰɑ tʃʰ: e

	CVC-root /kɑʃ-/	to cough
	[[kɑʃ i]=ɑtʃʰ-e]	cliticisation of the auxiliary
>	[kɑʃi-tʃʰ-e]	loss of initial vowel of auxiliary and clitic becomes suffix
>	[kɑʃ-tʃʰe]	loss of /i/ and no compensatory lengthening

μ μ μ   μ μ μ
| | | | | |
kɑ ʃi tʃʰe > kɑ ʃ tʃʰe

This analysis has been justified in more detail in Lahiri (2000). Our point here is simply that of the context of degemination. Since the progressive from the auxiliary /ɑtʃʰ-/ was reanalysed via cliticisation to a geminate /tʃʰ:/ on the basis of the CV roots, there is potentially a context where this geminate cannot be realised, viz. when followed by another consonant. Bengali does not tolerate trimoraic syllables. We find evidence for synchronic degemination in CVC roots.

(18) Degemination of progressive /tʃʰ:/

/ʃo-/ 'to lie down'	[ʃo-e]	[ʃo-b-e]	[ʃu-tʃʰ:-e] > [ʃutʃʰ:e]
/ʃon-/ 'to hear'	[ʃon-e]	[ʃun-b-e]	[ʃun-tʃʰ:-e] > [ʃuntʃʰe]
Degemination	[tʃʰ:] > [tʃʰ] / C-		

There is additional evidence that the underlying form of the progressive is indeed /tʃʰ:/. The causative verbs usually have the suffix /-ano/ such as /lek^{h}ɑno/ 'cause to write' where the root /lek^{h}ɑ-/ 'write-INF' is the host to all the other suffixes. Note that the vowel /o/ is added as a hiatus between a CV root and the causative suffix, e.g. /k^{h}ɑ-/, /k^{h}ɑ-o-ɑ/ 'eat-INF', /k^{h}ɑ-o-ɑ-no/ 'cause to eat/ feed'.

(19) Causative verbs

	VERB	ROOT-1P.PRES	ROOT-FUTURE-3P	PROG.2P. ORDINARY
a.	/lek^h-ɑ-no/	[lek^{h}ɑ-i]	[lek^{h}ɑ-b-e]	[lek^{h}ɑ-tʃ^h:-e]
	'causing to write, making someone write'			
b.	/k^{h}ɑ-o-ɑ-no/	[k^{h}ɑoɑ-i]	[k^{h}ɑoɑ-b-e]	[k^{h}ɑoɑ-tʃ^h:e]
	'feeding someone, making someone eat'			
c.	/ʃo-ɑ-no/	[ʃoɑ-i]	[ʃoɑ-b-e]	[ʃoɑ-tʃ^h:e]
	'putting someone to bed'			

Thus, the CV roots /ʃoɑno/ 'to put someone to sleep, to make someone lie down' and /k^{h}ɑoɑno/ 'to feed someone' must permit the geminate [tʃ^h:] for the progressive form. Had it been an initial CVC root such as /lek^h/, the degemination rule would not permit the geminate [tʃ^h:] to surface. We could then argue that given that consonant length is contrastive, one may expect both gemination and degemination; and indeed, both occur. In contrast, vowel length surfaces purely on the postlexical level and there is no occasion for any shortening.

CONCLUSION

A few conclusions can be drawn from our various productive rules in Bengali. First, vowel lengthening as well as vowel nasalisation both apply within a word. The nasalisation affects stressed vowels and since word stress is always on the first syllable of a prosodic word, nasalisation is not evident elsewhere. Furthermore, nasal vowels themselves only occur in stressed position and consequently, contextual nasalisation is always word-internal. Vowel lengthening too is restricted to a prosodic word. Our example with the emphatic clitics (cf. example 3) show that, in vowel-final CV words, the vowel is lengthened since the clitic is added to the prosodic word. In contrast, an inflectional suffix leads to a diphthong and there is no lengthening; compare $[k^h\text{ɑ-i}]_\omega$ > $[k^h\text{ɑi}]_\omega$ 'eat-1P.PRES' (where /ɑi/ is a diphthong) versus $[[\text{tʃɑ}]_\omega\text{=i}]_\omega$, 'tea=also'.

Regarding the phonological processes affecting consonants, we see a variety of patterns. We find both assimilation and dissimilation, both involving LARYNGEAL features which may or may not have quantity-related implications. Gemination is certainly feasible, particularly since medial underlying geminates are the norm. Degemination is more restricted since the usual context of this is syllable-final. Given that only medial geminates are contrastive, word based degemination does not occur. Nevertheless, historically, compensatory lengthening leads to a geminate-inflectional morpheme, which in turn may be syllable-final and therefore is in a position to degeminate. From the very few phonological processes we have enountered, we can also conclude that word as well as phrase level constraints operate in Bengali.

REFERENCES

Chomsky, Noam, and Morris Halle. (1968). *The Sound Pattern of English*. New York: Harper & Row.

Chatterji, Suniti Kumar. (1926). *The Origin and Development of the Bengali Language*. Calcutta: Calcutta University Press. (Reprinted in 1975, Calcutta: Rupa & Co.).

Clements, George N. (2001). 'Representational economy in constraint-based phonology'. *Distinctive Feature Theory*, 2, 71–146.

Dan, Mina. (1992). 'Some issues in the metrical phonology of Bangla: The indigenous research tradition'. Unpublished PhD Dissertation, University of Poona.

Dasgupta, Probal. (1984). 'Bangla emphasizers and anchors'. *Indian Linguistics*, 45, 102–17.

Fitzpatrick-Cole, Jennifer. (1996). 'Reduplication meets the phonological phrase in Bengali'. *The Linguistic Review*, 13, 3/4, 305–56.

Halle, Morris, Bert Vaux, and Andrew Wolfe. (2000). 'On feature spreading and the representation of place of articulation'. *Linguistic Inquiry*, 31/3, 387–444.

Hayes, Bruce, and Aditi Lahiri. (1991). 'Bengali intonational phonology'. *Natural Language and Linguistic Theory*, 9/1, 47–96.

Jakobson, Roman, Gunnar Fant, and Morris Halle. (1952). 'Preliminaries to speech analysis: The distinctive features and their correlates'. *MIT Acoustics Laboratory Technical Report*, 13.

Lahiri, Aditi. (2000). 'Hierarchical restructuring in the creation of verbal morphology in Bengali and Germanic: Evidence from phonology'. In A. Lahiri (ed.), *Analogy and Markedness: Principles of Change in Phonology and Morphology.* Berlin: Mouton, 71–123.

—— (2012). 'Asymmetric phonological representations of *words* in the mental lexicon'. In A. Cohn et al. (eds), *The Oxford Handbook of Laboratory Phonology*. Oxford: Oxford University Press, 146–61.

Lahiri, Aditi, and Henning Reetz. (2010). 'Distinctive features: Phonological underspecification in representation and processing'. *Journal of Phonetics*, 38/1, 44–59.

Lahiri, Aditi, and Jennifer Fitzpatrick-Cole. (1999). 'Emphatic clitics and focus intonation in Bengali'. *Phrasal Phonology*, 119–44.

Lahiri, Aditi, and William Marslen-Wilson. (1991). 'The mental representation of lexical form: A phonological approach to the recognition lexicon'. *Cognition*, 38/3, 245–94.

ABOUT THE CONTRIBUTORS

Josef Bayer, a retired professor of linguistics at the University of Konstanz, Germany, was trained in German philology, linguistics, philosophy and musicology. He was also Professor at the University of Jena and Visiting Professor at the University of Duesseldorf and University of Vienna. His interests lie in syntax and its relation to language processing. He has worked on Germanic (German and its dialect) and on Indo-Aryan (Bangla) languages. His research was funded by a number of grants from the German Research Council. Bayer is author/co-author of two monographs and seventy-six articles, and editor/co-editor of eight volumes on different topics in linguistics. His publications include *Directionality and Logical Form: On the Scope of Focusing Particles and Wh-in-situ* (1996) and *Case and Linking in Language Comprehension: Evidence from German* (2006).

Krishna Bhattacharya, formerly Professor of Linguistics, has taught in the Departments of Linguistics, Bengali Language and Literature, Sanskrit, and Comparative Indian Language and Literature at the University of Calcutta, Kolkata. Her interests include phonetics, phonology, applied linguistics and language-music. She has published six books and over sixty articles in the domain of linguistics and literature, and completed five research projects successfully. She has also edited/coedited books and journals. She has visited the USA, Thailand, Germany and Japan on academic work. She translates stories, essays and poems from Odia to Bangla. Her publications include *An Intensive Course in Bengali* (1994), *Bengali-Oriya Verb Morphology: A Contrastive Study* (1993), and *Oriya Galpodashok* (2000).

Probal Dasgupta, an Honorary member of the Linguistic Society of America, has taught in New York, San Francisco, Melbourne, Barlaston, Kolkata, Pune and Hyderabad. He retired as Professor from the Indian Statistical Institute, Kolkata. He writes in Bangla, English and Esperanto and has to his credit over ten books and four hundred other publications in the domains of linguistics, literature, translation and philosophy. His edited works include *Indian Linguistics*, the *Language and Development* series, *Year Book of South Asian Languages and Linguistics*, *Language Problems and Language Planning*, and *Beletra Almanako*. He is the president of the Akademio de Esperanto and the former president of the World Esperanto Association. His authored volumes include *The Otherness of English: India's Auntie Tongue Syndrome* (1993), and *Inhabiting Human Languages: The Substantivist Visualization* (2012).

Sandagomi Koperahewa, Professor of Sinhala and the Founder Director of the Centre for Contemporary Indian Studies, University of Colombo, has authored twelve books and a number of scholarly articles on Sinhala language, grammar and language policy planning in Sri Lanka. He has served as a consultant to the Presidential Task Force for a Tri-lingual Sri Lanka, Department of Official Languages, Department of Educational Publications, National Institute of Education and the Information Communication Technology Agency of Sri Lanka on various language planning projects related to Sinhala. Apart from his main research areas, Professor Coperahewa has been actively engaged in various research and other collaborative projects related to contemporary Indian studies. His books include *Remembering Rabindranath Tagore* (2011), and *One Hundred Years of Gitanjali* 1913–2013 (2015).

Aditi Lahiri, Fellow of Somerville College, Oxford, and Professor of Linguistics, University of Oxford, was a student of the Bethune College and University of Calcutta. She has taught at the University of Konstanz, Germany; and in the USA at the Universities of

California, (Santa Cruz and Los Angeles), Cornell, Harvard, Stanford and MIT. The fields of her scholarship are phonology, phonetics, historical linguistics, psycholinguistics and neurolinguistics. She has earned numerous awards and honours—the Honorary Life Member of the Linguistics Society of America 2013, the Fellow of the British Academy 2010, the Professor Sukumar Sen Memorial Gold Medal 2009 from the Asiatic Society, Kolkata, the Gottfried Wilhelm Leibniz Prize 2000, the Max Planck Research Prize for International Cooperation 1995, the Commander of the Order of the British Empire 2020—to mention a few. She has to her credit more than eighty papers and book chapters published in renowned international journals and books.

Carol Myers-Scotton, Professor of Linguistics, is presently an adjunct professor at Michigan State University in the Department of Linguistics and Languages and also a visiting scholar at the MSU African Studies Center. She retired from the University of South Carolina in 2003, where she was a Carolina Distinguished Professor. She has authored/co-authored over a hundred articles and book chapters in linguistics. She has published widely on language contact phenomena, especially code-switching. Her publications include *Duelling Languages: Grammatical Structure in Codeswitching* (1993a), *Social Motivations for Codeswitching: Evidence from Africa* (1993), *Contact Linguistics* (2002), and *Multiple Voices: An Introduction to Bilingualism* (2005).

Suniti Kumar Pathak, a renowned Indologist, was a Professor in the department of Indo-Tibetan Studies, Visva-Bharati, Santiniketan. He is proficient in Sanskrit, Hindi, Bangla, Pali, Prakrit, English, Tibetan, Chinese and Mongolian languages. He writes in Bangla, English, Hindi and Tibetan. He has to his credit over fifteen books and two hundred articles that have contributed widely to the domains of Tibetan, Himalayan, Buddhist and Tantra studies, Indic-Tibetan literature, Asian culture and world peace. He has translated Tagore's poems into Tibetan. He was the Csoma de Koros Research Professor of the Asiatic Society, Kolkata, and was awarded the Certificate of Honour by the President of India. His books include *Snyan Ngag Bsdus pa* (1961), *Tibetan-Hindi Dictionary* (1973), *The Indian*

Nitishastras in Tibet (1974) and *Buddhism: World Peace and Harmony* (2011).

B. N. Patnaik, former Professor at IIT Kanpur, taught generative linguistics, computational linguistics and English for more than twenty-five years. His areas of interest include generative linguistics, sociolinguistics, computational linguistics, communication, Odia folklore, Odia Purans, and protest literature. Currently he is working primarily on conversation analysis and medieval Odia literature. He has published research papers in theoretical and applied linguistics and the Sarala Mahabharata. He has written the first partial generative grammar of Odia. He has authored *Science and Tradition* (2000), *Globalization: Language Culture and Media* (2006), *Introducing Saaralaa Mahaabhaarata* (2012), and *Language Matters* (2018) to mention a few, and co-edited Noam Chomsky's *Architecture of Language*. He is an associate editor of the English-English-Odia Dictionary. He writes a blog on Sarala Mahabharata: saralamahabharat.blogspot.com

Tariq Rahman, is Professor Emeritus of Quaid-i-Azam University, Islamabad, and currently Dean, School of Education, and School of Liberal Arts and Social Sciences, Beaconhouse National University, Lahore. He was a Fulbright fellow, the first incumbent of the Pakistan Chair at the University of California, Berkeley, and received the Humboldt Research Award from Germany. He has authored eight books and over a hundred other publications, chiefly in the field of linguistics. He is well known as a creative writer, columnist and a literary critic in Pakistan. He is also the recipient of the titles of Distinguished National Professor, *Sitara-i-Imtiaz* and the Lifetime achievement award. His publications include *Language and Politics in Pakistan* (1996), *Language, Ideology and Power: Language-Learning among the Muslims of Pakistan and North India* (2002) and *From Hindi to Urdu: A Social and Political History* (2011).

Pabitra Sarkar, a well known name in the field of linguistics, was Professor of Bengali at Jadavpur University, Kolkata. He was also the Vice-Chancellor of Rabindra Bharati University and later Vice-Chairman of West Bengal State Council for Higher Education. He was trained in linguistics at the University of Chicago on a Fulbright Scholarship. He is a person with varied interests and is a linguist, grammarian, literary critic, columnist, writer and actor. He is associated with the various aspects of performing arts, and is also a singer of Rabindra Sangeet. Apart from authoring sixty-four books, he has also edited forty-five books and published numerous articles on various subjects in Bangla and English. His publications include *Bangla Byakaran Prasanga* (2006), *Bhasha, Desh, Kal* (2012), and *Katha ar Kahini* (2014).

Udaya Narayana Singh, formerly, Director of CIIL, Mysore, and Professor, Rabindra Bhavana, Visva-Bharati, Santiniketan, is currently Chair-Professor, Amity Centre for Linguistic Studies, Amity University. He contributed generously to the field of linguistics—published more than one hundred and eighty research papers, set up the Centre in Applied Linguistics and Translation Studies at the University of Hyderabad, and National Translation Mission in Mysore. He has visited and lectured in Andorra, Bangladesh, Belgium, the Caribbean Islands, France, Germany, Iceland, Italy, Nepal, Pakistan, Russia, Singapore, Sweden, Thailand and the USA. A reputed poet, playwright and essayist, Singh is also a recipient of many awards, grants and honours. A few of his books are *Language Development and Planning: A Pluralistic Paradigm* (1992), *India Writes: A Story of Linguistic and Literary Plurality* (2006), and *Translation as Growth: Towards a Theory of Language Development* (2010).